I'm Not Crazy
Just Bipolar

I'm Not Crazy Just Bipolar

Wendy K. Williamson

authorHOUSE®

AuthorHouse™
1663 Liberty Drive
Bloomington, IN 47403
www.authorhouse.com
Phone: 1-800-839-8640

This book is a work of non-fiction. Unless otherwise noted, the author and the publisher make no explicit guarantees as to the accuracy of the information contained in this book and in some cases, names of people and places have been altered to protect their privacy.

First published by AuthorHouse 11/5/2010

ISBN: 978-1-4520-6850-3 (hc)
ISBN: 978-1-4520-6851-0 (sc)
ISBN: 978-1-4520-6852-7 (e)

Printed in the United States of America

This book is printed on acid-free paper.

Because of the dynamic nature of the Internet, any Web addresses or links contained in this book may have changed since publication and may no longer be valid. The views expressed in this work are solely those of the author and do not necessarily reflect the views of the publisher, and the publisher hereby disclaims any responsibility for them.

Most of the names in the book have been changed to protect those people and the author.

Cover design by Kim Sillen Gledhill.
www.kimgledhill.com

For more information:
www.wendykwilliamson.com

For:

Mom & Dad

Bipolars Everywhere

Introduction

I was diagnosed with bipolar disorder my last semester at Virginia Tech sixteen years ago. At that time there was no book like this for me to read, only ones written by doctors or famous people. I thought being told that I had bipolar disorder meant I was crazy and abnormal and I wanted more than anything to be normal again. Of course, I know *now* that normal doesn't exist. Normal is a cycle on a wash machine.

Five years ago I hit turbulence. My friend died, I was downsized from my job, and I had to move back into my parents' house all within a short period of time. I went into a deep depression and struggled to find a purpose in my life. Why was I alive when my happy, newlywed friend was dead? Writing this book made sense to me. Maybe that was my unfulfilled purpose? So I set up a makeshift office in my parents' basement and began writing. However, my writing was fueled by sleepless nights of manic driven creativity and I couldn't complete it. I continued faster in my downward spiral.

I tried several times to commit suicide. I was in and out of the hospital seven times in fourteen months and ended up receiving over thirty ECT (electroconvulsive therapy) treatments. I didn't want to live which, needless to say, makes completing a book pretty tough.

Once I was finally stable and sober (that also was a big struggle), I felt inspired again but needed a sign. A sign from God, the universe, my angels, *something* to reassure me I was on the right track. I always wanted to tell my story, and thought I could help someone doing it, but who was I to think that I could? All I had ever written was a bunch of poetry, half of which I was too embarrassed to let anyone read.

Things began to shift when I started listening to those "you can do it" CDs all the time. I stopped thinking of myself as a waitress and called myself a writer. Pretty soon the right people and resources were put in my path and I finished this book.

My wish is that when you read this, you gain some hope and understanding as a result. Whether you have bipolar disorder or you're a family member or friend of someone who has bipolar. Maybe you are a professional in the field. Regardless of who you are, we can all use a little light to understand ourselves and each other. We are not going to get through this battle alone. And it *is* a battle. One out of every five bipolars commits suicide. We need each other to not only get well but, at times, to stay alive.

If you have bipolar disorder, your story, your details, will be different, that's true. However, some of the feelings will be the same because after all, our *brains* are the same. I hope this helps you feel less alone, less ashamed of some of the things that maybe you've gone through. None of this is your fault. You didn't ask to be born mentally ill. But since we've got it, we have to deal with it the best way we can.

I want you to know that I am rooting for you in your life, whoever you are. Yes, there will be ups and downs, mania and depression. Most of us suffer from both of these from time to time. Never forget to remember there is peace too.

Foreword

Public awareness often takes a very long time to catch up to the current scientific capability. Unfortunately, the average person often has an outdated and inaccurate understanding of mental illness. A few years ago a study on the public perception of the cause of mental illness demonstrated 71% felt it was emotional weakness, 65% felt it was caused by bad parenting, 45% felt it was the victim's fault and could be willed away, 35% felt it was a consequence of sinful behavior, only 10% felt it had a biological basis and involved the brain and 43% felt it was incurable. When viewed in this manner, the common advice is: Snap out of it! Shape up! Get over it! Buck up! Just do it! Get off the pity train! Don't feel sorry for yourself! Pull yourself up by your bootstraps! You have nothing to be depressed about! An analogy can be drawn with a fish that is hooked by a fisherman and is swimming wildly and erratically to fight for its survival. Other fish are puzzled watching the battle against the unseen and unknown threat.

We can't understand these conditions unless we see it through the eyes of the victim. Wendy was struggling against an unseen adversary. At times her illness was very menacing and overwhelming. The darkness and depth of her depression impaired her ability to appreciate there was hope to feel better as some point in the future.

However, within her she found an inner strength few know they possess until they are forced to deal with such a challenge. She persevered, recovered and is now leading a full and productive life.

Fortunately, there is much better mental health treatment capability now and the public needs to be aware there is help and hope. Conditions that once resulted in a lifetime of institutional care can now be treated much more effectively and cost effectively on an outpatient basis. Patients need greater awareness that such help is available and the public needs to recognize that resources allocated to improve care and access to mental health care are healthcare priorities.

When most recover they don't want to think about it again, less share their experience with others and very few are able to write a book about their experience. I hope Wendy's story will give hope to others with similar difficulties, understanding to their family members and greater awareness to the public. On behalf of those who may benefit, thank you Wendy for sharing your story.

Robert C Bransfield, MD, DLFAPA
Private Practice of Psychiatry
Associate Clinical Professor of Psychiatry RWJ- UMDNJ Medical School

Table of Contents

The Diagnosis

Diagnosis Disaster

She was The Enemy. The shrink at Virginia Tech whose intensity was making me uncomfortable in my chair. I remember her squinty eyes as she accused me with them. Her shiny, black hair was pulled tightly into a severe bun. I was supposed to be graduating in just six weeks, but here we were sitting with The Enemy.

My parents were seated in her office next to me, thanks to my roommate, who had alerted them to my bizarre behavior. I had no idea why we were there. I only knew her for two minutes, but I already knew two things: I did not like her and clearly, she was The Enemy.

My father was holding my Mom's hand, but not saying much. He had just finished making small talk with The Enemy about how nice her orchids were. The Enemy was trying to make eye contact with me, but I avoided her. I kept busy, looking around, reading her fancy degrees and the titles of all her books that looked horribly boring. I presumed they were about as dull as her personality. I spotted a video camera on a tripod in the corner nearby.

Her manner switched from semi-serious to acting as if she was telling my parents I was going to die. Then I heard the words I will never, ever forget.

"Your daughter has bipolar disorder," she said matter-of-factly. "She is having a hypomanic episode."

Wait, what? I went over those words again, but it did not sound good.

"I'm sorry, but could you please say that again?" My Mom gently and politely asked The Enemy to repeat the bomb she had just dropped on us.

"She has bipolar disorder." The shrink said slower this time. "She is having a hypomanic episode which *could* be drug-induced." The Enemy added.

My parents sat there listening as The Enemy continued talking, but I had already begun to tune out. I was staring at my Mom hoping, half expecting she would jump up out of her seat and declare this woman insane to be saying this about her daughter. Instead, my Mom just bravely fought back her tears. Why wasn't she screaming? Why wasn't *I* screaming? The Enemy had them in the palm of her hand. Mom was hanging on her every word. My father was quiet as usual and staring off into space.

Wait, did she just say drug-induced? What drugs was she talking about? I didn't do drugs. Well, I did smoke pot but that's not really a drug-drug. She continued talking to my parents while glancing over at me. I was not really a part of the conversation, but she included me because she had to; she was a professional, after all. I was smirking at her because I did not like her *or* her new terminology for me. I did not like these words she was using to describe what she *thought* I had based on her ten minutes of knowing me.

"Excuse me, but could you please explain to me again what is wrong with Wendy?" My Mom had such good manners, even at a time like now. I was not taking any of this seriously, although my parents sure seemed to be. I couldn't believe they were taking her every word to be true like she was God or something! My Mom waited for The Enemy's reply.

Meanwhile, I felt like I was in a dream. A bad dream. The kind where I'm in a glass box pounding on the walls, but it's soundproofed and no one can hear me.

The song "Comfortably Numb" floated in my head. *"Your lips move…but I can't hear what you're saying."* I sat back and watched their lips move, but they may as well have not been speaking at all. Every now and then I'd tune in and listen, but I preferred staying in my head.

"Bipolar disorder is the *newer* term" the shrink explained, "although manic depression is what most people have called it in the past." Ah, bipolar disorder was the *newer* term. She, of course, was on the modern side of medicine. I couldn't care less. At that moment, all I knew was that I was being told my brain was defective. I had a *dis*order. How could this be good? I played with the zipper on my jacket.

I was stuck on this term she mentioned, this *manic depression*. Since I'd never heard of bipolar disorder, the Jimi Hendrix song, "Manic Depression" came to mind and was the extent of my knowledge on the subject. What were the words to that? *"Manic depression's touching my soul. I want what I want but I just don't know…"* I kept going with the words then reluctantly tuned back into the nightmare…

I looked at my parents and then back at The Enemy. They were still talking, but it felt like I was a spectator at a tennis match, one with a long volley. I kept alternating sides, watching their mouths move on either side of the desk. I was going through the motions so they'd think I was paying attention. Geez, they looked so serious. This was not good. No, this was not good at all.

"I would like to videotape you," the shrink said, her eyes squinting again, like she was accusing me of something. "It really helps to show you how manic you are..."

"Absolutely not!" I shot back. They all turned to look at me. I would not be some lab rat for her stupid research. Sensing she wasn't going to get anywhere, she backed off. Without skipping a beat, The Enemy switched gears.

"I have diagnosed and treated over one thousand students here at Virginia Tech." She declared. *Wow, that's a lot of sick people*, I thought. I held onto that large number, though, and when I thought of how many *other* people were diagnosed with something, it made me feel slightly better that I was one of many at my school.

"I diagnose most students a few weeks or months before graduation. It's very common." She continued. "You are lucky. Not all universities have a psychiatrist on staff."

Did she say lucky? I was trying to figure out how I was lucky. For her to be convincing me that I was mentally ill and now lucky to have her, well *that* was pushing it. It was too much to digest in one session. Scratch that. It was too much to digest at all.

Then she asked about the videotaping again. *Are you kidding me?* What about the word *no* didn't she understand? I wished she would take her camera, tripod, orchids, fucking degrees and march it all on back to Cornell where she came from. Why had she even come to Tech anyway? Her stupid research, no doubt. I kept popping in and out of what she was saying, which was basically a monologue directed at my parents about how sick I was. Focusing for me was not going well. Then again, *none* of this was going well.

Bipolar disorder...it sounded so serious. Like I had lost a limb or had cancer or something. She did say that since I have bipolar, I had a very high IQ (finally some good news!) That's the only good thing I had to hold on to. Fabulous, I'm fucked up but at least I'm smart. Well, I guess it was better than hearing you're fucked up and dumb.

The shrink sprung into action giving my parents a list of what I was and was not to do, effective immediately. I was told to give them my debit card, which I protested, of course. As I reluctantly handed it over to my Mom, I thought I had at least $10 left in my account. (As it turned out, I was actually overdrawn by hundreds!)

"We'll put her on a few medications which should help her mania. Lithium is a good mood stabilizer for that. She'll need a tranquilizer too, so she can sleep. Then we'll add...."

Medications? As in plural? Mood stabilizer? Wait! Did she say... *tranquilizer?* I was getting really nervous that she was going to just drug me up and that would be the end of me. I was slowly adding everything up and not liking the total.

"You need to eat properly." The Enemy looked right at me, my parents followed. Was it me or was she scowling at me? I scowled back. My parents were looking at me sternly as The Enemy went through each item on her how-to-ruin-my-life-now checklist.

"What? I'm eating." My Mom's eyes looked so sad now. They were all red. "Well, okay I'm not eating a *lot.* But I mean, I am eating."

"Those bruises on your arm are from malnutrition." The Enemy said. She made me sound like I was a child from a third world country. Everyone looked down at my bruised arms, including me. Where did *those* come from?

I was subscribing to the theory that people could go without food for thirty days. I had read it or heard it somewhere. Hadn't Jesus gone for thirty days without food? Didn't it say that in the Bible? I was trying to do a mini-fasting thing, thinking it would cleanse my soul.

"The medication will help you sleep."

"What? I sleep!"

"Wendy, the car crash?" My Mom reminded me, obviously perturbed. The Enemy looked interested and leaned forward like she wanted details. I wasn't sharing any.

"It was an accident. That was *one* night." What we all knew (except The Enemy, of course) was that I had fallen asleep at the wheel less than a mile from campus on my way back from Richmond one weekend. I had to get back to Tech for aerobics and it seemed a perfectly plausible explanation for driving without any sleep to get there in time for my 8:00 am class. I couldn't miss one more aerobics class or I might fail and not graduate. That was the "clean" version. The one I might even have told The Enemy.

What I was leaving out however, were the not-so-pretty details of that night. I was up all night because I had gotten wasted with a guy I just met in Richmond who was twice my age. With no sleep, I attempted to drive back to Tech. My parents knew *that* was the real reason for my car accident. Without knowing all those details, they knew. At least, my Mom knew. She always knew my truths. *Dammit!*

I didn't want to sleep a lot. I mean, I had too many things to do! Now they were going to *drug* me to get me to sleep? There went all my ideas that come to me at night. And they *always* came to me at night. Now I wouldn't be awake to write them down. Great. Just fucking great. I was still on the sleep and medication thing when the next bomb was dropped by, you guessed it: The Enemy.

"You can't drink. Absolutely *no* alcohol or drugs!" The Enemy was shaking her head. What? I couldn't fathom graduating without partying. Plus, Halloween was coming up. I even had my costume ready. I was going to be Inga from Sveden. I had my sister's dirndl from her job at the German restaurant all ready to go.

"But I'm graduating in six weeks. I'm a graduating senior. We party. Are you serious? No drinking *at all?*"

The Enemy shook her head. "No alcohol or drugs. And you need to be in..."

I was still digesting those words, choking on them really, when I got nailed with:

"...the hospital."

Wait. *What?* Did she say *hospital?* I was still back on the no drinking thing. The word hospital hadn't sunk in yet. Hospitals were for people who are dying or having surgery. Was she for real? I was weeks away from the finish line! I would be getting my diploma in six fucking weeks and this bitch wants to yank me out and throw me in the hospital?

This was serious; there was no dodging it now. The "H" word was on the table. Nothing up to that point had come close or fully gotten my attention yet. She had it now. I shot a look at my parents.

"Here are your choices," The Enemy said. "You can take a medical leave, be hospitalized, and come back next semester." I couldn't believe it. She was so casual, like we were talking about changing a course or rescheduling an exam.

"No way." I kept shaking my head no. This going into the hospital idea was not acceptable. Nope. Would not work for me.

"*Or*," she continued, "you can take the harder route and stay in school. Take the medication and be watched around the clock by your family and friends."

I knew I couldn't withdraw from the semester this close to graduation with my diploma at stake. How would I feel about coming back? *Would* I come back? How would it look if I just disappeared? Plus, everyone in my major would know something was wrong with me. I didn't think I could come back when all my friends were graduating. Who would I even live with? I was *hoping* for a third option but it quickly dawned on me that it was only curtain A or B.

"If I leave, I'm not coming back." My diploma was the only ace in my hand. My parents looked at me and each other and they knew I meant business. It was all they needed to hear. We had to come up with a solution that didn't involve dropping out and going into the hospital. Our solution was not what she recommended. I stayed.

How the hell did I get here?

Virginia Tech

I'm A Hokie

I had decided I wanted to go to hotel school. Let me back up a bit. My parents' friends *suggested* it to me at their dinner party one night. It sounded like something I might be good at, seeing as I was passing around a plate of hors d' oeuvres. They said hospitality management involved hotels and restaurants and travel. It sounded exciting…like an adventure!

"You have the right personality for it!" They said enthusiastically, as the couples dunked their shrimps into the cocktail sauce.

"Okay." I shrugged, feeling kind of awkward. I looked down at the tray I was passing, shrimp tails everywhere, trying to figure out if I really just chose my college major this way.

It did sound kind of fun and surely it must be less academic pressure than most *other* majors. I didn't want too strenuous a major to ensure I'd get my diploma (or "my ticket to play the game" as my parents called it).

Out of those college guide books, my Mom picked out Virginia Tech because it was in the category of: "Best Education for the Least Money." I was concerned that my Mom was bargain hunting for my education. Slightly worrisome.

"Just apply. For me. Please? Humor your Mother." My Mom was not one to ask much of me or demand anything.

"Alright Mom. I'll apply." I did apply, but I had no intention of actually going there at the time. I was strictly appeasing her.

Although I was planning on going to another school, I got in late spring and ultimately decided to go to Virginia Tech. As it turns out, Virginia Tech did have one of the top schools for my major. Nervousness set in and I wondered: how was I going to make it through four years of rigorous academics? I had developed virtually no study skills in high school. (I did study hard in Spanish because our teacher was an ex-nun from Peru who scared the shit out of us.) I was well aware that I was in for a wake-up call in college. I wasn't sure how I was going to be able to balance academics with drinking. Little did I know, the scales were already tipped against me.

Academics were the last thing on my mind as we made our way through the Blue Ridge Mountains. I marveled at how spectacular they were against the bright blue sky. Engulfed in the beauty of the scenery, I was so excited I could hardly contain myself. Finally there was an end to our eight-hour journey from New Jersey! I felt like a sardine, cramped with Mom, Dad and my sister Samantha in our Subaru station wagon. At last, I was at the beginning of my new journey.

Naturally, there had to be a glitch to my new start. We noticed smoke coming from our Subaru's muffler, which had started somewhere between New Jersey and Virginia. It had gotten progressively worse and was now jetting out in an unusually strong velocity making everyone, especially me, extremely nervous.

As we pulled onto the university campus, through clouds of smoke, I saw tons of people everywhere. The lush green grass filled the seemingly endless wide, open spaces between the many stone buildings. The stadium was gigantic! It was impossible not to feel small. I tried not to feel overwhelmed, rather to revel in the excitement. The energy was in the air. You could practically see it.

"Dad, um, slow down. The map says it should be right… over… there?" I was half looking at the map and signs and half ducking, praying no one would recognize me in our smoke machine.

"I think that's it. West Ambler Johnston, right?" My sister spotted it first.

"Yeah that's it. That's it!"

"Wait Dad, go to the right. It looks like you can park in that lot over there." Samantha, my older sister was ever the practical one and the first to figure out where we could park.

Another person pointed to our car and yelled something to us. I ducked again. Then I popped up and turned around to check the amount of smoke coming out. It was much worse than before. Fabulous. What a way to make an entrance.

"God, I hope nobody recognizes me." I was starting to panic a little as people looked at our smoking car go by.

"It's a big school, honey. Nobody's going to remember you." My Mom sounded tired, but still positive.

"Your car is smoking!" A girl said with her hands cupped to her face. She repeated it and with each syllable, she pointed her index finger towards our back tailpipe. We could all hear her even with the windows up. Her eyes were wide in disbelief at how we could still be driving this obviously hazardous car. I slid down further in my seat, trying to avoid eye contact with her.

"Oh my gosh, we're at my dorm now. I mean, she could remember my face." I knew it was possible because she had a full view of my face right then. I wasn't in ducked down mode.

"No she won't Wendy. Relax."

Relax? Grrr! That word was right up there with "calm down." My sister and I despised that phrase and would pull it out of our dirty bag of tricks in our worst fights. "Relax" wasn't "calm down," but it was a steady second.

We pulled into a spot and parked. My family was getting out of the station wagon, all eager and ready for action. I, however, was not, still frozen, with images of that girl's face and wondering who else had recognized me. I got out slowly, also reminded of the next dreaded step. We had to get to my room without anyone seeing my bags.

Ugh. It was time for the Hefty bags.

You see, my family's favorite moving luggage was, yes, Hefty bags. They had done it like this for my sister, so I knew it was coming. I was just in denial up until the actual, dreaded moment of their unveiling. As we dragged my black bags into my dorm room, I wondered why couldn't I have luggage like *normal* people?

Some of these southern belles were really decked out, with perfectly matching sets. I was already feeling inferior and I hadn't even met anyone yet. (By the time we were done hauling all my stuff I decided it was a pretty practical solution after all. But couldn't they at least make these things in colors?)

"Hi!" A girl with a deep tan, huge green eyes, dimples and beautiful smile appeared in my doorway out of nowhere. She practically scared the shit out of me. The bubbly gal came over and thrust out her hand.

"Oh, hi." Keep it cool, I told myself as I shook her hand, nerves still rattling.

"I'm Mary," she continued smiling. Her energy radiated and could light up our whole hall. "We're neighbors!" Mary giggled. She was very tan and a little bit too peppy for me, I decided.

"Hi Mary. I'm Wendy. These are my parents. And this is my sister Samantha." Mary looked familiar. My parents shook her hand,

Samantha waved and everyone exchanged hellos. I kept trying to place her. Then I thought no, how could I know her already?

"Wait!" Her eyes widened. "Were you in the Blue Subaru? Oh my gosh…I thought who *is* that?" She let out a quick laugh. "Don't they know their car is smoking?" She kept laughing, apparently this was very funny.

I couldn't believe my luck! What was the chance that the girl who was pointing to us, and had made eye contact with me, would be *my next door neighbor?* I looked at my Mom who was busy talking to her and folding clothes from my semi-deflated, semi-torn, Hefty bags. Dad was looking around my room with his hands folded across his chest, clad in his khaki shorts, Docksiders and frown. Samantha was on the edge of my bunk bed listening in.

Nobody comprehended the magnitude of my misfortune. I knew I'd be hearing Mary tell this story over and over again. Fucking great start.

Thanks to our embarrassing smoking car, my parents were forced to fly home to get to their teaching jobs in time. My sister had to stay in my room for a week until the car was fixed. She needed it to take to college in time for her classes to begin. Needless to say, it made for an awkward start. That damn car!

Even more annoying was my new roommate and her nauseating, sappy boyfriend. They reminded me of Doug and Wendy Whiner from those Saturday Night Live skits. Everything that came out of their mouths was in "whine" form. No exaggeration. Everyone knew I got bagged with the worst roommate on the hall. Our room always had to be pin-dropping quiet so she could study and she marked all her soda cans in the fridge (we drank different brands, mind you). The Whiner's relationship helped solidify the belief that I didn't want to have a boyfriend early on.

Plus, the guys…well, never before had I *seen* so many hot guys in one place at one time. And their southern accents were new and sexy (it sure beat the Jersey accent). I thought I had died and gone to heaven! I mean, they were *everywhere!* I would stare out my window at the volleyball court (complete with sand and everything) and check them out, practically drooling. It was hard to concentrate on schoolwork on a nice day with that view. I'd look at them, playing with their shirts off, and think to myself: *college life is awesome!*

I was very insecure and couldn't believe that guys were flirting with me. But they were! Drinking fixed that problem and gave me the liquid courage I needed to flirt back. I wasn't used to this because in high school I never had a boyfriend. I mean, *never.* This was a whole new world for me. All of a sudden, I had found my playground.

I loved going out with all my new friends, the girls in my hall. I was in an all-girls dorm that was just over one thousand women. There were seventy-five women on my wing alone so there was plenty of drama and late night story-telling. Anything to avoid our studies! It was fun, exciting and I had a lot of girlfriends. You couldn't feel alone. It was virtually impossible.

Soon the football games started. I loved the tailgates. There were tailgates before the game and afterwards. We'd sneak in alcohol to the games in plastic Ziploc baggies and then add it to the sodas we purchased at the game. Instant Jack and Cokes! There were parties after the games all day and night until you passed out. It was an endless day of drinking. I loved the hype and excitement and drinking, so game days were favorites of many and certainly mine. Our dorm was the closest to the stadium. We had it made. We didn't even have to walk far!

My next door neighbor, Mary had quickly become my closest friend. She was a sweetheart. Mary also loved to party, so we joined forces early on. Her brother was a sophomore living in the nearby dorm called Pritchard Hall, which held over one thousand freshmen and sophomore guys. (That was too much testosterone under one roof!) Pritchard Hall was notorious for being the top party dorm on campus. And it was. By night we turned into fast forward partying fools thanks to Mary's brother, his friends and smelly Pritchard.

The boys of Pritchard would get rowdy. One time, some of them had thrown an entire soda machine from the fourth floor into the courtyard. On weekends it was typical to see the hallways wet with water, beer, mud or a slippery substance where the drunkest (or the stupidest) of the lot would do running body slides. A successful slide ended up in the bathroom, having made it all the way down the hall.

That's where we drank. It was disgusting, insane, wacky and unpredictable and I loved it over there! (Except that it smelled of stale beer and body odor, especially on the weekends.) I was always trying to figure which was worse: warm crappy beer or room temperature cheap vodka. Well, vodka worked faster anyhow.

That's the way my drinking started out. It was pretty hardcore from the start. I was off to the races the minute I stepped onto university soil. I never realized I had a problem with drinking because everyone I was friends with, for the most part, drank the way I did. I was in college and that's what college kids did. Okay not *all* college students, but certainly the ones I hung out with.

I was headed right for Greek life, where my drinking got worse and I blended in even more. Combine dorms, apartment parties, bars downtown, block parties, fraternity parties and that about summed up my description of college heaven. I loved life. There's no question that I was having a hard time balancing the sudden social freedoms of college with the pressure of an academically challenging university.

I was launched into very challenging courses and in way over my head. I did spend some time studying and almost always went to class. I took good notes, but the tests and quizzes were very hard. I wasn't doing too well in Chemistry, and Calculus was kicking my ass. (I ended up failing Calculus and had to take it again, although I did okay in Chemistry.)

I was drinking more and more and before long, I wasn't just going out on Friday and Saturday nights. It had turned into Thursday, Friday and Saturday nights. Then I discovered there was a fraternity that had a couple kegs and really good, loud music in their basement every Wednesday night. My partying schedule quickly morphed into Wednesday, Thursday, Friday and Saturday nights. Then on Tuesday nights there was "Ladies Lock Up" at a favorite bar. From 7:00-9:00 p.m. it was ladies only and beers were only a dime! The only time I *wasn't* drinking was on Sunday and Monday nights, but even that would later change on occasion.

Don't get me wrong, I did not drink Tuesday through Saturday night every week. I don't want you to get that impression, but it didn't take long for me to drink many of those nights. One could find a way, an excuse or a place to drink, every night of the week. And have lots of great company doing it.

Drinking and guys went hand in hand. The thought of an actual relationship with any of them occurred to me but seemed like a bad idea. I knew I was incapable of making any real commitment. I especially loved the ones that drank like I did. I remember this nice guy who adored me but didn't drink. I ran from him like the plague. There were many others, however, that I ran towards.

The great thing about college was that I could always think of, and point the finger at, people who were more extreme than me.

The downside was that blending in with those people made my own behavior nearly impossible to identify.

I did go through formal rush. I wish I could say it was just about making good, solid friendships. Surely at a university of over twenty-two thousand students I knew I needed a little family. I'd like to say that was my main motivation. There was, however, the equally, if not more important motive of the social benefits of it all: the parties, socials and formals. I ended up pledging a great little southern belle sorority. I didn't like that they were all gorgeous and intelligent; I felt inferior and self-conscious. But, I put aside my insecurities and pledged them.

My sophomore and junior year were a blur of classes, exams and of course progressively more drinking. I was the only woman in my sorority who owned a monogrammed silver flask, given to me by my little sister. That's how my drinking was. And everyone knew it.

In hindsight, I recall a very lonely girl who was missing a chunk of herself. Yet, despite this, you would never know it at the time from the outside. I did have a lot of fun. I went on every spring break to warm destinations with friends. I spent a semester abroad in London and backpacked around Europe. I even went to Mardi Gras. My college years were the best years of my life.

Until my last semester.

That's when the shit hit the fan.

Mania Strikes

Semester from Hell

Although it was sixteen years ago, by typical memory standards, I fall short. Some of it is probably a case of selective memory, but I can remember things on the rare occasions if I let my mind go there. Memory lane of my last semester is not exactly a friendly place I care to visit often. My illness made a black mark on my college years, like a bad ending in a movie that was good up until the end. Those months my mania tarnished became a painful twist of wreckage whose disfigured parts took away the beauty of the whole.

I was already doomed because of my shenanigans from that summer. I had spent it in Colorado on a hotel internship required for my degree. I lived with a bipolar woman, dated a bipolar man and was caught in a spin cycle of insanity. We revolved around daily drunkenness, gambling and pot smoking.

It caught up with me and got shuffled into my manic deck. It blended in with the events and the hectic pace of any graduating senior's schedule, thereby making it hard to detect. It didn't take long for my brain to turn on me though, making it the strangest few months of my life.

I had one last semester to get through. I could practically *touch* the finish line. It was a close race for not only my diploma, but for my sanity as well. Somewhere in between my summer in Colorado and graduation in December of 1993, I lost my mind.

The hype of my final semester heightened because it was fall and our little town of Blacksburg transformed. It always came alive for our home football games. It was the usual blur of games and tailgates, beers and shots. I hid behind fake smiles and laughter. Not too far into the semester, it had become clear to those around me that I had lost my ability to make sound decisions of all sizes. I felt I was living an ever-present odd, uncomfortable and isolating existence. Never in my life had I felt so alone, even while surrounded by tens of thousands of people. I felt unable to connect or talk to people. I became very withdrawn living inside my head most of the time. Nothing and no one could have been in alignment with me for very long. I was in my own world and orbiting alone.

I was trying to do too many different things on so many levels. Although I was relatively active throughout my college days, there was a uniquely pressing need to accomplish more that semester. More than was possible even by most over-achievers' standards. All of a sudden, I felt it was my last semester and I should try to make dean's list. (Previously, I had never *cared* about it, much less thought about trying to achieve it.)

I also thought I should try to start a small catering company. Why not put to test what I'd been taught? I should become more involved in the H.M.A. (Hospitality Management Association) group and go on even more marketing and convention trips. Our sorority needed a new house to live in and I started my own personal crusade (which I'm not sure I told anyone about) to help research possible locations. In addition, I was working part-time.

There were a lot of shoulds that I did, or tried to, make happen.

While they sounded reasonable, when you added them up and threw in a touch of paranoia, it could no longer be labeled ambition. Intertwined with all of those shoulds were the ever present addictions that had always plagued and followed me.

Plus, it was tailgating season! The apartment I lived in was right behind the football stadium. It was the perfect location for tailgates that were before and after the games, as long as you *and* the keg lasted. I thought life and its responsibilities would soon take over, so I intended to make my last semester count.

I was going to parties, bars and tailgates which was a pretty normal occurrence during fall semester, except I was going alone. In fact, I preferred it. I once went to my neighbor's party after a football game and talked to no one. I sat outside on the railing of their balcony and was spitting over the side on purpose, in order to keep people away from me. They would look over at me and wonder what the hell I was doing. They only came near me because they had to. I was a few feet from the keg.

When the keg ran dry, I bought two more for these people whom I'd never met, at a party where I knew no one. I wasn't trying to be nice; I just needed a place to drink. (Naturally, I charged them despite the fact that I didn't have the money in my account to cover it. I had no concept of what was in my bank account.) I spit again to make sure no one came over to talk to me. I knew it was excessive, but I did it anyway. I didn't care.

"Hi." This blonde girl with dark roots (who was obviously *not* a blonde) came over and stood next to me while I sat hunched on the railing. Couldn't she see I was busy drinking and spitting to keep everyone away? I said nothing in return. Apparently my spitting trick was not working.

"I'm Kelly." She continued. *Kelly go away,* I thought.

"Hi." I had to say something, but made sure she knew I was not enjoying her presence by keeping it short.

"Do you know Chris? Or Scott? Or Mike?" I gathered these were the names of the guys for whom I just bought the two kegs.

"No."

"Wasn't it you who just bought the kegs?" She looked confused.

"Yeah." I offered no explanation and asked her no questions.

"Oh." She paused, trying to hide her confusion. "So what year are you?" She was trying to appear to be someone who rolled with the punches by keeping the conversation going. Much to my annoyance, she wasn't catching on.

"Senior."

"Graduating in May?"

"December." My one word replies weren't stopping her. I twisted around and spat off the balcony. That ought to give her a hint. I'm spitting even *while you're talking to me.* However, she barely flinched and kept the line of questioning going. I just wanted to be left alone with my beer. Which didn't seem to be getting me drunk enough (even though I'd already had quite a few).

"Oh wow! Good for you. You must be a little sad though. I'm only a junior. Where are you from?" What part of my body language saying *fuck off* was she missing? Should I spit *on* her?

"New Jersey." This was getting personal. I should've said *I'm from Fuck-off-Ville* and watched her face.

"Really? Meeeee too! What's your major?"

"Hotel Restaurant and Institutional Management" I replied in monotone. This was such a boring conversation. I felt like I was at sorority rush on the first day where nobody gives a crap what you say because it's all kind of bullshit anyway. Except she wasn't moving on to the next person fast enough.

"I'm a psych major." She nodded and looked at me without smiling, knowing full well that I hadn't asked. Of *course* she was a psych major! The weirdest people were psych majors because they were trying to figure out other people. All of which was just code for trying to figure out what was really wrong with *themselves. Well you can't figure me out, bitch. I'm just fucked up. Now leave me the fuck alone.* I said nothing back. Obviously, my internal dialogue must have showed that I was annoyed, bored and no longer playing along.

"I was just trying to be nice." She said under her breath, obviously disgusted, as she walked away.

I thought, *of course, you're the only bitch crazy enough to want to talk to me because you're a psych major!* It all made sense.

She disappeared inside and I was safe in my corner again. My kegs were keeping me company and would hopefully deter me from further intruders. Luckily, it worked. Nobody else tried talking to me. I could tell people hated coming over for refills by the look they gave me. I didn't care. That was the goal anyway.

Then I saw him. I could pick him out of any crowd with radar eyes. I recognized him instantly from his lacrosse hat worn so low it almost covered his eyes. It was this asshole who sexually assaulted me the previous year. We had met at my favorite bar, gotten stoned in the parking lot, and went back to my place.

While fooling around he went too far, hurt me and wouldn't stop. I should've woken up my roommates and their boyfriends. But he kept shushing and trying to pacify me like a hysterical little child. The bastard got away with it. Probably because I was high. Plus, I distinctly remember not wanting to wake everyone up and cause a scene. When I didn't wake anyone up, he knew he had me. Maybe deep down, since I had already been assaulted (at age fifteen), I didn't care.

Every time I had seen him since, a little alarm went off inside my body and today it was too loud to ignore. I couldn't stand to be near him. The scumbag was coming towards the keg and I had to get the hell off the balcony.

I blew past him, through the living room and headed for the door. Everything built up inside of me and I couldn't stop the tears that were welling up. When I started to cry on my way out, someone followed me outside. His name was Scott and as it turned out, it was his party.

"Hey." He called after me, confused. But I had already whizzed past him, out the door and down the stairs.

"No no no." I muttered underneath my breath and tears. I was worried I'd trip on the stairs as I could barely see them through my tears.

"Wait!" He persisted as he followed me down the stairs, almost as fast. I was already around the corner.

I broke down. The tears came flooding like a dam that was long overdue to break.

"Hey, are you okay?" He said as he approached me. I was half hoping he wouldn't find me, half hoping he would. His genuine concern relieved me instantly. Still, I felt so lost. I was beside myself, confused and borderline hysterical.

Unbeknownst to me, what was really happening was a complete unraveling. This was a chunk of my episode and only partly due to seeing the scumbag. But I couldn't put my finger on it. I had no idea what crap was going on inside my brain.

I leaned with my back up against the brick wall of his apartment building. It felt completely safe to break down alone but I had a feeling this guy was not letting me go.

"Are you okay?" He repeated as he tried to look into my eyes. I was scared to look up into his. My face was buried in my hands in shame.

I didn't reply, only nodded, cried and tried to gather myself, but it wasn't working. I put one foot up against the wall for support. I felt completely ashamed that I had broken down in front of this total stranger.

"Hi, I'm Scott." He extended his hand. It remained there, mid air, until I removed my hands from my face and shook it lamely. I felt depleted of energy, zapped of any feeling other than sorrow. The sound of his voice relaxed me.

"Hi, I'm Wendy. I live over there in #3. Look, I'm really sorry it's just that..."

"Shhh, it's okay. Don't worry about it." He didn't even need my explanation as he pulled me close. I remember feeling that it was the best hug I'd had in years. I felt everything was going to be okay and that he was safe.

"I'm sorry about your shirt." I apologized, embarrassed that I had just gotten snot on it.

"Ah, don't worry. I've got another one." We both started to laugh a little, and it was the first time I remembered doing so in a long time. He had such a gentle and funny way about him and I was grateful he made me smile.

I eventually pulled away and was drawing in the dirt with my shoe to avoid looking at him. I felt so vulnerable and stupid for crying. I was not one to cry and when I did, tried not to do it around anyone.

We started talking. We talked for hours and hours about everything that day and into the night. It was to be a bit of a foreshadowing that, even before my diagnosis weeks later, he and I got on the subject of mental illness. Scott told me his brother was mentally ill, had dropped out of college and randomly decided to join the circus. They didn't know what was wrong with him, but Scott thought he had heard his Dad say he was schizophrenic. He got kind of quiet about it but also seemed relieved to be talking about it openly because he said his family never talked about it. I learned he was from upstate New York and an engineering student. I knew Scott was intelligent. It was obvious he was also a straight up, good guy.

We hung out and kissed that night. He became my boyfriend, which was a blessing because I was lost. Scott was very good for me and I was lucky to have met him when I did. He made me breakfast and told me corny jokes to make me laugh. He bought me funny greeting cards that cheered me up, drawing cartoonlike pictures in them. He gave me mushy cards and told me he loved me. I was so far out there that I didn't have the capacity to fully love him back at that time, the way he deserved, but I tried to. He was the shelter in my storm, as in the Bob Dylan song.

We had endless conversations and I was constantly at his apartment. Scott and I played a lot of pinball at our favorite hangout downtown to blow off steam. Time spent with him was always a welcomed diversion from the chaos of my mind. He was a healthy influence on me and grounded me during a very unstable time.

Despite my instability, I managed to work part-time at an environmental company for some extra cash. I was photocopying, making phone calls and doing light computer work. I photocopied manuals and documents that had highly sensitive information in them.

The company I worked for collaborated with the EPA on its findings about radiation and contamination levels of various locations. I tried not to look at where these contaminations were, but I felt like I had super smarts and could quickly scan the information during photocopying. I began to *feel* like I had a photographic memory (even though I did not).

Photocopying and organizing the pages (although they were in order the whole time) became difficult and stressful as the semester went on and my mania grew. The other part-timer would make comments under his breath about contaminated sites when we were in the photocopy room together. It freaked me out. I would look at the documents more closely and it made me increasingly paranoid.

Also, one creepy engineer (who I didn't like) needed flowcharts made. He had me go through the program's tutorial since I was unfamiliar with the program. It was supposed to be an easy program and even had "ABC" in its name. I felt stupid and restless and useless. I had to start it over and over and wanted to rip my hair out. It was impossible to concentrate!

The skeevy engineer kept popping his head in his office (where I sat at his computer) saying, "You think this is *hard?*" or "You started it over *again?*" or "You'll be a college grad soon. Surely you can do *this!*" He seemed to be enjoying the fact that I was struggling. I remember his quizzical look as if I were a puzzle he could not solve and that bothered him. The fact that he couldn't was the only satisfaction I got.

I felt an internal eruption building and told the office manager Linda I had to quit.

"Linda, I can't work here anymore." I said, disappointed in myself. Why couldn't I handle this easy job? "I'm under too much pressure. It's just too much."

"It's not doing rocket science, Wendy. You're just photocopying." Linda said perplexed. I predicted she wouldn't understand.

"I'm sorry, Linda. I can't."

"You're not doing that many hours. Do you need to cut back more?"

"I'm sorry. That's not it. I just can't handle one more thing right now." To her, I was simply photocopying, doing flowcharts and it was only ten hours per week.

Why bother going into how photocopying made my head feel like exploding. That it was sheer torture trying to concentrate on anything. Or how much I detested the creepy engineer who basked in some sick delight as he watched me struggle, inept at the program he could do blindfolded. I certainly couldn't explain (even to myself at the time) my inability to do simple tasks or my increasing paranoia. I didn't need the aggravation for the little pay I was making. I quit.

In the meantime, I got a catering gig. Let me rephrase that. I *started* a catering gig. I decided it seemed like a fabulous idea to try to put everything I had learned at Tech to good use. Could I pull it off and make a high enough profit margin? Let's test it out, I thought. I persuaded my roommate's boyfriend to let me do a lasagna dinner for them at their fraternity house.

It was a *disaster*! While in line, one of the brothers noticed I had the rolls in a plastic container that said "cat box" on the side. (It was a *new* cat box of course, that I bought in a flurry at the grocery store but forgot to remove the label... it was the perfect size for the rolls!) How could they have known it was a *new* cat box? I was mortified.

Needless to say, it was my one and only gig in the catering biz. I paid my two assistants most of my profits and felt a slight satisfaction that I did pull it off with a higher than average profit margin. If it weren't for the cat box label mishap, it wouldn't have been so bad. I think.

It didn't help matters that I went away on little marketing trips wherever and whenever possible with the hospitality club. I was always active in my major in this respect, going on many trips ever since my freshman year to gain experience for marketing different hotels and resorts in Virginia. They gave us free accommodations (always midweek when they had lower occupancy) and in return, we did marketing blitzes for them, mostly cold calling and some telemarketing.

There were also trade shows that semester. In between classes, football games, and the part-time job (before I quit), I was dashing off on those trips every chance I got. It was another excuse to party, and a free pass to do so. It always got me out of class with a valid reason. I was in all hospitality classes, so the professors understood and excused my absences if I made up the work. I got behind though. Of course it didn't help that we always partied wherever we went, digging me further into my episode.

At a restaurant convention in Richmond one week, trouble followed me home. After I had stayed up all night partying on the last night there, I drove home with no sleep. I had to get to get back to Tech that next morning for, of all things, my one credit step aerobics class. I could not afford to miss one more class or I would fail. If I failed, *I would not get my diploma*. It was a race down to the last class, the last credit. I *had* to make it back in time!

I was minutes from campus when I fell asleep at the wheel.

I felt the ground change.

I suddenly awoke, jerked my head up and saw I was headed right for a huge, grassy dip in the center of the highway. Straight for the bushes and trees.

I swerved to get back on the road and crossed both lanes with a screech.

Somehow I ended up safely on the shoulder, on the other side of the highway.

There wasn't a single car on the road.

The car wasn't drivable, but I was okay and didn't hurt anyone else. Thank God. I sat there for a few moments in shock. The impact of what had just happened, or what had been narrowly averted, hadn't hit me yet.

The next thing I knew, there were tons of cars in both directions. It was rush hour traffic and had it happened one minute later, even thirty seconds later, this would have been a different story. I knew God or an angel had saved me.

Within what felt like seconds, but could have been minutes, an older pickup truck pulled over. The man leaned over, rolled down his passenger window, and asked me if I was okay. Still in shock, but already at ease with this man, I said yes.

He told me to jump in, and just like that, I did. I trusted him instantly, sensing he was somehow special. Like a person who, although a stranger, was someone I once knew. This man was mystical in some way and held some kind of unmistakable spiritual link to me. Although it was bewildering, his presence simultaneously calmed me.

"Be careful now." He gave me a stern, concerned look, tipped his cowboy hat, and drove away.

I felt confused as I stood there watching him leave and decided he must be an angel. I was feeling more connected to God and my angels than ever.

I realized I was lucky to get out of it all unscathed. It was the first time it occurred to me that maybe I should've slept a little the night before. Yet, it was more a fleeting moment of clarity, rather than the temporary arrival of sanity. Even right after a near accident of epic proportions, I dismissed it as quickly as the thought came. My judgment was way off, although I had no idea how off it truly was.

Things *truly* took a turn for the worse that semester when I started hanging out with a seemingly decent fellow we all knew as K.C.

The K.C. I knew prior to that semester was a nerdy accounting major. A very bright guy who I met way back during freshman year. K.C. (which stood for "Kurt's Cousin") wore plaid button-up shirts and outdated glasses. K.C. often smiled a shy, nervous smile and I got the impression that he liked me by the way he acted goofy and weird around me. I had even met his parents walking on the drillfield one weekend and they too seemed like nice, southern folks. I think he would have *remained* harmless were it not for his bad influence, drug-dealing, derelict cousin Kurt. I knew nothing about Kurt until my horrific last semester when I met him.

One night, I brought a backpack full of books and homework that I intended to work on to Kurt's house near campus. K.C. had work that night too, so the plan was to do a little work, then play. It was the first time I had gone to Kurt's house and it was scary. It was also the first time I met Kurt and *he* was scary. Kurt was one shady dude and didn't go to our school, despite living in Blacksburg. Nor did he go to any college in the area, for that matter. He only preyed upon college kids to sell them drugs.

Instinctively, I knew it was not a good idea to be near Kurt, much less at his house. But K.C. was a good guy and willing to get me stoned for free. He wouldn't do anything to harm me. Or so I thought.

Despite my heavy pot smoking and drinking, this particular night was significant because up until that point I'd never taken or done any other drug, besides pot. I had a healthy fear of acid and all types of harder drugs. (The occasional party acquaintance who offered it here or there, always got turned down.) But this one night, everything took a turn for the worse and catapulted my condition. I believe now that the weed K.C. and Kurt gave me to smoke was laced.

I distinctly remember they insisted I get high first. This not only confused me, but the abnormally excited, creepy looks on their faces freaked me out as well. Not at all the typical stoner look of someone simply waiting for a toke. There was something almost anticipatory about them. Like they were waiting for my *reaction*, which I sensed, and it made me nervous. I felt uneasy, but chalked it up to being with K.C.'s derelict cousin, in his very shady drug house.

After taking a few hits, I immediately felt very weird. It was a different high. I'd never experienced this before. I looked over at them, feeling really odd, and saw them exchange looks and laugh. I felt like I was on the outside of a joke. It was making me uneasy. I had changed from Wendy into this strange, paranoid girl. Clearly, I was already headed into the eye of the storm: destination episode. However, I'm convinced that whatever the pot was laced with (it was probably angel dust) was the gasoline that added fuel to my episode's fire.

Kurt had a pet iguana that suddenly fascinated me. I knelt by its cage and studied it. The eyes on the iguana scared me with each, slight flicker. I was transfixed on them and couldn't tear myself away. I kept waiting for it to move even though it rarely did. I didn't mind though, as I ended up sitting next to the cage on the floor for a long time.

The next memory I have is standing in the kitchen and staring at the floor. It was one of those black and white checkered tiled floors. It seemed to be an intricate pattern that I had to figure out, despite the fact that there was nothing to figure out because it was perfectly symmetrical. That's the last thing I remember that night.

After that night, things got *really* weird. My memory was becoming like Swiss cheese - full of holes. I was staying up all night regularly. Since I couldn't do this at my boyfriend's place (he was always busy studying for his big engineering exams), I would stay up at my place or other places. I didn't want to be at my apartment. Anywhere, but there.

There was an apartment full of guys whom I knew and it was safe to hang out there. They were close friends of my friend, George. They told me I could come over anytime and watch cable and hang out. I hated staying at my apartment and as my mania grew that semester, so did that feeling. I liked being out, roaming and not sleeping, wherever possible.

I went to their apartment one night. It was unlocked and I let myself in. All their bedroom doors were closed and I plopped myself and my backpack down on the couch. I found MTV using the remote.

I stayed up all night watching MTV. The song "Everybody Hurts" by R.E.M. came on. I was so grateful they made the song that helped me feel better. It told me someone else knew exactly how I felt. I was hurting and lonely and sad. But it gave me hope, to hold on despite my loneliness. I watched the music video on MTV and identified with the characters. It made me want to cry and I needed to cry, but tears weren't coming.

Music was always doing that, giving me hope and making me feel. I needed not only to *hear* it, I also needed to *see* it. That night, I really did need MTV so I could do both. I connected with music because I wasn't connecting with much else, believe me. I could barely talk to people. I was talking *at* them.

The next morning, I wanted to get out of the apartment before everyone woke up. It wasn't dark, but it was the time of morning just before the rest of the world was awake. I took a shower and put last night's clothes back on. While I was in there, I heard two of them talking. Shit! I was hoping I could shower and leave unnoticed.

Now they were really gonna think I was weird since I could've and should've showered at my own place. I left my shoes and backpack there. Why? I don't remember exactly.

I walked to campus barefoot. On the way, I saw a leaf pile and decided to lay in it. I felt unusually free. Free of rules, shoes, books, restrictions. Free like a hippie. I was in charge of my own destiny. I knew if people drove by and saw me there, they would think it was weird, but I didn't care. Nobody was driving or walking to classes yet, it was still early enough. Why not do what I want?

I studied the sky and how cool the clouds looked. Like bunches of cotton candy against the bright blue sky. I stayed in that leaf pile for a good twenty minutes just thinking. Although I felt a little cold, I thought it was okay to be barefoot with wet hair in the late fall. Why not? Most people would say that was wrong, but was I out of my mind? I hated shoes. I was defiant. In my mind, I was just being original, unique. Certainly not crazy or manic.

Suddenly, I was bursting with energy, like I had just awakened from a deep sleep and been given a thousand cups of coffee. I had to get out of this leaf pile and get to campus fast! I had to tell Eldora my epiphanies...

Eldora was the manager for the floral department where I worked in special events the semester before. We still kept in touch and I would drop by from time to time to keep her up-to-date. She was a motherly figure to me during my last two years at Tech and reminded me of Thelma, my first babysitter. Eldora would hear about my shenanigans of the night before and shake her head. She used to give me advice (which I never took), then tell me what to do for the work shift. She could get quite bossy, that Eldora, but I loved her anyway.

Eldora wasn't there that day so I talked to Cruz, who I ran into just outside of Eldora's office. It wasn't an office, rather a space in the basement of the dining hall.

Cruz was a divorced, middle-aged guy, real nice, with a big, thick, out-of-date mustache like they used to wear in the seventies. I always thought he had a cool name. It sounded like the name of a stuntman or action guy from a would-be C-grade mini-series. I always thought Cruz could do so much more than just be a dining hall supervisor, but having benefits and working for the university was a good job in a small town such as this, I kept reminding myself. This was no metropolitan area where you had your pick of the litter. And there were no seventies series scouts looking for fresh meat in these here parts.

I cornered him and began professing all my ideas about life. All the while, he looked at me with big, wide eyes like he was scared of me.

"Where are your shoes?" Was all he could say after I paused. He looked down at my feet like I had no toes. He turned and entered the huge walk-in refrigerator with a clipboard in his hand. I assumed he was doing inventory and followed him in. He turned around, alarmed that I was now inside the refrigerator with him, with no shoes on.

"I don't need them." I realized it must've looked funny to him. But Cruz could not think outside the box. He was not one of those kinds of guys. He couldn't appreciate a hippie like me.

"Wendy, *where are your shoes?*" Cruz spelled it out slower for me. He was alarmed and even getting slightly angry at me. I was sensing by his reaction that he just wasn't *understanding* me. He looked at me, then down to my feet again then back to my head. He was ignoring what I was saying, all my great *ideas* that I was going on and on about. He looked at me like I was a martian.

"I left them at a friend's house. Listen Cruz, I was thinking,

41

maybe I should look up my biological father. I mean, do you think that's a good idea? I think I want to write a book and it might be crucial that I..." I was jumping from one topic to the next, going on and on, when he stopped me mid-sentence.

"And your hair! Why is your hair wet?" His eyes were wide open and he had a look of terror on him. As if he spotted a tornado heading right for him.

"Because I don't care. Cruz, you're not *listening* to me!" I was getting really frustrated with him.

"But it's *October*, Wendy! It's *cold* out." I couldn't believe he was so fixated on everything physical. It's *cold* out. You need to wear your *shoes*. Dry your *hair*. He was completely missing everything and not listening to what I was saying. He just kept staring at me. I started to follow him upstairs.

"I never blowdry my hair! I hate hairdryers! I don't even *own* one!" He stopped climbing the stairs and turned around. He was visibly upset, looking down at me with concern. This was a man who used to flirt with me. I used to think he was a dirty old man. Now he had switched to the concerned fatherly type. (His reaction towards me scared me a bit that day, I have to admit. Just a little, but not for long.) As I looked at him, I wondered if he had kids, the way he was acting so fatherly towards me and all. He turned around and started climbing the rest of the stairs.

"Wendy, go home...and dry your hair." He called back at the top stair. He opened the door to the dining hall halfway and turned around.

"But I have to..." I was right on his heels, a few steps from the door.

"And find your shoes!" He slammed the door.

I walked back to my apartment where I began pacing. I had

to figure everything out! My roommate stood there, watching me with a concerned look. I kept pacing back and forth, back and forth, thinking, ever thinking and I began ranting. (She later told me that I had been pacing for hours, though the way I remember it, it seemed more like ten or fifteen minutes.)

Her eyes were wide, her fingers curled loosely near her mouth like she was trying to concentrate and solve a problem. She was simply watching me, but not talking to me. I was not talking with her or anyone. I was incapable of holding a conversation. It was more of a diatribe with the air aimed at God only knows who.

Wheels In Motion

Before long, my roommate called my parents and said, "Something is wrong with Wendy." Eldora was onto me, too. I had gone to her house one afternoon and was ranting and raving. By this point, nearly all my emotions and expressions had turned into anger aimed at my parents for no real reason. While I was pacing and spewing nasty things about them, Eldora had a friend on the phone who was a doctor. He stopped Eldora mid-conversation and asked her what was going on in the background. He listened in, alerted her and it prompted Eldora to call my Mom. My Mom called her friend, who was a therapist, and repeated what Eldora and my roommate had both said to her.

"I don't like the sound of this, Barbara," my Mom's therapist friend said to her. "I would get down there right away."

"Okay. I have to get a hold of Jerry." My Mom said to her friend.

"Where is he?"

"He's up hunting with his friends at Val's cabin."

"Can't you call him?"

"There's no cell phone coverage. They're way up in the mountains."

My Mom finally got in touch with my Dad, told him something was wrong with me and that she was leaving the next day for Tech.

She told him she'd received calls from two different people saying how strangely I was acting. Her baby cub was in trouble and mama bear was coming.

"I'll leave right away, too." My Dad left immediately and drove down. The troops were rallying, although I had no idea I was even at war. I actually thought it was a social visit, although I did find it slightly peculiar that they were coming now. Why now, since we were only six weeks away from graduation? I was the last to know what was going on. I was right in the middle, my brain was the very cause of all of this, yet I was the last to understand.

Meanwhile, Eldora had me go to the on campus counseling center. She made the emergency appointment for me and made me promise I would go. I went to humor her since she went through the trouble to make the appointment. I had no idea that her doctor friend told her I needed help *or* that she had called my Mom. It was a covert operation.

When I got there, I was told to fill out this questionnaire while I waited to be seen. The lady who handed it to me was the receptionist. I filled it out with lots of details. I made it very confusing. I did this to make sure they understood I was complex and deep. One question said "Who referred you?" I responded "my friend: thank God."

I had all the warning signs. That questionnaire was so marked up by the time I got through with it that it didn't take a psychologist or anyone with any training to ascertain that I was in deep trouble. (Despite my feeling at the time that she didn't have much training, she may have for all I know. I'm grateful now they even *had* a counseling center. Most schools back then did not.)

Counselor Lady looked at me with those same wide eyes that everyone else did. You could see the fear in them. But at that moment (through my manic arrogance goggles), all I chose to see was her presumed inexperience. It looked at first like she was reading off my answers and simply going down the list. She looked up at me as if she was about to ask me something, then paused.

"I'll be right back." Counselor Lady said nervously bringing my paperwork with her. I thought she must need to ask someone how to proceed, not because I was a code red.

While she was gone, I soaked up my surroundings. It was a good thing I wasn't claustrophobic because this place was as small as a shoebox. And why was every office always painted white? Would it kill them to splash a little color in here? I mean, you know, spice it up a little and give us something to *look* at? I looked out the one teeny tiny window but there wasn't much of a view. Geez, a shoebox office with a view of nothing. It tells you where Counselor Lady ranked in the big scheme of things.

I sat there with my great stack of books in my lap that I'd been carrying around that day. It was my shield of armor. I was there to do battle. I had to prove to them and Eldora that I didn't need them *or* their help. My books provided comfort. (Not that it occurred to me to crack open a single one of these books that I *had* to have with me.) She returned.

"It says here you were referred to us." She was quick, this one.

"Yes."

"And who referred you?" Keep reading lady, I'm not going to spoon feed you all the answers. Okay, let's get these boring basics out of the way. I tried to be compliant but this was going too slow for me. I was horribly bored.

"My friend Eldora." I saw Counselor Lady's eyes widen and I knew she had seen the "thank God" part. I wondered if she saw my Bible amongst the many books I was carrying. Maybe she thought I was a religious freak now, too. Whatever lady, just move this along.

"Okay, friends. I see it here." Yes, then why ask me these stupid questions? I remained quiet, anticipating the next question on the list but couldn't remember what it was. I think it was the 'plans after graduation thing.' No, maybe it was the 'why are you here' thing. This is lame. I don't need help. What the hell am I *doing* here?

"You have down that you are graduating in December?"

"Yes." Come on already. This was really getting annoying. Tick tock. Didn't I have anything better to do? Unfortunately, I couldn't think of anything.

"Wait one moment okay? I'm sorry, I'll be right back." Well, at least she apologized, I thought.

"Okay." I said. She was still wet behind the ears, poor thing. Counselor Lady had to be new, probably fresh out of some two-week training course. It was clear she didn't know what the heck she was doing. She seemed afraid of her own shadow; I didn't think Counselor Lady was cut out for this kind of work. Then again, how hard could it be to regurgitate answers to the questions I'd already answered? I sat there alone patiently but kept thinking there *had* to be something better I could be doing with my time. She came back. Marvelous.

"So what are your plans after college?" I was getting tired of these questions...blah blah blah. Why was I even here? Eldora said she had made an appointment for me to "talk" to someone at the counseling center. That was all I was told. This woman was not really talking to me. She was reading these questions aloud and it was annoying me. This was getting soooooo old fast. This wasn't helping me, but I was humoring Eldora, I reminded myself.

"I don't know. I thought about law school. I'm not sure yet." I tossed around the idea as if I had a bunch of options. I mean, I did get an A in my Hotel Law class and our professor said, "If you get an A in this class, you would make a good lawyer." So maybe I could be a lawyer? Why not? I was just throwing it out there. I wanted her to know I was smart enough, that I *could* go to law school if I wanted to. I had options. I had choices. I was going places.

I looked down at the book on the top of my heap. I had just bought it a few days ago at the bookstore on campus. It was a collection of speeches by Dr. Martin Luther King, Jr. It was on sale, of course, so I couldn't pass it up. Counselor Lady saw I was off in my own world and followed my glance down to my books. I know she had to wonder about them. Was she looking at the titles? Was she impressed?

"That's quite a stack of books you have there." She nodded her head slowly. Was that a slight smile? I think I did impress her, or at least I had her interest maybe? Or was this all part of the act of sizing me up. Maybe she'd be writing all of this down. I was ready to explain my reason for each book and was hoping she was going to ask. She didn't of course.

Counselor Lady had said something I missed. I was in my own world and not being present for Questions 101. This was *such* a drag.

"I'm sorry, what did you say?" I felt slightly bad asking her to repeat herself. It didn't take a genius to figure out I checked out of this conversation.

"I said I want to make an appointment for you." She repeated. "Will you come outside with me? No, actually can you wait just another moment?" Counselor Lady disappeared again, this time for a little longer. I was starting to wonder about this disappearing act. Did she have a manual in the bathroom or what? She returned.

"Okay, thanks again." She greeted me with a smile. This looked like a smile of relief that our session was coming to a close. I'm with you on that, sister. "I have an appointment for you to see our psychiatrist on staff." *Psychiatrist? What?* I missed something here. Counselor Lady handed me one of those official doctor appointment cards.

"A shrink? Seriously?" I laughed. I couldn't believe her assessment of me ended in an appointment to see a shrink.

"So, here's your card for that." Counselor Lady was all business like, and turned to write something down in my file.

"Great. Thanks." I said confused as I put the card in my Filofax. I couldn't believe it had escalated so quickly from this appointment to seeing the school shrink! I noticed the card said tomorrow on it. Wow, that was fast, I thought. What's all the rush? She's obviously a *bored* shrink. Her schedule must need filling up or something.

"You mentioned earlier that your Mom was coming down for a visit?"

"Yeah, she told me this morning she's coming down. I'm picking her up tomorrow."

I was very confused. I didn't see that I was there because of any problems I was having. I was not putting the pieces of the puzzle together at that point. I thought I was just there to pacify Eldora. I thought this lady was just following protocol. Sign 'em up, get 'em out.

"Well, good luck to you Wendy." Counselor Lady said with a nervous smile. *She had to lose this nervousness if she was gonna make it,* I thought. She held my file close to her body and walked me out.

"Okay, bye. Thank you." I said as I walked away. What was I thanking her for? Wasting my time? Referring me to a shrink? Counselor Lady was nice though. She tried.

Without missing a beat, I popped by that afternoon to see a management professor I had my sophomore year whom I loved, just adored. Everyone who had him loved him. He was voted favorite professor in several informal student polls. People took his class just to be in his presence because there was something unmistakably special about him.

He taught dry management courses in the business school, but spiced them up and made them fun. His personality was what really made the boring material bearable. We loved watching him erase with his shirtsleeve out of passion. His eyes always lit up in excitement during his stories. (During one class, he actually showed the film "Casablanca" and served popcorn. He was famous for that move.) Dr. Rubinsky would always apologize in advance before handing out tests and quizzes. He said he felt badly that he had to grade and therefore, judge us. He muttered to himself a lot. We all knew he was brilliant. By far, he was the greatest professor we'd all had at Tech.

I ran over to go see him and knocked on his door, which was all the way at the end of the hall. Everything was so spread out at Tech. I was starting to get shin splints from all this running around.

"Hello, Dr. Rubinsky?" I saw him seated at his desk. He was almost always at his desk; we all swore he lived there. "Hi, can I, um, talk to you?" He had a zillion books in his office, so much that there was barely any room for anybody or anything else. He was rumored to have lived in a trailer with just as many books and no TV or phone. I could believe it. This guy was a genius.

"Hey, Wendy, how are you?" He whirled around in his chair, all smiles. I had his class three years earlier, yet he still knew my first name which always amazed me. I popped in once in a while because he was a person you never wanted to say goodbye to. He saw the look on my face, even still, his smile did not wane. "What's the matter?"

I told him how confused I was and everything that was happening. I said a lot of shit was going down. Although I didn't say my mind was in turmoil, he seemed to understand it. He, unlike Cruz, knew me a little better and took time out for me. After I was done ranting, he looked up at me and gently responded.

"Wendy, you're like Job." He chuckled.

"What?" I had no idea what he was talking about.

"You know, Job. The book of Job in the Bible."

"Oh," It was starting to ring a bell, but a very faint bell. "What happens in the book of Job?" I asked him.

"You should read it." He said, face still beaming.

"Tell me. I won't be reading it anytime soon."

"Read it." He saw my face and continued. "Well, okay, basically everything happens to him. All this crap, horrible stuff, one thing after another. But he comes out fine. He has faith. You're going to be alright Wendy. Just like Job." He chuckled to himself again. "You're just like Job." He kept smiling, shaking his head and laughing.

"Everything works out for him in the end, though?"

"Yes, you'll get through this. It'll all work out okay. Have faith." This was interesting because we had never talked about anything like this before. Dr. Rubinsky and I had a deeper connection than I had ever had with any other professor. Yet we had never before spoken of anything spiritual or religious. He did make me feel like maybe it was going to be okay. Could he be right?

"Well, you see, I *think* I'm supposed to write this book. You know, about everything I'm going through. I don't know what exactly. I even chose a pen name this summer." Most people, by that point, would have smiled and said something half encouraging, but you knew they were thinking 'yeah okay kid. Good luck with that.' Not him. He was listening sincerely and not laughing at the idea. He didn't say "you're crazy", or "go talk to someone." He took me dead serious.

"What do you know about publishing?" I continued. I knew he had written a book, so it was worth a shot.

"Not much, but I can give you the name of my editor. She's more into the scholastic book type stuff though. She's real nice, Linda, you'd like her. She just left for London, I think, but she'll be back soon. Here's her name and number. Call her when she gets back. Just tell her you know me." He wrote it down on a scrap of paper. He always had scraps of paper everywhere. He handed it to me and smiled again. It was like he had all the faith in the world in me and I felt it. Even in the state I was in. Even in the state he could *see* I was in.

"Thanks Dr. Rubinsky." I slipped the paper into the compartment of my Filofax and zipped it up.

"No problem. And I'm sorry, Wendy."

"Sorry for what?" I had no idea what he was talking about.

"Sorry if I wronged you with your grade when you took my class."

"You didn't. Don't worry."

"I hate giving grades. I hate judging minds. Sorry, sorry." He was always muttering and repeating.

"I think I got a B. Maybe a C. I don't know. It doesn't matter. Really, you didn't wrong me, honestly." He was always apologizing to everyone about having to give us grades.

"Okay. Well take care of yourself."

"Thanks Dr. Rubinsky. You too."

"Keep in touch, let me know how you are." He chuckled. It was almost a nervous chuckle or something.

"I will."

I was not laughing. Everything was serious to me. Even Dr. Rubinsky hadn't made me smile. He made me feel *better*, but I was *not* smiling. My sense of humor was long gone.

The whole time I felt chosen by God. If you asked me how, I wouldn't have had a clear, exact explanation to give you as to *how* exactly, except to say I knew I had to clean up my act. I felt like I was an example of why you should not smoke pot. That if you did, you could end up like me. Maybe it was my guilt and shame for all of the pot smoking I had done and was doing, especially that summer. Maybe it was my remorse over the collective promiscuity of my college years. Maybe it was the car accident.

In hindsight, I think it was all of it. It was a remote, vague feeling of not so much punishment, rather I should straighten up and fly right. I was translating this collective guilt into merely wanting to be better. I wasn't willing to stop drinking. But I realized I *should* quit smoking pot. That was my big epiphany.

I set up camp at a bar that I hadn't frequented prior to that semester. A dumpy bar called the Underground. It had better beer on tap, which was what it was known for, and probably its only redeeming quality. For a few weeks, that was my hang out.

I would carry around a large drawing tablet, the kind an artist would use, in which I wrote down all my ideas. I always sat at the same table in the window and people knew to find me there. The underclassmen in my major who would party and get high with me (prior to my stop-smoking-pot epiphany) would come sit with me. They'd listen to me, although I have no idea what I talked about — probably just boring, rambling bullshit. I thought I was prophetic, that what I was saying was quite the opposite of bullshit and somehow very important. I had a mini-audience, which made it worse and fed my hungry ego.

Those few underclassmen were buying my bullshit. *I* was buying my bullshit. Suddenly, I felt like I was some super smart college student who was too good for studying and preferred to converse at bars. Not get wasted at that point mind you, just talk in endless dribble about God knows what to God knows who.

One day, I had gotten back from being at the Underground and my roommate, Linda was in her room watching her soaps. I could never understand how she was so addicted to them. Hers was the only TV we had in the whole apartment, but she wouldn't put it in the living room. She swung outside her bedroom door when she heard me in the hallway.

"Is your car still at Kurt's?"

"Yeah." She knew it was because it wasn't parked outside our apartment. I had gotten a flat and had to leave it at Kurt's.

"And it has been how many days?"

"Like three or something. Why?"

"You know, my father is in the FBI. They have offices all over, even in small towns. *They know what's going on, Wendy.* Especially with drugs. They *watch* what goes on," she said looking at me suspiciously. This was a vicious move on her part, I thought. Linda knew all about K.C.'s cousin and what went on over at his house. I was pretty sure she was trying to scare me. How could the F.B.I. possibly know about what was going on at that stupid little house? *In Blacksburg?* We were pretty good friends, so her springing the FBI thing on me seemed kind of mean.

"What are you talking about?"

"Your car, at Kurt's house? He's bad news, Wendy."

"It's just my car there." She was successfully scaring me. I mean, not everyone knew he was bad news, surely. I'm sure a good number did, though. Paranoia was setting in. I was starting to believe her. The longer I let my car stay outside Kurt's house, the greater the chance there was of the local F.B.I. putting me together with them. Linda never mentioned her father was in the F.B.I. What did I know about her anyway? She could be fucking with me. But if she wasn't, I mean, were the neighbors aware of what was going on there? Surely they *could* have a clue. My car, my plates were there in plain sight.

"That's all I'm saying. The F.B.I. is everywhere, Wendy. My father has been in it for twenty-seven years. They'll think you're involved with him. *Think* about it." She closed the door, turned up her TV and left me staring at her closed door.

Linda had me thinking now. *Was* Linda telling me the truth about what she knew about the F.B.I. in small towns? *Did* she have my back? Was this paybacks or the truth? Hard to tell. It rattled around in my brain like a lotto ball, driving me nuts. F.B.I. or no F.B.I., I had to get my car out of there. And fast.

We had started out on the same team, amicable. It was me and a sorority sister, plus two other roommates we had found from a list at the housing office. We weren't all best buds, but it worked. Now it was World War III and I had no allies. Linda had instilled in me a microchip of paranoia. Or was she still an ally? The worst thing was I couldn't tell. I felt so alone.

The reason I wasn't getting along with the last one, the grad student roommate, was my fault really. Still, it didn't help that she was retaliating. You see, she was having sex, really loud sex one night with her annoying boyfriend. Actually, it was *more* than one night but this one night was obnoxiously loud, like I'd never heard before, except in the movies. I thought, how rude!

Well, one weekend her sister was visiting and I somehow managed to make a very inappropriate comment about it. It was wrong of me, but it flew out of my mouth before I knew it. Everyone just looked at me. After that incident, she was out to get me. The war was on.

She knew at the time I was losing my mind before *I* knew (because I was the last to know). From then on that semester, she would take every opportunity to play with my head.

One time, she took a phone message that she had retraced every other letter really well, darkening it over and over so that it looked really weird. Maybe to anyone else it would've looked just funny or as if she was doodling, but to me, I swore she was playing with my mind. I swear, to this day I believe she did it on purpose. She wasn't one to sit around and doodle on phone messages — if you know what I mean. And it happened right after the sex comment that I made to her sister. I kept that message to remind myself that she was an enemy. I taped it up in my room.

It was not only her. I felt like almost *everyone* was against me. It was paranoia all the way around. I wasn't popular around the apartment and I didn't want to be there. I liked to be out roaming around. I wanted to be *anywhere* but there. I didn't even like being in my room, but if I ever was in the apartment, that was the only place I'd be.

My sorority sister roommate was the first one who called my parents to say I needed help. At the time, I was not appreciative of her efforts. I felt betrayed. (It was only after that semester was over and I had distance from it all that I could see how much her intervention helped me.) But then, to me she was an enemy. That semester, nearly *everyone* was an enemy. The list of allies was very short, indeed.

Always an ally was Eldora. I called her up and told her about my visit to the counseling center. She brought me to a fast food restaurant that afternoon, before I picked up my Mom.

"You need to eat something."

"I don't wanna eat."

"Please?" She was on my case.

"No Eldora. I don't feel hungry."

"You have to eat *something*. Come on now. How 'bout a baked potato?" She had gotten in line and was calling out to me. "What do you like on your baked potato?"

I said nothing. I felt badly, but I really didn't want to eat. I wanted to fast. She came back with a bunch of greasy food.

"Come on, you got to eat, Wendy." She bought me a baked potato, despite my protest and put a glob of sour cream on it.

"Thanks, Eldora."

"Fries?" She continued. "How 'bout some fries?" She had a cute southern accent. She tried hard to get me to eat and was so kind to me. I felt badly and took a few bites. "I got you a small shake too!" She was excited and started eating. My grandmother loved those things, also. Maybe it was a grandmother thing.

"I don't need to eat. I'm fasting." I declared. I knew Jesus fasted. I knew that I was not Jesus or at all Jesus like, but I did have a sense that I was trying to reinvent myself. A cleanse-the-soul if you will. I needed some sort of purification after stopping my pot use and knew I could go without much food. "Where's your car?" Eldora asked me where my car was because I hadn't ever walked to her house before.

"I got a flat tire. It's outside this guy, Kurt's house."

"Who's Kurt?" Eldora did not know the ins and outs of my current life. She wasn't my boss anymore. I used to tell her about my shenanigans when I worked under her. She could never keep it all straight, but boy did she give my parents an earful when she finally did meet them a few weeks later. (She nearly gave them a heart attack!) I told her that I'd gotten a flat outside the drug dealer's house, who was the cousin of the guy K.C., who I knew. She was following along but listening with half an ear, concentrating on her food. Eldora liked her food.

I told her that I thought his cousin spiked the pot I was smoking one day with something else, which caused a strange reaction. She was looking at me now, chewing with her mouth open. I was thinking I said too much.

"Drugs, Wendy? You know, I don't even want to know." Eldora was shaking her head. "You're a smart girl. What's *wrong* with you?" It wasn't a question; it was more of a statement. It was hard to miss that she was disgusted. But Eldora was no stranger to problems. She had kids and grandkids and I knew they weren't all angels.

"Which one has the house? K.C.? Kurt?" She was trying to follow.

"Kurt."

"I'm confused. It doesn't matter. Where is your car now? And *how* did you get mixed up with these two? Girl, you have *got* to keep your legs closed." She was frozen, mid fry. Then she shook her head, resumed eating and reached for her drink. I was pissed off. She liked to talk to me like I was a whore sometimes.

"First off, I never hooked up with *either* of them. And second, well um, it's a long story."

"Um hmm. It always is." She finished her fry and grabbed a few more. "Well, when we're done here, we'll go get your car." Eldora was eyeing the dessert on her tray. It was making me sick looking at all this food.

"Eldora, my car has a flat. How are we gonna get it to the station?"

"Well, where's his house?"

"Off South Main." I described where the house was.

"Well then it's only two blocks away from the Gulf Station. Drive it on your flat to the station slowly. It'll be fine."

"It's okay. My Mom's flying in tomorrow."

"Suit yourself."

Then my mind flashed to what Linda said about the F.B.I. Damn her! What if she was right? Then I *should* get it out of there today. But I was done with Eldora and her lectures about eating and whom

I should and shouldn't hang out with. And her comments! No, I'll take my chances and wait until my Mom comes down. Oh, another explanation for Mom tomorrow. Why was everything such a fucking mess?

She snarfed the rest of her burger down. My potato sat there pretty much intact. I felt badly, so I forced a few spoonfuls at her urging.

The problem wasn't food though. The problem was me and my bipolar brain. Unbeknownst to me, this was about to change. Help was on the way, and I was about to be restored to some semblance of sanity.

When my Mom flew into Roanoke Airport the next day, I remember picking her up and spilling my guts to her on the way back to my apartment. I told her I was sexually assaulted when I was fifteen. I just blurted it out. I hit her with the details, cursing out the camp counselor out who did it. (I had never mentioned that I was raped to *anyone*, except my boyfriend Scott that semester.)

Everything had turned to anger inside me and now I was spewing it out like hot, molten lava erupting from a volcano. I also included my biological father Bill on that list, who we rarely spoke about. It was under the surface, since I never talked about him, and she probably assumed he and his existence didn't bother me very much. But now I was angry, so *everything bothered me.* (She told me later that I even cursed her out, which I don't remember doing.)

The theme for that semester was shame. I was ashamed of myself in so many ways for what I had done. I felt I had let myself and my parents down. I was becoming unglued and beginning to realize it. I couldn't fully comprehend my behavior though, or connect the dots. What had I done to *cause* my downfall? I still had no idea. And I was *completely* in the dark at that point that I was suffering from mental illness.

I was offering up anything and everything to explain what was going on. Which tells me, in hindsight, I must've known that something was wrong. Still, I was looking at other people who had wronged me in life. I had no clue something was deeply wrong with *me*.

Wrong? Yes. But as bad or deep as it was? No. Absolutely not. I thought it was emotional stuff from my past haunting me. I had no idea why my Mom was really there. I had no idea she was there because an illness had taken control of my brain. Or because I was having the worst manic episode of my life.

"Daddy is coming tomorrow." Mom said calmly while watching the road. I was still telling myself this was only a visit. My Mom's mood was very serious though. This was not a visit that was scheduled, as graduation was six weeks away. I knew Dad was at his friend's cabin hunting with the guys. It wasn't adding up, but I wasn't capable of, or attempting to, break down the math.

"Okay." I responded, slightly confused. I continued my ranting and spilling my guts out on that ride home. Mom was quiet as I went on and on.

The next thing I remember was being in the shrink's office. I don't even remember the details of my Dad getting to Tech or how he did. I was so out of it.

What my Mom didn't know at this point, was that I didn't want or feel the need to eat. And it was really hard for me to sleep. I felt like I would lose all my great ideas and not be able to remember them if I did. (What brilliant ideas? I have no idea, but I was terrified of not being awake to write them down.) I was listening to really bizarre music over and over, like a broken record, that I wouldn't ordinarily listen to. Plus, I was broke. Not a dime in my account. I remember buying things I had no need for, like a TV stand and I didn't even have a TV! But when I got one, I thought, damn it, I'll have a great stand for it!

What my parents had yet to learn, but were about to get a crash course in, were my manic behaviors that all pointed to having bipolar disorder. In hindsight, there were so many clues we missed until it was too late. (See "To The Parents and Families" at the end of the book.) The problem is one's first manic episode (and diagnosis) is a complete shock to everyone involved. And no one, no one, is prepared.

The Finish Line

The day at the psychiatrist's office was a day I'll never forget. I can remember it like it was yesterday. It was there I was handed down a label that has since caused so much pain and struggle and depression and mania. I was just in the beginning stages then.

It was crucial to me in my life's plan that I graduate on time that semester, so I showed up and tried to keep up. I knew I would never come back, that it would never be the same. I stayed and fought the fight. I was fighting my illness, my brain, myself, my limitations, my paranoias, my medications and my alcohol and pot addiction. It helped to know that my family was on my side deep down, but at the same time, I felt very alone.

Initially, I felt my parents had sided with the shrink I hated. I did come around when I saw they were there day after day, holding my hand through everything. They supported my decision to stay and graduate rather than drop out and be hospitalized, like I really should have been. Thank God I have an incredible family because there is no doubt in my mind I wouldn't have graduated without them.

My Mom, Dad and sister Samantha were all right there for me. They dropped me off, picked me up and/or walked with me to class each day for six weeks. They made sure I took my meds. They made sure I ate and slept, sometimes sleeping on my couch because the hotels got expensive. They made sure I didn't drink or smoke pot. If I went out, which was rare, they talked to the person and made sure they, too, knew the rules. They played nurse 24/7 and if they were any less dedicated, I would've had to have been hospitalized. I really *should've* been hospitalized.

I had already been diagnosed, but begged my Mom to be allowed to go out for Halloween. I wanted to be "normal" as much as possible, even though I couldn't drink. My life as a graduating senior was *so far* from normal at that point. I had to get top clearance to go anywhere unchaperoned.

I dressed up as "Inga from Sveden," getting my inspiration from the movie "Trading Places," when Jamie Lee Curtis' character was dressed up on the train. I had a coat hanger in my hair like those crazy, broken arrows that Steve Martin used in his skits. I had braided my hair over them. I wore my sister's dirndl that she wore when she worked at a German restaurant back home. I wore my "knapsack" which was my backpack and walked around saying, "Hi! My name is Inga from Sveden...von't you help me with my knapsack?" I quickly stopped saying that phrase, wished I could drink and went home early. The party was over and Halloween affirmed it.

My notes in class had become undecipherable from the tranquilizers I was taking. They looked like an EKG readout. I had no legible notes to study from when finals came. Only pages filled with scribbled lines. I was tired of the side effects and of being so tired. I did not like being in slow motion.

I decided I wanted to finish out my college career on my own, without *any* pharmaceuticals. Naturally, I took a turn for the worse in this effort to try and take back control. I said I didn't care, that I was going to know that I did it myself, without any pills. I had to do it for me, I justified.

I would *not* recommend this route to anyone, but it's what I chose to do. I was certifiably out of my mind. Only, I was out of my mind *and* supervised. My parents and sister used up their vacation time at their jobs and all their energy to get me through. That made all the difference. Two of my professors admitted to me they knew people who had gone through similar times with deep depressions and were very kind and sympathetic.

One of them was a professor who was an expert in his field, traveling all over the world with his consulting business. I really respected him, even though I thought he was a pompous ass who cared more about his business than our class. Still, I did think he was a pretty sharp guy and he seemed to know an awful lot about my new label. I sensed that someone very close to him had bipolar disorder or some mental illness. He told me that I must be very smart. Coming from him it was high praise. This was not The Enemy telling me in her stiff, impersonal manner. This was someone who I respected, telling me face to face.

It was my first glimpse of relief. Just a little bit, but I took it. He knew someone and it was okay because, despite this major defect, overall I had a good brain. I had hope again, that maybe I could achieve good things after all. I began to see the silver lining of my clouded brain.

My best friend in my major was an A-student and took great notes. Julie was the *only* person in my small major to whom I told the truth. She let me use her notes to study for the finals. (I did not do well, but I at least passed.) In fact, Julie confided in me that her mom had been in and out of sanitariums (as she called them) all her life. Her sadness and introversion made sense to me at that point. She helped me get through academically. That and the understanding of my professors whom I had taken aside, one by one.

It was remarkable how God surrounded me that semester with people who knew other people who were mentally ill. Each person who I was close to (my boyfriend, my A student friend Julie and each professor I spoke to) all knew someone and/or understood. It made me feel like less of a freak. I did not feel good about myself. I did not like having my family all there babysitting me. It was not a good ending to my college career. I did not like being labeled a dented can. However, being connected to all these people was comforting and softened the blow.

The fact that Scott studied so hard helped me because he was so often inaccessible that I didn't feel like I was missing any big parties. It made it easier for me to attempt to study. Without being on medication by this point, I was fighting my mind to concentrate. Focusing wasn't going well. Studying was next to impossible, but I had Julie's notes and I tried. I gave it my best.

I ended up doing poorly that semester as predicted, but still finished college with a B- average overall. (I also managed to get three very small scholarships along the way.) Not too bad for a difficult school and a *very* disruptive illness.

The day of graduation I overslept and was almost late to my own graduation. I missed breakfast at the B&B where my family was staying. I have a picture with them there (I ate nothing – shocker) with my wet hair (another shocker) and no makeup on. I was not exactly a vision for success, like my fellow classmates. My cheekbones were sunken and for the first time in my life, I was looking gaunt from my lack of eating. My boyfriend, Scott stood next to me in my graduation pictures. He was also a huge help in keeping me going, quietly there encouraging me, in addition to my family, who were beyond amazing.

At graduation, I scribbled notes all over my commencement

program. Most people kept theirs all neat for a keepsake. Mine was all marked up.

"It's over Wendy, you can stop taking notes now." Ted, my classmate, joked with me. My classmates kept looking at me. I made them nervous. I made *everyone* nervous. Even I was aware that I was nuttier than a fruitcake.

I don't like looking at pictures of my graduation because I see how awful and sick I looked. I see the strain of my illness on our faces through forced smiles. We all barely made it through. But, I did make it and I got my piece of paper. Lots of love, patience and support from my family, friends, professors, shrink, the kind community at Virginia Tech (and let me not forget divine intervention), got me through.

And that, believe me when I tell you, was nothing short of a miracle.

My Roaring Twenties

Start Spreadin' the News

Instead of setting out to conquer the world as a new college graduate, I was forced into the reality of my situation. It had been recommended, by The Enemy, due to my manic episode at school, that I take a low stress job for the time being. I was pissed off! Being told I had to come in for a pit stop right away, at the *beginning* of the race? I don't know if I was more upset about not having the chance to set the world on fire as I always imagined it, or the fact that The Enemy was making decisions for me even *after* I graduated.

I didn't have much of a choice at the time other than to just accept where I was. I went back to the employment agency where I worked during holiday breaks while back in college. Immediately they sent me out to work at a large insurance company as a file clerk in their auto personal injury claims department. If it sounds boring let me assure you, it *was*. My photocopying and filing skills were put to the test as I wasted away day after day, hour after hour, performing meaningless tasks. Not only was I not climbing the corporate ladder, I wasn't even *on* one.

My only consolation was knowing that at least this was not my destination; I was lying low for a few months doing this horribly boring job. I kept reminding myself, once my new doctor got my medications right and I was stable, I would be onto a more exciting and lucrative job. (Then again, *anything* compared to that job would be more exciting and lucrative.) Unfortunately, I did need the green light from my new psychiatrist because I was living with my parents and had to do things right.

The new doctor I went to seemed to be The Enemy's long lost twin: Dr. Von Enemy. I came up with this nickname not just to entertain myself, but mainly because her last name began with Von. Her husband was Norwegian and also a shrink in the same office. She was short with a dark complexion and long black hair; he was tall and blond. They were an odd looking pair, so opposite. But I thought it was cute they were a shrink couple. I figured if they had kids they must be mutant smart. Probably that and really fucked up.

I sat in the waiting room anticipating my first visit. Before she came out to get me, it was a bit eerie, sitting there alone amidst the dull browns and mustard yellows. It reeked of bad seventies décor, and not the cool retro stuff. Rather, it was more of a stale this-doctor-hasn't-updated-their-office-since-it-was-rented-from-the-last-ten-other-cheap-doctors-down-the-line, type of bad. The fabrics that covered the chairs and couches were a mish-mosh of pathetic plaids and tightly woven deep browns.

The carpet looked original, and made you wonder where the door-to-door carpet installation man was with his swatches for the past three decades. Clearly, she and her husband were out to lunch if he had come by at all in the past few years since they'd been there. Maybe I should put a call into a carpet installation company, one with those annoying ads and give them her address for a quote. Something *had* to be done about this waiting room.

I waited longer than usual noting she was late. Once she emerged from her office, no patient came out with her. There was no apparent reason why she was eight minutes late for our appointment. Had there been any signs of a crisis? Perhaps on the phone with a patient who needed her? No, I decided she was just late. I soaked in her appearance as she held the door open for me. I distrusted her instantly observing her smile and those big, outdated glasses. I expected her to at least make something up, but she made no apology despite the fact that we were now beginning ten minutes late.

This was not a good start. It was as if she was setting it up from the beginning who was going to be in the place of power in this relationship. She held my file, the RX pad and the knowledge that could get me better. From where she stood, I'm sure she thought *she* was the one in power. But from where I stood, I was paying her and she needed my money to pay her bills. I concluded that she needed me more and that *I,* in fact had the upper hand. The power struggle had begun.

I dreaded meeting this new doctor after my experience with the first one at Tech. I knew she was judging my appearance and formulating a set of mundane, yet specific, set of questions that I did not want to answer, but would have to. I was uncomfortable with getting to know another professional in the clinical sense while at the same time trying to pass it off as a pseudo-caring relationship. She would be taking notes about our little meeting. What would they say? Undoubtedly, she'd also tell me how I needed to live my life and behave and take this or that medication so that I didn't have another *episode.*

That word, episode, had become a dirty word in our house. I dreaded hearing it from my Mom. It was always in the context of: "You better do what the doctor said because you don't want to have another *episode.*" After much resistance to that word, my Mom gave up using it. It became like the "f word." A curse word you wouldn't say no matter what. (Unless Dad cut his finger while chopping vegetables, then it was okay. Especially if blood was present.) They knew I'd freak out even if I heard it in reference to a TV show. It was a horrible word and avoided at all costs.

Dr. Von Enemy's office was not much better than the waiting room. The same carpet that had no color category spilled into it as well, making me wonder how many other patients were disturbed at how ugly these offices were. Couldn't this be viewed as encouraging depression?

I found it a good distraction from what was really going on: I didn't want to face this woman. I must have been preoccupied because it hit me all at once that it was absolutely *freezing!* Once she sat down at her desk and I had my seat, I saw she put on a mink coat over her shoulders. *Mink coat?* Here's a novel idea: turn up the heat and lose the coat, lady.

It didn't take long for me to despise her, sitting there in her mink coat while I froze my ass off in my cheap, old chair. I was distracted by the size of her gleaming rock-sized diamond earrings and decided I liked her even less. Those had to be over a carat. Maybe she didn't have enough business and kept the heat off all the time. (I never did run into a single patient while I was there.)

We got down to business. I answered her questions, bored but getting used to the protocol with each new doctor. So far I was not getting a good feeling, but tried to keep an open mind. Maybe she was a good doctor and that was all that should matter? I went back to her a handful of times and continued my boring temp job. I was doing okay, I suppose. We were focusing on getting my medications worked out.

One day, I brought my Mom with me. I was building my case to find another shrink because we weren't hitting it off. It just so happened that Dr. Von Enemy was in rare form that day. She had a pizza right there on her desk and proceeded to grab a slice. She began chomping on it at the beginning of our session, asking how the medications were making me feel. I tried not to look at my Mom because I would've burst out laughing. Then she blindsided me.

"Do you drink?" She had her slice in her hand, awaiting my reply.

"A little on the weekends, but not much," I wondered if she was going to offer us a slice.

"You know, you can't drink on these medications."

"I know." I was hoping there might be a little leeway there, but apparently not. There was no harm in drinking *a little*, I thought.

"I'm sorry, I never had dinner." She apologized.

"It's okay." I looked at my Mom. We were horrified.

"You can't drink at all while taking these medications."

"I can't drink? *At all?*" I was in shock. "Not even a little? But I'm twenty-two years old!" I said emphatically. I thought of my plan to work in New York City and couldn't imagine not going out after work to the bars and clubs. Not drink at all? My life was over.

"You mean, you can't *not* drink?" The look on her face taunted me, instead of showing concern or care. She took an above average interest in me all of a sudden and leaned forward.

"No, but I don't want to *not be able* to drink!" I started rattling off the names of all the events I'd need to drink at in the future: weddings, holidays, concerts, going out with friends. Then my mind jumped to my wedding someday. Why, what would I do for the champagne toast? (I wasn't engaged, or even had a boyfriend but that was beside the point!) She cut me off before I could finish my list.

"Well, if you *have* to drink then you're an alcoholic." She said matter-of-factly.

"I don't *have* to drink. I just want to be able to, if I choose to do so. Besides, that doesn't make me an alcoholic." What an idiot! She was calling me, a twenty-two year old, an alcoholic! *Me!*

"I'm telling you that you can't and you're saying that you have to." We were going around in circles and she was getting on my last nerve.

"I'm *not* an alcoholic!" A teeny tiny voice inside of me questioned it, but I remained indignant.

I looked at my Mom and she was shaking her head too. We quickly got out of there. Thank God! I didn't like her anyway. What did she know about me with her stupid mink coat and diamond earrings anyway? What did she know *about me?* Besides, I was *too young* to be an alcoholic! On the way out to the car, my Mom and I agreed.

"I mean, how dare she call *me* an *alcoholic?*"

"I know! *You?*" We laughed as we got into the car.

I never went back to her as a result. I simply switched and found a new doctor. I mean, the pizza and being frozen to death, that I could handle. Being accused of being an alcoholic, that I could not.

I simply couldn't handle one more label at that time. Dealing with my bipolar disorder was all I had room for on my plate. I was, we both were, in serious denial. Mentally ill, that's one thing. But an alcoholic too? That was too much to face. Denial runs deep.

Impossible not to deny, however, was where I was at in life. Rather, where I was not. In my world of not climbing the corporate ladder of success, I was commuting every day in my crappy car to this five story depressing mecca of metal desks, metal chairs, metal file cabinets, and papers and files galore. There were no smiles to be seen. *Everyone* was miserable. Of course, there wasn't a lot of money spent on the décor, either. The only color in the place was the overdone makeup of the lady who I reported to and the snacks in the vending machines. Surely this job was working against what my medication was trying to achieve. I avoided slipping too far into depression by getting the hell out of there.

I wasn't convinced the medication I was taking was working, but I *was* convinced that if I stayed too long at that company, I would've gone backwards. It motivated me enough to want to kick ass in life and get on my way. I was getting ready for the big city. But first, I needed a new doctor and the right meds.

Thankfully, one of my doctors told me about the UPenn Bipolar Disorder Unit in Philadelphia. It was the best place to go nearest to where I lived. I had no health insurance, but they did free treatment for people who enrolled in their drug studies and met the criteria. Having no psychiatrist at that point, I decided to investigate and went there to see about the drug trials. I wasn't thrilled about being a guinea pig, but I was a broke college grad without health insurance. The price was right.

As fate would have it, they were doing a new drug study. I would be receiving free care from a top psychiatrist specializing in my disorder. It seemed like a no-brainer of a decision, so I enrolled in the trial and commuted to Philly for over a year until it ended. It wasn't a convenient commute, but I was lucky to have found them. And the cheese steak man in the truck outside the building was a highlight. (Sometimes I even got two!)

I remember Judy, the doctor's assistant, who was helping the psychiatrist with the clerical parts of the research. She was a nurse, recording information and administering the medications for the trial. Judy was very kind with a soft voice and big, blue, sad eyes. She had neat script handwriting and traditional, but obviously expensive clothes. I especially loved her rings and all her jewelry. I had a lot of time to look at and admire her jewelry while she wrote everything down. She rotated everything each week so I would always see new pieces. They were all unique, the kind you'd see in museum catalogues, very expensive ones that I would dream of someday owning. I was so bored by the questions that repeated every week and sick of talking about my feelings. But Judy was always patient and understanding with me, accepting whatever I said. She just took it all in stride, writing it down.

The study forced me to rate how I was feeling for data collection purposes. I did not like doing that; it became very mundane. It was the first time I really had to *think* about how I was feeling. It was a matter of doing the on-the-scale-of-1-to-10 thing. I found it increasingly annoying. She tried to be helpful by suggesting something different.

"Wendy, have you ever journaled?"

"No, not really." I had written poems here and there, but that was about the extent of my writing.

"Hmmm…I think you should try it."

It sounded like a lot of work. I didn't jump on it, but her soft, non-threatening demeanor made me think I could handle it. Then I panicked a little. Did she mean every day? The thought of a commitment to do something new like that scared me.

"Do you mean, like, *every* day?"

"No, it doesn't have to be every day but I think it might help you." She had such a gentle way. She could have said, "Spear a frog in the creek," and I would have said "Okay," despite not having any idea *how* I was going to actually spear a frog in the creek, let alone find a creek. Or a frog. I pictured sitting alone with this new journal thing, much like sitting alone on a rock, waiting for the frog. It was just the way she suggested things that made you want to try.

"Here." She handed me a journal, watching my face for a reaction.

I looked down and had flashbacks of the little test booklets we used in college for essays. It was the same kind with only paper, two staples and a flimsy, makeshift cover. I had my spear — had to catch my frog now.

"Thanks." I set aside my feelings of nervousness at the prospect of filling up those lines and pages. Instead, I focused on my gratitude towards Judy and realized that she had become the first professional who showed me a human, caring side to this whole, complicated process of wellness. Judy didn't have a fancy degree, just a big heart. She spent a lot of time with me, recording feelings, doing the scales and reading my journals. The little booklets (despite my initial fear of them) became a nice change and unleashed some truths for me. I found it easier to put my feelings into words than numbers; it had been a long time since I'd done that. It felt good and definitely helped me.

When I got out of the elevator onto the 2nd floor, I knew without a doubt, I was in the right place. I even learned a new tool (journaling) for my virtual toolbox. Three train changes and two and a half hours one way later, I also learned to go to any lengths to get well. There were many lessons gained by my positive experience at UPenn. The most important was: wellness didn't always have to cost a lot of money (my treatment there was free), but I had to work for it.

Pretty soon after I started going to UPenn, I began working in NYC. I worked for a large hotel in Times Square as a front desk clerk on the 3-11pm shift. My drinking really took off. Working 3-11pm was the ideal drinker's shift. I had plenty of time to sleep off my hangover, yet still had enough time get back into the city to start my shift. There were a few hours after my shift was over to hit the bars and *just* enough time to make the last train or bus home. I was working in a city with a zillion bars and clubs. I got off work when the city was alive and beckoned me to drink. It was an alcoholic's paradise. I had arrived!

It didn't take long for the allure of the city, with all its sections and different bars and clubs, to wear off though. We drank mainly within a stone's throw of the hotel. The bar we became flies at, almost nightly, was called "JL's."

JL's was like our "Cheers" bar. And for all the money I spent at that bar, I still couldn't tell you who JL was or if there even *was* a JL. But I knew all the songs in their jukebox. I knew they had three bottles of Jaegermeister on tap and my favorite beer was on ice in a tub on top of the bar. They had amazing chicken fingers (which was the only food I ever remember ordering at JL's). We congregated around the tall tables with bar stools and wasted whatever money we didn't blow on alcohol on keeping the same old tunes rocking in the jukebox.

The bartenders, Maggie and Emily, could look at me and know what I needed and had it ready immediately upon arrival. They knew *all* of our drinks and we knew all about them. Well, all that they disclosed to us anyway. I liked calling Maggie "Mags." It was a habit I learned from my Uncle Rick. He worked on the floor of the New York Stock Exchange and everyone there had nicknames. Mags was tall, lanky and had curly hair. She was my favorite, much peppier than the jaded Emily. Emily ("Em") was older and a little surly. You could tell Em had been a bartender much longer than Mags. Mags was my girl and I was always happy when she was on.

On New Year's Eve, which would've been their greatest revenue night, JL's actually closed their doors to the public and threw us hotel employees (and their other best customers) a party. Free alcohol, food, DJ, the works. We gave them enough of our money all year long that in thanks, they threw *us* a party. That's how much we drank there.

Occasionally, we'd stray to other places to mix it up. These weren't fancy cocktail lounges at five star hotels or bars one might brag about.

No, these were dive bars, pool halls and the once-in-a-blue-moon large dance clubs.

One such hole-in-the-wall was called "Sweeny's." It was owned by a couple of Irish guys with authentic accents who made sure the beer was Ireland's finest. And that was the bar's *only* asset. Located on Eighth Avenue, it was a rough, small bar in Hell's Kitchen which consisted of a bar, a few side tables and a pool table that, invariably started fights. One night, we were the ones who actually started one. Needless to say, we didn't go back there for a while.

On rare occasions, we'd also venture off and play pool. We were a bunch of drunken fools who infiltrated the pool halls of Eighth and Ninth Avenues. These were seedy places where you could bring in a forty ounce of beer in a brown bag and nobody cared. The only noises you heard were the clank of balls, the roar of the subway and the muted bullshit we all spoke. Some were hustlers, some were drunk novices spilled over from the bars and some were simply good players there to get better. When the subway came, it sounded like it was running right through the place. It made it impossible to concentrate or talk, which was fine. Nobody gave a shit, from the looks of it anyway.

"Let's go shoot some pool!" Gil always shouted at last call.

Gil was one of the other front desk clerks. He would yell to everyone with his cigarette dangling out of his mouth. He never dropped it even though it always seemed, and we half expected, like he was going to. As Gil got drunker, the angle of his dangling smoke would grow steeper. There was also a direct correlation between his level of drunkenness and how narrow his eyelids were. He'd try to rally people to do something, such as play pool, as everyone was leaving the bar to go home. Gil always tried to keep the good times rolling.

"I don't know." I said. If there wasn't a crowd joining us, I really had to be in the mood to play to be alone with him.

"You can bring beer in." Gil said, his eyes suddenly wide open. He said that every time, as if I forgot. No matter how drunk he was and squinty his eyes were, they always got real wide when he mentioned this fact. He'd throw in that we could bring in our own beer. As if we had forgotten from the last ten times.

"I know, but it's late. Who else is coming?" If the gang was scattering and going home, I rarely went alone with Gil. I didn't feel comfortable because I didn't trust him. It was mainly due to the employee party that had been thrown by management when we'd all gotten a hotel room to crash. After getting back from the club where our party was held, I went to the room to pass out. Gil said he would walk me back. I was too drunk to go back alone safely, and I said okay. When we had gotten there, nobody else was around so it was me and him in the empty hotel room. In no time at all, he had put the moves on me. I stopped him immediately. I never trusted him before that night, and I certainly didn't trust him afterwards. This was one of the reasons why I avoided playing pool alone with Gil.

Gil was the kind of guy who was a wheeler and dealer, but only for show. He could schmooze at work with the customers or with his friends, but you sensed that he would not exactly make it on the street if he tried selling drugs or something. Gil would be killed in two seconds for doing or saying something dumb. He was not very trustworthy, even though he was a nice guy. He once threw a party in his Queens apartment. It was a really bad section of Queens; it felt like the projects. Gil was dancing close and grinding on me. He did it to the single ladies. It was annoying how he thought he was quite the ladies man, when in reality, he was just a gangly, overly confident and unattractive man. But he did have charm, you had to give him that.

"Where is your *wife*?" I said to him. I loved to say the word *wife* to married men who acted inappropriately. But trying to get Gil to come up with a conscience was impossible.

"We have an *understanding*." He smiled, slowly bobbing his head to the music, keeping rhythm. I understood that to be code for: she knew he cheated.

Also familiar with Gil's moves were some of the other hotel employees. Three other single front desk clerks and I eventually teamed up and rented a house in North Jersey, just fifteen minutes from the city. I was out of my parent's house and now the drinking was really taking off. It was a crazy time, working at that huge, nineteen hundred room hotel. We saw all kinds of interesting people come and go at that hour and we worked with people from all walks of life. When I got off work, Times Square was lit up. I felt like I was at the center of the world and alive. It was my manic playground.

Sometimes we would go dancing at a club like Webster Hall, where we could get into for free. They wanted us to promote their place to our customers, so all we had to do was give our names to our concierge and they would fax them down. We skipped the lines and admission and walked right in. Life was good. I remember going there and getting lost in the dancing. There were three different floors with all different themed music. The first floor (or sub floor) was reggae so you could go there and get your groove on with someone. Then leave once they got too close.

I'll never forget the main floor. It seemed like a sea of a thousand people and I'd get lost in the music. There were people dancing in cages and on stage. There was one woman who hung from a trapeze.

She swung going back and forth hooked only by her ankle. Nothing else. I'd stare in amazement wondering if she'd ever fall.

There were men, cross-dressers or transsexuals (I'll never know) in the ladies bathroom. Wigs on mannequin heads lined up in front of the mirrors. Once, when I tried on one of the wigs for fun, this man with a shaved head and tank top got feisty.

"Don't try it unless you're gonna buy it!" He snapped at me all nasty.

"Don't be in our bathroom unless you're a woman." I said under my breath. Then I thought, how do they expect you to know if you want to buy it if you can't try it on anyway? Apparently, he was not a very good salesman.

When 11:00 pm rolled around each night, we counted our drawers, changed out of our uniforms and unleashed our leftover energy onto the city scene. However, more often than not, we'd go to the same bar around the corner and not make it to the clubs. It was not as glamorous as one might think.

I had entered a dangerous world because I was earning decent money and could afford to drink more. I was smoking cigarettes now and felt grown up. It was my first job with benefits. Although I didn't feel I had truly arrived, I knew I was doing okay. Young, earning more money than I ever had (spending every penny I had on a good time) and in the big city.

The bottom started to fall out. Within a year and a half of the same routine at the hotel, drinking almost every night, my job was in jeopardy. I was in trouble because I was always late, whether it was because I was hungover, irresponsible, or both. Eventually, management (including one of the managers who I was dating and drank with) told me to take a day off. It was a paid day off to think about my commitment to the company.

I was sick. Not only sick mentally and physically because of the alcohol, but the medication I was taking was not working. It seemed to be working for a while. But eventually, the medication didn't have a snowball's chance in hell. All the alcohol I was drinking was blocking its effects. I was depressed. I was tired of the job. I didn't want to be a front desk clerk anymore.

On that paid day off, I went on a shopping spree and opened three charge accounts at large department stores. I bought nice clothes, a pair of Birkenstocks, three hundred dollars of expensive makeup and a thousand dollars worth of television and stereo equipment.

Looking back, clearly I was manic. It goes along with excessive spending that I'd become more and more familiar with each passing manic episode. Not just excessive, but "in the red" spending. The kind where after my episode has subsided, I am on "cleanup" and staring at my bank account statement wondering what went wrong. It would not be for a long time down the road until I put two and two together and realized all the plastic in my wallet was obtained at the same time. There is no room for reality and a manic episode to co-exist. It takes a while to piece together the truth puzzle.

Then Jerry Garcia died. (I had been to a lot of Dead shows and was a big fan.) The day Jerry died, I didn't want to go to work. In fact, by that time, I didn't want to go to work *at all*. I was heading downwards and depression had taken over my canvas with speckles of mania splashed in. It was not a pretty picture. Alcohol, I would later learn, was my brush.

My Uncle Rick was aware of this and tried to help me stop drinking around the same time. He was a recovered alcoholic and understood what I was going through. I was in major denial and, up until that day, had no idea anyone had a clue that I had a drinking problem. I thought my only problem was that I was mentally ill.

One day while at his house for a family barbeque, Uncle Rick took me aside, Diet Dr. Pepper in hand as always.

"Wendells," he said very seriously, "I think you have a problem."

I felt blindsided and stared back at him blankly. I thought he was going to make one of his usual jokes or ask me something trivial. I wished he was talking about my job, car, finances or the boyfriend (all of which were usually problems). Based on his serious tone, however, I knew he was not talking about *those* problems.

We looked out over his backyard. The kids were playing in the pool. My aunt was at the grill smiling, talking to my parents. Everyone was having fun. It was a beautiful summer day. Underneath it all, I already knew what he was talking about. It had crossed my mind, but I *certainly* did not think anyone from my family thought this. Until that day, when he hit me with it. I was in denial up until that very moment.

"And you need help," Uncle Rick continued, scaring the shit out of me. Because he knew me so well and I respected him, I had to pay attention. Coming from anyone else in the world, I would've walked away. But from Uncle Rick, I had to stay and listen.

"Do you think I'm an alcoholic, Uncle Rick?" The words flew out of my mouth. Never before had I put "I" and "alcoholic" together, except to deny it.

"Here. Go see Bob. Tell him I sent you." He took out his wallet and handed me the business card of a CADC (Certified Alcohol and Drug Counselor) named Bob. I was not ready to pay a professional to talk about this. Then again, I was not ready to talk about this at all. To anyone.

"So you think I'm an alcoholic?" I pursued. I still couldn't believe anyone in my family even knew that I drank a lot. I mean, I was always careful not to drink too much at family functions. Wasn't I?

"And Wendells, I can't tell you whether or not you're an alcoholic. Only *you* can determine that." Rick said gently, then walked away. I stood on the deck looking at the card and quickly shoved it my pocket. I hoped nobody had seen him give it to me.

How could I be an alcoholic at age twenty-five? Washed up at only twenty-five? I was too young. It wasn't possible! That word alcoholic was haunting me.

I wasn't ready to face the music, so I simply changed songs.

My French Connection

New York City had bled me of my sanity and many brain cells, so I switched gears and embarked on a new career. I took a job I had planned on taking after graduation, before my episode from hell. It was a small consulting company in Maryland, specializing in computer network conversions and training for hospitality companies. When I called my contact Cheryl in Human Resources, she was thrilled to hear from another foolish person willing to get paid a low salary, live out of a suitcase and survive on a skimpy expense account.

I arrived in Maryland to begin training. The company made the *catastrophic* mistake of making me the technical manager for the project. Out of everyone on our team, they believed I had the most computer experience. I didn't have the first clue of how computer networks actually operated, nor did I have any idea how I was going to pull off upgrading and changing out old systems. I knew it was going to be a struggle. Right off the bat I had to pretend to know what the hotel company's (the client's) I/T people were talking about. (Ironically, the client was the same hotel company that had nearly fired me the week before.)

I followed along in the manuals and kept my game face on. It was a nightmare.

Thank God for Tom. My new friend Tom, the catering training manager on our team, was quite a colorful character. He sat next to me in our claustrophobic training room at the client's company headquarters. Tom told me he lived in DuPont Circle. How he could afford to live in D.C. on this pathetic salary was a mystery to me. Then one day he mentioned a rich boyfriend and it all made sense. Tom wasn't shy about his sexuality. Not that it took a rocket scientist to figure out he was gay in the first place. I loved how flamboyant he was. So did he; you could tell he amused himself.

"Tom..." I whispered.

"Talk to the hand 'cause the face don't care." He stuck his hand out like he was a crossing guard. Meanwhile, he kept his head buried behind his *Unix For Dummies* book. Tom had his own little language that took getting used to. He provided much needed comic relief. I loved him to pieces and couldn't imagine how dull our group would've been without him.

"Tom!" It was my loudest possible whisper. People were looking over at us. The snobby team (from the hotel company) knew that our team, the "consultants," were really just a bunch of frauds. I tried to maintain some dignity about it all because we were getting paid to know something.

"Wendy, *stop* it!" Tom teased. "I'm trying to learn here." He added sarcastically. Of course he was not referring to our big, useless manuals that lay open. He was talking about his stupid cliff notes. Although he was trying to make a joke of it, you could see he was cracking under pressure. Beads of sweat were dripping down his forehead. It hadn't fully sunk in yet that we were about to go into these huge hotels, some of which had almost one hundred computers, and completely change everything. And *I* was going to be the one screwing up everything up. I put my pen down. I needed that damn book.

"Tom! Can I…uh…borrow your book?" I reached for his copy of *Unix For Dummies*, while hiding from the geeky technical manager on the hotel company's team. Appearing knowledgeable was becoming increasingly difficult. The geek, who sat only two seats down from us, looked up and grinned. Shit! Had I been caught?

"Um hmm. Sure thang." Tom handed it over as I snatched the bright fluorescent-yellow-announcing-help-I-don't-have-a-clue-book and stashed it in my briefcase. Could they have made this book look any more obvious? How about a nice, pastel cover?

I looked over at the geek nervously. Luckily his little, greasy nose was back into his binder and my secret was safe. Phew! I realized I was now pages behind in this mega binder of bullshit. My bigger realization was hitting me: I was regretting my decision to take this job. I was in way over my head and we weren't even out of training yet.

Although screwing up computers, in the grand scheme of things, was the least of my problems. I couldn't help compare where I was at, or rather *not* at, in life to my college friends. I felt like a complete failure because I was so far behind the success curve and carrying on like I had been in college. Plus, I was still single. My jealousy made it hard to be around them. I also felt ashamed because I was mentally ill and knew that had also gotten around.

Pretty soon, the lack of sleep (we were working around the clock on the computers at night when the employees were off them) started to gnaw at my bipolar disorder. I know *now* that sleep is so vital to keeping the lions of mania at peace. But back then, I didn't know and didn't care. I was living on the edge.

My drinking and blackouts kept me from looking at my mental health or guarding it. I wasn't always on my medication at that point in my life. There were no direct consequences (yet) for my behavior and not taking my illness seriously. After ninety days, once I had medical coverage with that company, I did go see a shrink and get on medication. But how could it have worked?

I was getting ready to leave the traveling/computer consulting job because it was wearing me thin. On my last project there (working for a chain restaurant out west) my company had teamed me up with another heavy drinker. His name was Pierre. And he was trouble.

Pierre had moved to the U.S. when he was ten years old with his mother and siblings, but was as French as he was American. He still spoke French fluently. Pierre and I started spending more time after work together. We were isolated; there was no one else. I had no friends or family on the road and knew no one but him. Whether we were in small towns or big cities, on my days off there was only him to explore with. Late at night when I finally got to eat dinner, he was my only choice for a partner. We meshed together out of convenience and loneliness. Soon, we started living as a couple on the road, pooling our housing allowances together, getting suites instead of individual rooms.

Pierre introduced me to red wine. I never liked the taste of it or any other alcohol for that matter, but I drank it with him. I felt less guilty drinking wine (versus other kinds of alcohol) because it seemed more sophisticated. When I drank, I usually felt lonely, but that problem was solved because I wasn't lonely with him. We were lonely together.

Occasionally, we would come off the road and go home to NJ for a little break. As it turned out, Pierre's parents lived one town away from my parents. One day, while on break back home, we went out with his friends. One of his friends was this loser I knew from high school.

We were smoking cigarettes at his loser friend's place with his loser friend's roommates, when a guy I didn't know pulled out a mirror. Then he poured some white powder on it and chopped it up with a razor blade.

"Here," he said and gave the mirror to Pierre's friend. He took out a dollar bill and rolled it, snorting what I presumed to be cocaine. I felt uneasy sitting there and witnessing this. This house was a dump. The furniture was old and I was the only woman there, which also made me uneasy. But, at least I was with Pierre.

Next, his friend passed it over to Pierre. Pierre repeated the process and soon he had a big smile on his face. He joined his friend and was on the same plane. I could tell. I wondered who had bought the stuff. Had Pierre?

"Try this." Pierre said to me with a grin on his face, like he knew the secret to happiness and this was it. He pushed the mirror over on the coffee table so it was in front of me. His friend looked at me, also grinning. I saw how they both looked so happy after they each did a line. I didn't want to do it because I had always been dead set against doing anything but pot. That conviction vanished as I sat there looking at how happy my new boyfriend was. I wanted to be happy, too.

Without saying a word, I took the rolled dollar bill and I did my first line of cocaine. I had opportunities in the past to do hard drugs like cocaine, but I never took them. I wanted to be on the same level. I wanted to feel what they felt. I did the line and could taste it going down the back of my throat. I didn't like the taste, but I was in love with how it instantly made me feel. Now the three of us were all feeling the same way, the same high. Nothing mattered. Nothing mattered at all.

For someone who was pegged and had pegged herself as more of a leader, I quickly became a follower. I fell hard. Hard for him and now hard for cocaine. First it was just a little coke, here and there. It started off slowly. We didn't have access to it when we were out on the road for work. We would be in different towns and didn't know anyone or where to get it. We couldn't very well travel with it and risk going through airport security.

Back in Texas for work, somewhere near Deep Ellum, Pierre found us pot. We got stoned and talked about quitting our jobs and moving home because we were tired of living out of our suitcases. The hours were horrible, the pay pathetic, the expense account was a joke and we were worn out from that lifestyle. We had no future plans, we only knew we had to get out.

One night, I was really high, really fed up and decided to quit. I did it in a forty-five minute stoned, rambling voicemail message to the CEO telling him *exactly* what I thought of him and his company. Pierre quit too and we decided we had earned ourselves a vacation.

"Baby, where could we go?" I asked Pierre. We were always calling each other "baby" which annoyed the crap out of everyone around us. We couldn't help ourselves. It was a habit.

"I don't know, where could we go? When are our tickets home for? Next Friday?" Pierre was always asking me organizational questions. (We were supposed to be there working until the following Friday.)

"Yeah."

"So we have the rental car until next Friday too then, right? You don't think they'll come after us to pay for the extra week. Do you?" He asked, worried.

"I don't think so. There's only one woman in the accounting department. She's overworked as it is and approves all the expense reports unless anything looks suspicious. It'll match our flight date, so why would they check it, baby?" I was lying on the bed with my head on his chest. We were master plotters.

"Okay, so where should we go?" Pierre asked, clueless. But, I had this one covered.

"There's this place called South Padre Island. A bunch of fraternity guys at Tech went there one spring break, so maybe it would be cool." I had no idea where it was, but thought it was on the Gulf of Mexico.

"Do you know how *far* that is?" He asked. "It's probably pretty far, baby. I mean, Texas is a huge state. Maybe they have a map in here." Pierre got up to look through the desk for the room guide. We had pooled our housing allowances and had gotten a suite at the Hilton. Luckily, we were in Dallas at the moment, so lodging was above par here. He handed me the binder of information he found.

"There's no map."

"Really? Damn. Keep looking." Pierre kept rummaging through the desk, but came up empty handed.

"Nope. We'll have to get a map tomorrow. I wonder how long it will take us to get there." I was bummed we couldn't plan everything that instant.

"Who cares how long it'll take." My excitement returned. "Roadtrip!" We got high some more, pleased with our idea, and planned on leaving the next day.

When we got to South Padre Island, before checking in, we immediately went to a tattoo parlor we found. Pierre wanted to get a tattoo around his arm; more importantly: we wanted to score some drugs. We had half a pizza left, so we offered our unfinished slices to the two tattoo artists there. The hope was that by being nice, they'd tell us where to get drugs. Although skeptical, once they determined we were cool, they told us. We bought three kinds: pot, 'shrooms (which they enthusiastically informed us were picked fresh yesterday) and of course cocaine. I was excited to do coke again. We hadn't done it since NJ.

Locked in our room the entire week, we did all the coke we could afford, drank wine, got stoned, ate 'shrooms, played cards, ate a little food and listened to CDs. (I can barely listen to the Sheryl Crow CD I had bought in Dallas, because we listened to it over and over again.) We never even lied in the sun, despite our oceanfront room inches away from the beach.

One sunny day we rented a jet ski after throwing down a few Long Island Iced Teas. We rode one together because they were so expensive.

"I want to ride alone." I protested after we had fallen off. "Let's get another one and we can ride side by side." We floated there contemplating getting a second one, but knew we couldn't afford it.

"No, go on baby," Pierre said. "Take it by yourself. Come back and get me in a few minutes." I felt badly leaving him and it seemed a little weird to leave him there floating. Still, I was excited at the thought of riding it alone.

"Are you sure?" I checked.

"Yeah, I'll be fine." He said, bobbing in the water.

"Okay!" I accelerated and waved, leaving him behind me floating in his vest.

I headed for the bridge. I loved going fast and feeling the power of the jet ski. I could really get used to one of these, I decided. When I came back around, I couldn't find him. I must've gone much farther than I thought. I kept circling around looking, but he was nowhere to be found. Was it possible? Had I lost my boyfriend?

It didn't help that right before downing those Long Island Iced Teas I had taken my medication. I was beginning to feel woozy from the heat, my meds and the drinks. It dawned on me perhaps that wasn't the brightest idea. The thought came and went quickly as I continued my search. I needed to find Pierre! I looked frantically, but couldn't find him anywhere! If I looked straight ahead, I might miss him to my left or right. As I rode the jet ski, if I looked left or right, surely I could run him over. It was a nightmare! I kept circling around and around, terrified that he'd drowned. I was in a complete panic.

Twenty minutes later, I gave up. I rode the jet ski in and slowed down at the dock. The jet ski employee was on there waiting, to my relief. I swung my leg around.

"I can't find my boyfriend!" I shrieked to the guy as I stepped onto the dock.

"What?" He looked at me confused, like I had two heads and was speaking Swahili. Perhaps he didn't understand the severity of my situation. My boyfriend was out there floating around somewhere and I couldn't find him! This man before me was obviously programmed to receive the jet ski and simply end the transaction.

Disregarding this, I gave him the short version of the story while he was tying it up. He stood there like he was waiting for something else, not the rest of the story, when I realized he wanted the vest back. I twisted, unclipped it and handed it to him.

"...I thought I knew where he was, but when I came back I couldn't find him. Have you seen him? You remember what he looks like, right? Has he come back?"

It wasn't busy, only a weekday after all. Hell, we were probably the only renters they'd had all day. Was he staring blankly at me because he couldn't believe I lost my boyfriend? Or maybe he just didn't give a shit. I was thinking: *earth-to-jet-ski-rental guy*, when I heard Pierre's voice.

"Where the fuck did you go?" Pierre was furious. At least he wasn't cursing at me in French.

"Oh thank God, there he is." I spun around, thrilled to see him.

"He's pissed!" The guy walked away, laughing. *Finally, he talks*, I thought. *Before he was acting like a mute.*

"Why the hell did you take off like that?" He demanded.

"You said to take it. You told me to go alone and take it for a ride." I defended.

"Yeah, I meant for a few minutes, not for *a half hour!*"

"Come on, Pierre. That wasn't even fifteen minutes!"

"Bullshit! It *was* a half hour. What the fuck were you thinking Wendy?"

"I don't know. I went straight and just headed towards the bridge." I realized I'd gone too far, too long but I wasn't going to back down. Not all the way, anyway.

"Yeah I know. You went *all* the way to the bridge. Do you know how far that was?"

"Look, I'm sorry. I got carried away and went too far. I guess I just wanted to…"

"I mean I was waving and waving! I kept thinking, surely she's gonna turn around and come back to get me!"

"I'm *sorry*, I couldn't find you anywhere! Did you swim back?" That would've been a pretty far swim. I didn't think he was that good of a swimmer.

"No, a *boat* came by and rescued me!"

"Oh my God, are you serious? Baby, I'm so sorry."

"When they helped me on board they said, 'What happened? You two get in a fight?' and laughed their asses off."

"I am so sorry. I feel like total shit."

"They did offer me a drink though. And some food." He lightened up a little.

"Did you take it?"

"Of course I took it!" We finally had a laugh and shook off what could've ended much worse.

Pierre and I headed off to get some fast food before barricading ourselves again in our hotel room. Another night of getting wasted, listening to music, playing cards and staying up all night. We took pictures of ourselves with our disposable camera. (I recently found them and was shocked at how disgusting I looked. Even with a smile, it was clear I looked miserable. Yet, we thought we were having the time of our lives.)

At the end of the week, we drove back up to Dallas and flew home to New Jersey. Not only were we jobless, there was no job on the horizon. The only plan we did have was another brilliant scheme we had formulated back in Texas. We decided to go to France that summer, stay with his family and travel all over the country. This *would* have been great if we had any money. Instead, we applied for credit cards — in my name of course — because he had already gone bankrupt. Naturally, we spent God-only-knows-how-much before we left on cocaine and alcohol. My addiction still wasn't that bad. Yet.

We arrived in Paris and stayed in a town called Saumur in the Loire Valley with his grandmother and aunt. I loved them instantly, even though I couldn't communicate very well with them. Pierre constantly had to translate and I felt badly. I was seeing his patience wear thin and the stress of us not having any money made things worse. His grandmother called us the "lovebirds" in French, which couldn't have been farther from the truth because we never made love. Alcohol and drugs had become our only "loves."

We drank countless, I mean *countless*, bottles of red wine with Pierre and his relatives. Most of them had no labels, were at least twenty years old and got pulled out from their cellars. As they got us drunk night after night, my fear of drinking these unmarked bottles of mystery wine vanished. We played card games for hours drinking wine with his Uncle Guy. I was relieved to have an activity (besides drinking) where I could occupy my time. Uncle Guy was an artist who had lost his wife.

Uncle Guy's wife was also manic depressive and died from liver complications that Guy swore stemmed from taking lithium. This made Pierre even more opinionated about me taking my medications. I said things were different now, that they do blood tests and they have all kinds of medications. But Pierre was convinced (as was his uncle) that lithium had killed her. I tried to reason with him saying maybe they had her on too high of a dose. Maybe they didn't test her levels enough or, most likely, at all? Maybe she was an alcoholic and had cirrhosis of the liver? He refused that theory, although we don't know the real story. We had endless arguments and the medication issue was one, giant revolving topic.

In fact, a theme for our summer in France (and our relationship), was our fighting. One day Pierre and I had a massive fight in the middle of a tour. He accused me of having a thing for his brother.

"I see you looking at him all the time. Just admit you have the hots for my brother, Wendy."

"Oh yeah, that's it! You got me, Pierre."

"Just admit it!" His eyes had turned into mini-blazing fires.

I don't think that it was only the coke that made him so paranoid. His father was a cheater. That was the reason his mother left France with the family when he was ten. She was trying to escape and start a new life without her cheating husband.

"You're unbelievable!"

"Just admit it, Wendy!" He screamed.

Sensing it was going to get ugly, I ran down the stairs and out of the tour place. I wanted to leave him (and for him to stay with his family), but he followed. We argued all the way down the stairs and were now out on the street. His family was still upstairs, unaware of what the fight was about, but they knew we were fighting. People a block away probably knew we were fighting.

"You paranoid son of a bitch! I can't look at someone? He's gay! How would that work Pierre? Tell me! Huh? How?"

"Admit it! You think he's better looking than me. I always catch you staring at him. Just admit it!" Was this a pissing contest about who I thought was better looking? Or was he really so crazy that he thought I had the hots for his brother? Something was seriously wrong with Pierre and I was finally beginning to see it. He was paranoid and insecure. This I knew before, but I couldn't take it anymore.

I ran across the road and kept running until I was out of sight and breath. I stopped and looked around desperately for a phone booth. I spotted one, tucked away inside and closed the door behind me. I was safe! But wait! I had no money and couldn't speak French! I couldn't even work this damn pay phone! And how could I push my flight up and leave immediately with no resources to stay in a hotel, no ability to speak French to even change the flight, nothing? (My plane ticket home wasn't for a few weeks.) Then reality set in: I was stuck here. Even worse: I was stuck here with *him*. Broke, in a foreign country where I didn't speak the language, and 100% trapped!

Luckily, it blew over and his relatives were all very kind to me. That got me through. (Well, that and lots of red wine!) We played more cards and drank more old French wine from the cellars of his relatives. We toured vineyard after vineyard. We fought the entire time, every day, about every little thing. We drove to the South of France and Monaco. Yes, the countryside and beaches were beautiful, but everything else was horrible. Summer in France. The idea *sounded* like a good one, but it ended up being my summer from hell.

As if it wasn't bad enough with our constant fighting and being broke, it got worse. I got sick. Very sick. My last few weeks there I was so sick that his old football buddy (soccer to us Americans), who was a doctor, examined me and said I should probably be in the hospital. I had bronchitis, which was turning into walking pneumonia. I spent most of the mornings and part of the afternoons in bed coughing. We were on the 3rd floor (which was more of a functional attic than anything else), so it was very hot up there in August. I often wanted to jump out of our tiny little window and looked longingly at the pavement!

There was no air conditioning because it was very expensive. I couldn't shower for very long because it, too, was costly. Anything that could provide comfort cost too much, so I suffered. It was torture!

To this day, the only French phrases I remember how to say are: *I am sick, I am tired, I am sad* and how to order two packs of cigarettes. That tells you how my summer in France was. A nightmare.

We got back to the U.S. in one piece, but we were broke. I was physically, and worse, *mentally* broken. I knew deep down that being with Pierre wasn't right, just like I knew doing cocaine or smoking pot or being drunk wasn't right. But I wasn't facing up to the facts at that point.

I hadn't connected the dots and studied the picture to realize that Pierre was a jealous, paranoid, cocaine-addicted alcoholic who had taken me down to his low level. True, I was also addicted to those same things and going down that same hill. But with two people, there is a snowball-down-a-hill effect: you gather speed. It wasn't that he was forcing me down that hill; I was headed there anyway. I'm grateful now he introduced me to cocaine because it got me to my bottom faster. I truly am.

After a small loan from both our parents, we moved into a rented house. I had gotten a job working for a bank and Pierre managed to land a decent computer networking job for a major contractor. We had our old '72 BMW that we'd gotten before we left. With a new paint job it looked snazzy on the outside, although it was really a rundown piece of crap on the inside.

It's funny, our lives matched the car because on the outside we *seemed* okay, but everything was really a mess on the inside. We had our families down for a house warming party. I cooked quiches and made Dad's special recipe salad dressing. That happy couple façade was there. The happy couple was not.

We were doing cocaine on the weekends and drinking constantly. Before too long, I started smoking pot during the week to try to come down from the high of the coke. I was terrified of the bank's random drug tests. I was miserable at my job. I was miserable at home with him. I just was plain miserable. Nothing was going right.

Pierre made matters worse by convincing me to stop taking my medications. I was tired of fighting him about it. I was still taking my meds as prescribed, but our medical insurance would be up in a few months, so that battle was about to end anyway. Although deep down I knew right from wrong, having someone tell me I didn't need them was all I needed to hear. I didn't really want to be on them in the first place. I wanted to believe I could function on my own. I thought if I wasn't taking my meds and I didn't go under, it would prove I was okay. Plus, the money we spent on my medications we could've spent on more drugs and alcohol. That was the bottom line. I wanted to be high more than I wanted to be well. We both wanted that.

My life was bad news and I wanted to run away. Pierre was always controlling me. He had become so paranoid that he wouldn't even let me go to the grocery store alone. (He thought I would be flirting with the stock boys.) Funny thing is, I never flirted with *any* guys, cheated on him or gave him any reason to think that. Our cocaine use was increasing, making his paranoia worse, but it was also making it unbearable to live with him. He forced me into a dependence upon him that weakened me and made me afraid to leave him.

We had no sex life. This was especially ironic because we always held hands and acted very lovey dovey in public and around our families. Everyone assumed we were sexually happy too, but we were not. Behind closed doors nothing went on except sleep. I believed he wasn't attracted to me anymore. I thought, *I guess this is what it's like to be married*. I tried to keep it going with little romantic gestures. Once or twice a week I started putting little post-it notes in his lunch bag saying "I love you" and other endearing things like that.

"Why didn't you put a note in today?" He asked later as we ate our fast food dinners.

"What do you mean *why*?" I responded in return.

"Are you mad at me or something?" Pierre probed.

"No," I said. "Just because I didn't put one in, doesn't mean I'm *mad* at you."

"Well, I looked for it today at lunch and there wasn't one there. I was disappointed."

"If I put one in there *every* day then it's an obligation. I do it to be spontaneous and fun. They wouldn't mean as much if I did it every day. Would they?" No answer. I felt I could never please him. Even when I was trying to do something nice, I was not doing it right, or enough, for him.

Every Friday night our ritual was to cash our paychecks, go to the liquor store and get a few of his favorite thirty dollar bottles of French red wine. We would also get liquor to do shots and a case or twelve pack of beer for when we were desperate and had nothing else left. (I remember Sunday nights feeling ashamed that our recycling stash looked like we threw a party every weekend. It looked really bad, even our denial couldn't deny that.)

Next, we would go to a seedy part of a well known local drug town. Pierre had a friend, Pat, from a computer class he had taken. Pierre (like most of us addicts) had a knack for searching out other addicts to score from. Pat's boyfriend, "Shorty" was his nickname, got us coke and we did that almost every weekend for about eight months.

In the beginning, I kept saying I only wanted pot. I didn't want to be a coke addict. I knew we could never get enough coke to keep us as high as we wanted for as long as we wanted. And honestly, it scared me because it seemed hard core. But I was an addict and I took what we could get. Everyone else preferred coke so I was outnumbered. It didn't take long for me to get addicted to it, too. Now I was one of them.

Pretty soon cocaine turned into crack cocaine. Pat or Shorty would cook it for us. We would stand in their kitchen, talking and watching them to see how they did it. Prior to meeting them, I had never done crack, but Pierre had. I didn't even know what it was until after I got sober. All I knew was that we bought the cocaine, added some things, heated it up until it got hard and we smoked it. I still thought it was cocaine. Crack was supposed to be cheap. Yet we were blowing every cent we had! *I had no idea this was crack cocaine.*

We went to Shorty's and Pat's apartment almost every Friday night. We'd sit at their table for hours upon hours into the early morning. We'd talk and play cards and smoke cigarettes until there was no crack cocaine left. It didn't take long before Pierre began to get paranoid and think Shorty had the hots for me. (That didn't come as a surprise because he was paranoid about everything, especially men and me.) I had to make sure I was not too friendly with Shorty because it would invariably start an argument on the way home.

Sometimes a straggler would come into their apartment and plop down in their living room, ever so conveniently when we were there. The other tenants sniffed us out, like dogs sniffing out drugs at the airport. They'd pretend to be nice to us just to get a hit or two. They didn't want to get to know us. No one asked our names or anything about us. They weren't there to sit at the table and talk or play cards. They just knew we were there and if they showed up, we would share. We always had the generous Christmas-like giving spirit, because we were slightly better off. But not by much. We had the income, but we spent every penny and then some. We knew better than to expect to be put on their Christmas card lists. They were addicts just like us.

I always had a hard time focusing on the drive home. I was terrified we would get pulled over. Pierre would make me drive (the jackass that he was) because he already had a DUI and I didn't. Even though I understood his logic, I thought it was selfish of him to throw me under the bus. We were almost always the only people on the road at 4:00 am. I felt like a target, though surprisingly enough we never got pulled over.

Come Monday we had nothing left. I wouldn't even have thirty-five cents for the toll to get to work. Those weeks that I had to travel on the parkway to our bank's headquarters a few exits away were the worst. I'd throw pennies just so the cameras at the toll plazas would see me try to pay something. I figured I'd be less likely to get a ticket than if I threw nothing.

I loved the rush, but there was never enough and it always wore off sooner than I wanted. To make matters worse, we had a speckled, black and white countertop in our rented house. When we did lines, and had nothing left, we would scrape the countertops to see if we could get one more spec. Just one more taste of numbness. That's what this drug did to us, to me.

One night, or I should say early in the morning, I was sitting on a metal folding chair in the middle of the kitchen. I hugged my knees inside my college sweatshirt and questioned myself: what had I become? I looked sideways over at the burners where we had just cooked the last of our cocaine and I felt like the scum of the earth. I felt so alone. And rather than stop myself, all I wanted was more cocaine, which made me loathe myself even more. I wanted to keep the high going because it was wearing off and I hated how real I was feeling.

"Go get us some more, baby!" I was yelling and crying at the same time.

"Baby, we don't have any more money."

"I don't care. Get me some more!"

"With what? We have no more money. What do you want me to do?"

"I don't know. Do a cash advance. Don't we have anything left?"

"Baby, our cards are all maxed out. There's nothing 'til next Friday. You know that."

I was quietly crying. I think it was at that moment when he realized he had helped turn me into a coke addict. I was already an alcoholic and smoking pot, but cocaine had catapulted me into a whole new addict category.

"I *knew* I shouldn't have gotten you into this! I knew it! Dammit!" He cursed in French as he walked out of the kitchen.

I remember seeing myself outside of myself. Was it an out of body experience? All I know is I saw myself sitting on that chair as if I were standing in the living room looking into the kitchen at myself. I saw my knees hugged into my chest inside my sweatshirt. It was impossible to ignore how low I had sunk. I was disgusted at myself.

My mania was out of control, my depression was right there with it and I wanted to run away. I was broke and addicted and had never felt so alone. I was ashamed of myself for so many reasons. I had become distant with my closest friends and family (although they never deserted me). I ceased caring about anything. I wasn't suicidal, but I wanted it all to go away. I wanted to leave Pierre, the house and my job. None of it felt right anymore. At that moment, I found my solution: I was going to leave NJ.

"I'm going to Colorado." I announced to him, holding my breath for his reaction. I loved Colorado and had close family out there. I could live with my cousins, clean myself up, get a new job and get away from him.

"What?

"I'm going to Colorado, Pierre."

"When?"

"Friday, right after I cash my paycheck."

"Well…when are you coming back?" He was concerned but must've sensed it was coming. He didn't know how long I planned to be out there, nor did I. I was making these decisions as I was going along.

"I don't know." I replied.

"You *are* coming back, right?" His confidence was waning. Pierre knew that he had to let me go and didn't put up a fight. I was leaving with or without his consent.

"Yes. I plan to…soon. I'm not sure when, though."

"I hope so, Wendy. I mean, you're not *leaving* me, are you?" Pierre was more concerned that I might be breaking up with him than physically leaving. Leaving and coming back, he could handle. Breaking up and leaving, he could not. I was doing both, but sensed he couldn't handle that truth at that moment, so I stuck with only one.

"No, I'll be back. I just don't know when."

He was sad. I suppose I was sad, too. But I was mourning the loss of my drugs and alcohol more; not so much him. I knew it was time to get sober again, and get squared away with my bipolar disorder. I also knew I had to start living right or I would eventually die. Living this way was hell. It was a constant fear of not having enough, of being caught at work or by the police. I knew if I didn't get away from him we both would've kept on existing like that until something really bad happened.

Since I knew Pierre wouldn't leave me, leaving him was the only solution. I would find my happiness in Colorado. I would get sober in Colorado. I thought it would be much easier to run away than to stay and deal with everything.

Pierre helped me load the car the next night and I planned on leaving Friday, which was payday. We barely spoke, but at least he helped me. He filled up the tank for me and was kinder to me than he had been since I couldn't remember when.

When Friday came, I was to get my meager four hundred dollar paycheck, which was all I had for my journey out to Colorado. I had my paycheck money, an old BMW and a tank of gas. I made the mistake of letting my plan slip to my sister. (Maybe that was subconsciously so I could be rescued?) I wasn't exactly thinking clearly. Looking back, I was in a mixed episode of depression and mania. Clearly, my decision-making process was not exactly sound. My parents were out of town in Charleston, South Carolina on vacation but due back the Friday I planned to leave.

At lunchtime, right after I cashed my check, I walked into the lobby and there they were: all three of them. My mother, father and sister stood there with serious looks on their faces. The gig was up. I knew I wasn't going anywhere.

It was intervention time.

I was and felt completely washed up, but wasn't ready to throw in the towel. That is, until the dynamic trio stepped in for the big intervention to foil my plans.

They came back to the house I was renting and helped me pack up the rest of my things. (Almost everything was already in my getaway car so it made that easy.) Pierre was still at work so it made leaving even easier. I tried to stash my bongs (both of which I had broken that week, which I saw as a sign from God I should quit). Our house looked like a drug den. They had to have known what had gone on there. At best, if it was totally cleaned up, it still looked like a dark hole or cave. All the windows were set up for permanent "weekend drug mode" with sheets, blankets or towels over all the windows. We were up all night and slept all day.

It was the end of the French Connection.

Immediately, I moved back in with my parents. I filed for bankruptcy. I had over eighteen thousand dollars in credit card debt.

By age twenty-seven I was, without dispute, washed up. I had bottomed out in just about every area of my life. I felt like driftwood that had washed up on a beach: broken, useless and lost. I went back to my Uncle Rick and he helped me get sober again. I had no money, not even for cigarettes, so Uncle Rick bought them for me. I knew I was going to be screwed for a long time because of the bankruptcy, but at least the financial monkey was off my back.

I began to see a new psychiatrist and went back on medication. I was on the road to recovery. I went back to the employment agency that I'd worked for on college holiday breaks. Luckily, the manager liked me and when there was an opening, she hired me as a supervisor. Ah, benefits again!

Vegas and Bust

I was doing well, seeing the same psychiatrist, stable on the right meds, sober and getting promotions at my job. So of course - I needed a vacation! Newly sober and scared to go away alone, I searched for someone to go away with me. (I worried that I would drink again if I went by myself.) A very straight-laced friend and her fiancée, both of whom didn't drink, were going to Vegas in a few weeks. I thought Tony and Tina would keep me straight. Perfect!

I booked the trip to Sin City (that should've been my first clue, the *name*). I tagged along with my pals. The only problem was their hotel was sold out, so upon another co-worker's recommendation, I stayed at a much cheaper hotel just off the strip. But when my friends went to bed by ten o'clock every night...

I was up late gambling back at my hotel. I mean come on, this is Vegas baby! You stay up late, wake up late, lie in the sun, eat at buffets, catch a show if you want to, gamble and party 'til the wee hours: Vegas.

Meanwhile, they were doing the elderly tour version: get up early, eat at the breakfast and lunch buffets, gamble the nickel slots, catch the free outdoor daytime shows then go to bed early (they even wrote down their wins/losses for the nickel slots!) I should have guessed.

Despite their elderly approach to Vegas, it could not insulate me from myself and the inevitable.

I'm a night owl. The lights, the action, the gambling - it was all right up my alley. Vegas seductively whispered my name and within two days I couldn't ignore its call. I had unexpectedly gotten an eight hundred dollars tax refund back before I left and saw it as my "Monopoly Money." The gambling was just another intoxication, another addiction to do while trying to avoid drinking or drugging. There it was again: gambling. Except this time it wasn't pocket change like it had been during my manic summer in Colorado. This time I blew through *all* my money. And in no time my internal clock got all messed up. My mornings turned into days and my nights stretched into early morning. With my lack of sleep and the intoxication of gambling, my mania had awoken.

My problem in Vegas (aside from getting sucked into mania) was a man named Ron. Or as I nicknamed him later: Moonraker. (He was the guy from the James Bond movie with the metal teeth.) Well, that was Ron. I was gambling all night at his craps table. He was one of the craps dealers at my hotel. Eventually, he made the first move. If I had seen his Moonrakerish teeth, I would have shot him down immediately. But he never smiled, so I never knew.

"Do you want to have a cigarette with me on my next break?"

"Okay," I said. We went outside through a side door off the floor. Out by the dumpsters, he pulled out a cigarette from its box and we sat down on a brick ledge.

"Hi, my name is Ron." He stuck his hand out to shake mine.

"Hi, I'm Wendy." I lamely shook his hand in return, feeling extremely awkward. I felt like I was at the beginning of a bad interview, rather than meeting my craps dealer at this shitty hotel.

"Sorry, do you want one?" He paused, just before lighting his cigarette. It was more an afterthought than a clear moment of chivalrous thought.

"No, thanks. I've got my own." I reached into my purse and got mine out.

"So...where ya from?" He paused as he leaned over and lit my cigarette with his match. *Match? Why didn't he have a lighter? This was not a good sign. Hmmm...red flag here.* (Scary thing was, this was my *first* red flag, before I processed the implications of the obvious *dive* he worked in!)

"New Jersey."

"Ah New *Joisey*, huh?" Ron chuckled, proud of his trite joke.

"No, New *Jersey*. Nobody I know actually says that. It's so annoying that everyone thinks that. But whatever. That's where I'm from."

"So... are you staying here at the hotel? With friends?" He was probably confused because he had never seen me with anyone. I always gambled at his table alone. In fact, my friends hadn't even stepped foot in this hotel the entire time. Why should they? It was almost depressing. There were no shows, great buffets or rollercoasters here.

Ron began counting the tip money he had with him like a seasoned pro, flipping open his big wad of mostly one and five dollar bills. He was simultaneously smoking and counting with his two hands. I winced, thinking of the smoke that would invariably go in his eyes.

"No, they're at a hotel on the strip. It was sold out, so I'm here. Plus, I couldn't afford to stay on the strip alone." Then I realized that spelled out: that's why I'm staying at your crappy-B-rate-hotel.

"Shit!" He started his count over, mid bundle, and I realized this couldn't be easy: holding a conversation, counting and smoking. "I keep losing my count," he said, shaking his head.

"I'm sorry." I felt guilty. All my chatter couldn't help.

"Nah. It's not you, it's me." He started putting the money in piles. Luckily, there was no breeze so making piles on the ledge between us worked. *Wow, some system they got here,* I thought. At least they must trust him if they're giving him all the money to count. That says something positive about his character. He must be trustworthy and honest. (What I overlooked was that we were in a dump of a casino and there must be a story there.)

"I'll stop talking. Sorry. It must be hard to count and talk." I felt a bit awkward, talking to a total stranger, but I felt a weird connection to him already. We had an undeniable bond that I couldn't explain. (In hindsight, I realize I was manic and lonely and there wasn't a bond other than the one I imagined. It's hard to trust what your feelings really are until a manic episode has subsided. When I am in a manic episode, I usually insist there's an incredible bond with some new guy.)

"It's not your fault," he said. "I'm just nervous around you."

"Oh." I didn't know what to say, feeling silly.

"Twenty-five…twenty-six…twenty-seven…" Ron started to re-count his little piles, this time out loud, so he wouldn't lose his place. I sat there silently smoking and when I was done, wondered if I should light another one. I was smoking a lot, just blazing through them. I couldn't drink or do drugs, so what the hell else was there to do? Gambling, smoking and talking to strange casino dealers by the dumpsters kind of went hand in hand.

"It's such a nice night." I remarked, looking around. The weather was beautiful, the view was…well we *were* at the employee entrance staring at the big red dumpsters that smelled. Not much of a view, or smell, but at least we had the nice weather.

"Yeah. Hey, do you want to go out to this bar we all go to after my shift is over? I'm done in less than an hour. Me and my buddy are going over there." He put the tips for his co-workers into little brown envelopes and waited for my reply.

"Okay, but I don't drink or do drugs. I'll only be drinking Coke, just so you know. As long as you're cool with that, sure I'll go. Oh, and I only smoke *cigarettes*." Poof! I agreed to go to a bar with a stranger — just like that! I was working so hard on staying sober. I mean, I could still do that at a bar, couldn't I? (Apparently, I thought I could.)

"No problem. It's cool. Hey, do you play pool?"

"Well, I haven't played in a long time...but I like to." I flashed back to the Pierre days. We used to play a lot.

"Great! Wait for me in the lounge. I'll be off in forty-five minutes or so."

"Okay." I wondered which lounge, and was about to ask, when I realized there was only one. I waited in the lounge, sipping my Coke and smoking, until they were done working. Off we went to their favorite bar down the road: me, Ron and his shady looking casino dealer friend.

All night long, we played pool and I drank Cokes with him and his friends. The first night I was okay being there. It felt good to be back in the bar atmosphere with the songs on the jukebox, playing pool and enjoying the camaraderie. In a way, I felt alive again. Intellectually, I knew I was playing games with my sobriety, but I was more confident than I should've been. I thought I could handle it. It didn't take long before I was back to my old ways and I drank.

My friends left Vegas as scheduled, but I stayed. I made the executive decision to call work and extend my vacation on my last day there. I called Regina, my boss, to tell her I was staying three more days. Regina was furious and it took a lot to get her mad.

"It's *not* okay, Wendy. You can't just do that! It changes everything here. I have meetings scheduled!"

"I'm sorry."

"Sorry is not okay. You have to come back as scheduled on Thursday, Wendy. I'm counting on you to be here to cover the office so I can go up to region on Thursday for my monthly managers' meeting!" That was a big meeting she would be missing. I knew she was going to be pissed off.

"I'm sorry Regina, but I'm staying in Vegas. I'll be back on Monday."

"We're going to have a talk about this." She hung up the phone. I knew there was a chance I was going to get a "verbal warning." I also knew they meant nothing unless you got two of them. Two verbals equaled one written and I wouldn't get two of them. Even a written warning meant nothing and I never aspired to be a branch manager anyway.

I always did what I wanted when I wanted. I played by my own set of rules and nobody else's rule book. My self-will was coming back and nothing and no one else mattered. Except for my quest for happiness. All bets were off when it came to my happiness.

I changed the return date on my plane ticket and checked out of the hotel. I could no longer afford it. I was broke, having gambled every last dollar away at Ron's craps table. Ron offered me to stay at his place my last three nights. We were hitting it off and spending a lot of time together, so I thought, why not?

I was drunk and stoned in no time. We spent every night at his dive bar getting drunk, playing pool and getting high. It was a loser magnet bar. This was no Cheers bar. This was the place where B Rate Casino Dealers and rookie pool hustlers hung out. Where girlfriends with bad hair and gaudy makeup went hand in hand with their guy's drink. To them, I was a fish out of water. To me, I was fitting in again. Sober, I never would've held a conversation with these shady characters. Yet drunk, they were my peers. I had come a long way from the jovial college bars to here. I drank, I sunk, and the amazing part was, I wasn't ashamed of who I instantly became with my drink and joint in hand. I played pool and imagined myself as his girl. I became her, as scary as that is to me now.

Three days later, I flew home and went back to work. Plans were in motion to move out there if things continued to go well. He was an active alcoholic. I was an alcoholic *trying* to recover. However, all I saw then was he and I in love in Vegas. That's it.

Things had gotten more serious with us from a distance and I had gone back out there to see Ron on my second trip to Vegas. I was trying to picture myself in that lifestyle…could I live there? I could find a job because there were a lot of hotels there and I majored in Hotel Management. My company also had a branch in Vegas, so I could probably transfer if a position opened up.

I relapsed with him in a bar. Again. No, he hadn't pressured me to do so, but I *missed* drinking. Especially in a bar. I was instantly sucked in again and drinking like I hadn't skipped a beat or been sober in NJ since my last trip. Instant downhill.

When I came home, I had to get sober. Again. Ron and I kept in touch but I was anxious to go back and see him. I was nervous about relapsing because it had become my pattern each time I visited him. My friends and family warned me and knew what I would do. I knew it, but I didn't care. I thought I was in love. Love became more important than my sobriety.

One day in particular, Ron and I had gotten into a huge fight on the phone. It was our ongoing fight about being committed to each other and the distance thing not working out. I wasn't sleeping well, and I felt like I had to get out there and show him how much I cared about him. We *had* to be together. I had no vacation time pre-approved but I would figure all that out later, I decided. He was pressuring me to get out there but of course, I had no solution on how to pay for the ticket.

I looked around my room. What could I do? I spotted my guitar in the corner that I hadn't played in years. Sell it! I went to the music store and they said they'd give me seventy-five dollars for it. I couldn't do it. No, I needed a new plan. Who could help me? Who was on my side? Nobody in my family would give me money to go see Ron. They didn't want me to keep going to see him and get swayed to move out there. They thought he was no good for me.

Melinda! Melinda was a flight attendant for a major airline and, although we weren't very close friends, I thought she might help me. I knew about their "friends and family" program. That was it! I called her. She wasn't thrilled, but she helped me. I went to Newark Airport and flew standby. I slept at the airport in my suit. They had a seat open flying into San Diego.

"I'll take it!" I told the ticket agent. I just wanted to see him (and get off the airport floor)! San Diego would do.

I had no clearance to take a vacation, but there I was on that plane. I called my boss after I was buckled in and we had pushed out of our gate. I didn't care about the job, the office or anybody else. I just saw that I had to get to Vegas. Was I manic? I must have been. This was not rational behavior.

"Regina?" I was hunched over trying to hide the fact that I was on my cell phone, as our plane was making its way to the runway for takeoff. If I was *lucky* I wouldn't get yelled at because the flight attendants were already seated. I was getting a few looks from passengers, though.

"Hi Wendy...wait, where *are* you?" she asked. She could tell it was no ordinary call from, say, my apartment where I should have been calling her from to say I was late for work. Getting a call from me saying I was late was pretty typical. Getting a call from a *plane* that I was taking a sporadic vacation, was not.

"Regina, I have to go to Las Vegas." I heard a beep overhead. I had to get off this phone.

"Well, put in for your vacation time. You have some left." Regina was very sensible and methodical. She made a great manager.

"Preparing for takeoff." The pilot had finished taxiing and we were momentarily stopped in take-off position at the end of the runway.

"Well... I'm...uh... leaving today. Actually I'm leaving...ah... right now."

"No...Wendy! You *cannot* leave!" Regina started yelling and in between, you could hear the plane beeping those pre-flight, last minute beeps. She must've heard them. Regina launched into the reasons why I couldn't do this. I heard the engines being throttled and I knew I had only a few seconds left. It was getting harder to hear.

"Um, Regina, I'm sorry but we're about to take off. I have to turn off my cell phone now. I'll call you when I land. I'm sorry."

"Wait! Wendy, no...you can't..." Click. Nothing mattered to me. I made these horrible decisions that I thought were so romantic. I was risking my job. Still, I didn't care.

I landed in San Diego and rented a convertible. I figured I may as well do this in style and I had just enough money, so I blew it on the upgrade. I did not call my boss right away, in fact, I don't remember when I called her exactly. It was not a high priority. I just wanted to get to Vegas to see Ron and what I didn't want was to get yelled at during my road trip there in my cool car. My judgment was completely off. I ignored everyone who was saying what I didn't want to hear. They just didn't understand my love for him, I told myself.

I should have known right from the beginning that it would never work when I saw where he worked, how he drank, his lack of teeth and how he treated his teenage son, Jeff. I should have known when I saw the hole-in-the-wall bar we walked into. I should have known when his friend took me aside and tried to explain how Ron was not right for me. There were a lot of signs I didn't want to read.

When I was in New Jersey, Ron would call me up drunk at all hours of the night, depressed, talking about the songs from his America album like "Sister Golden Hair." How we should meet in the middle of where we lived and just start over. Just the two of us, without any friends or family (although I always had enough sense to know that was a bad idea). He was the most romantic when he was wasted, so I would stay on the phone, despite how drunk and depressed he was. And it was *always* hard to hear him because he'd call from the payphone at the bar.

We did have some good moments. A few. We went to the Bellagio a few times, once standing there for an hour, watching as they rotated the fountain show. I thought that was one of the most beautiful things I had ever seen. He talked about cleaning up his act and trying to get in with a better casino to earn more money. We could get a better apartment together. I saw his potential. He needed me and I liked feeling needed, I suppose.

Going to the Bellagio, those rare sober talks and an occasional fun pool game were pretty much it for good times, though. He was always too drunk to have sex. Ron was a classic "bad drunk," often yelling and nasty. His son and I would just exchange looks and I felt sorry for the boy. I always gave Jeff money to get food because there was nothing in the apartment to eat and Ron never had any money. His son wanted to live with his mother, who was in Idaho with his other brothers and sisters. (Ron had five kids altogether.) The sad part was he was scared to leave his father. He was more a parent to Ron than Ron to his son. It was wrong, we were wrong, for a whole list of reasons that are crystal clear to me now. But back then, all I did was make excuses for him.

One night, we were shooting pool at his favorite hole-in-the-wall bar. We were taking on his friend and girlfriend and winning. She and I were taking a bathroom break and pretending to get along. I was worried about one detail. There was *one* thing that wasn't adding up. If Ron was always broke because he was always drunk and could barely pay his rent, how did he pay his child support? And, if he *didn't* pay his child support, shouldn't he be in jail? I began questioning this woman to figure this all out, since Ron never talked about it.

"Sally, can't they throw Ron in jail for not paying his child support payments?"

"Well, they can't throw him in jail since he's not divorced." Sally stopped dead. She saw by my expression in the bathroom mirror that I had no idea *he was still married*.

"*Whaaaaat?!*" I screamed. She looked back at me afraid.

"Oh my Gosh. I thought you knew." Sally put her hand up to her mouth in horror that she had just leaked the big secret.

"That lying asshole!" I yelled.

"Wendy, please don't tell him I told you. Shit!" She quickly put away her lipstick as I stormed out.

I pushed the swinging door open so hard it hurt my hand. I

looked over at him and he smiled his drunken, euphoric smile back at me. He tried to catch eyes with me, to share a moment, but I wouldn't look back at him again. I wanted to scream so loudly that it would've cleared out the bar and woken up all of Las Vegas. I mean here I was, ready to give up everything: my family, friends, a stable job, doctors, therapists and recovery network. Leave everyone and everything and move to the desert. All for this guy. Yet he was lying *the entire time about being married!*

I sat down next to his friend, a guy named Dusty with red hair who was shorter than me. Dusty was the only person I knew at the bar besides Ron and his host of lying friends. I considered Dusty as close to neutral as there was that night. Ron was snarling at me, having no idea why I was sitting with his friend and ignoring him. As he threw back drink after drink, his sneers grew nastier and nastier. My looks got equally as nasty. I should've figured his friend's girlfriend wouldn't admit to letting the cat out of the bag. Ron had no idea why I was mad.

Ron got so annoyed that he finally left. I assumed he was going back to his apartment. Not long afterwards, I walked outside. The sun stung my eyes (it was now daylight) and I put on my sunglasses. I went over to my rental car and grabbed the stupid America CD that he'd given me, the *only* thing he'd ever given me. I flung it across the parking lot like a Frisbee. Instantly, I felt a little bit freer. I planned to go back to his apartment, get my stuff and get the hell out of there. I was back on track and had snapped out of this madness with Ron.

Sanity had returned.

I enlisted Dusty to help me. I thought he seemed like a decent guy, in a I-have-no-other-option-but-to-pick-you-out-of-this-seedy-bar type of way. He was my *only* choice at the time. The rest of them were all liars. Ron's other friends had played game after game of pool, drank beer after beer with me and never said a word about Ron still being married. I didn't know Dusty very well, but at least he wasn't among Ron's close knit group of lying buddies. He was an acquaintance, another barfly from what I gathered, but not someone who had lied to my face.

"Can you come with me back to his apartment? I'm kind of scared." I asked Dusty.

"Sure." Dusty and I got in my rental car and drove to his place. Wow, he's so nice, I thought. I pulled into asshole's apartment complex and luckily found a spot close to the stairs to his second floor apartment.

"Stay in the car, but come if you hear me yell for you, okay?" I instructed Dusty.

"Okay." He replied.

"Actually, can you come up if you hear *any* yelling?"

"Sure, no problem." Dusty reassured.

"But don't get hurt. I mean, you know just be ready to call the police if it sounds really bad."

"Got it, I'm here. Don't worry." By the look on his face, I was feeling less reassured by the minute. He was starting to look nervous. It was starting to make me feel even *more* nervous.

"Okay good. Sorry to have to ask you all this. Thanks." I felt a little better knowing Dusty was there, even if he was much smaller than me. I decided he was beginning to remind me of the geek in *Sixteen Candles*. I quickly realized I was on my own. This guy wasn't going to help me.

With my heart pounding hard, I walked along the walkway to the stairs. When I turned the corner to the stairs, I saw a bunch of Mountain Dew cans that had been thrown at the bottom of the stairs. They were opened and had sprayed everywhere. I had a feeling those were the ones I bought his son; it was his favorite soda. Then I noticed a cake smashed up against the side of the next building. That was *definitely* the birthday cake I bought Jeff the day before. Now I was furious! Why bring Jeff into this? He was innocent!

I knew this meant that Ron was not only very angry, he was also really, *really* drunk. This was not going to be good and looking at everything smashed up like that, I got scared. When I looked to my right, I spotted my best suit, strewn all down the stairs. My best suit? How dare he! Now I was ready for war!

I had flashes of those trashy talk shows. The ones with all the bodyguards that hold back their guests. What had I become with this man? I felt like white trash. It was another moment of clarity, like the time I was in the kitchen with my knees to my chest on the chair, wondering how I had gotten there. I had to get out of here. First, I had to get my stuff.

I knocked on the door, not sure what to expect, but figured it would probably be his son. He always slept on the couch.

The door finally opened a crack and I saw Jeff's scared face hiding behind the chain. I was relieved when I saw it was Jeff and not asshole, but I wasn't surprised. I knew asshole was passed out. He made a quick motion to shut it, but I was already prepared; I wedged my foot in the door.

"Open the door Jeff!"

"No!"

"Op-en-the-door!" I said slower with more force. My foot was starting to hurt. I had to get him to open the door. And fast.

"Go away!"

"Jeff, *please* open the door?" I tried the nice approach, asking gently and slowly.

"My father said not to let you in." He sounded confused and hesitated slightly.

"Why not?" I couldn't wait to hear what his father said to him. This ought to be entertaining.

"He just said not to." At least he wasn't yelling now. I knew he must be able to tell I wasn't drunk. He knew his father was though. His father *always* was. I couldn't *believe* I was in this situation. What the fuck was I thinking?

"Would you please open the door? I just want to get my stuff. Then I'll leave. I promise." I took my foot out and he immediately slammed the door, of course. "*Why* won't you let me in? I don't understand. What did your father tell you?" There was a long pause.

"My father said you slept with his friend."

"*What?*" I couldn't help laughing. "*Are you kidding me?* Who are you going to believe, me or him?"

Silence.

"I didn't sleep with his friend, Jeff. I wouldn't talk to your Dad, so I *talked* to his friend. He lied to me about being divorced. Now open the door...come on. Please?"

At last, I heard the chain jiggle and then slide across. He turned the lock on the door, let me in and stood aside as I walked in.

"Thank you." I said as he quickly shifted his gaze to the floor.

I walked past him and into the bedroom. I didn't want to go in there, but I had no choice. That's where my stuff was. Luckily, Ron was still asleep and snoring like a champ. When I was midway through packing my stuff, he rolled over on the bed (which was just a mattress on the floor).

"Come here, baby. Gimme a kiss." He crooned, semi-coherent. He patted the tiny space next to him, half asleep, still wasted and obviously clueless that we'd been in a fight. I should've known: he was in a blackout. By the way he was acting it seemed he didn't remember a damned thing. I couldn't be with this man. I was so done.

"I'm leaving, Ron." This would've been obvious to anyone, seeing I was packing and still scheduled to be there a few more days. But we were dealing with Ron here, so I felt I better spell it out for him.

"Mmm…come here, baby."

"Do you even remember what you did?" I turned around to look at him, busy picking up my clothes and packing.

"Whaddya mean? Come gimme a kiss."

"Goodbye, Ron." I zippered my bag shut and slung it over my shoulder. I didn't turn around to look at him.

"Where are you going?" I heard Ron say, still confused, as I left his bedroom. I walked down the short hallway into the living room.

"Goodbye, Jeff. Good luck." Jeff was back on the couch, with cartoons on. Poor kid. He had a miserable life. He ate meals from 7-11. He babysat his Dad. He slept on the couch. He barely had any clothes, certainly no decent ones. His Dad drank away every dime they had. This apartment was disgusting. I marveled at how long it took me until that very moment to realize how stupid I had been.

I walked out.

I got back out to the car where Dusty was waiting. I hadn't slept that night, so I wanted to check-in to an inexpensive hotel and sleep a bit. I dropped him off at his place and checked-in to a hotel. By this time, it was already 7:00 am and checkout was at 11:00. Still, any sleep would do. I was anxious to sleep then get the hell out of Vegas. Far away from Ron. Far away from this nightmare. If I never came back to this town, it wouldn't be too soon.

Later that day, I got in the car to leave Vegas for good. Ron had since sobered up and called me a zillion times on my cell phone begging me to come say goodbye. (I had turned my phone off because it was non-stop.) I knew he was at the pay phone because his home phone was shut off. He guilted me into saying goodbye. He cried. The only other man that has ever cried to me was Bill, my biological father. I can't handle a man crying. Against my better judgment, I agreed.

We parted on decent terms. I said, "I hope you get the help you need Ron." I genuinely hope he got sober, but I doubt it. I hope he made a better man and father of himself, but he was not my problem anymore.

Oh and that saying "What happens in Vegas stays in Vegas?" It's bullshit. Unless, of course, you had a good time.

The Last Relapse

Back in Jersey I was feeling extremely guilty, although not as guilty as I should've felt, about everything. Not just about my relapse, but my unannounced vacation. There was also the matter of my letter of resignation. Prior to leaving for Vegas my last time, I gave up my job because I planned on transferring to a branch out in Las Vegas. This was, of course, prior to learning that Ron was still married.

But when the Ron deal fell through, they ultimately took me back. I lucked out because Regina decided to unhire the person they had just hired to replace me. I thanked her profusely, thinking Regina was being loyal to me. I thought it was because I was such a good employee. She let me know it was otherwise.

"I didn't want to have to train someone else." She stated flatly when I returned.

"What?" I was confused. I thought I was such a valuable employee.

"That's the only reason you still have your job, Wendy." Okay, so much for valuable. For the most part, I was a good employee. I knew she was angry for a long time. It took her a while to get over my unannounced vacation. She had to recruit, interview and hire someone to replace me. And it couldn't have been much fun to convince her bosses to allow her to hire me back. Then to have to be the one to unhire the person she'd just hired.

"I'm sorry." Sorry wasn't enough. I had to work extra hard to earn her trust back. It didn't take too long. She was so nice. A saint too, I swear.

I was getting sober again and, more or less, back on track. I was taking the same combination of meds and seeing the same shrink. (That hadn't changed over the Vegas period.)

Then one day everything changed when a telemarketer from Florida called to sell me a new cell phone carrier. I needed to change carriers anyway, so I listened to his pitch. And the trouble soon began. After the transaction for my new phone with his company was completed, we ended up talking for twenty minutes until his shift ended.

"I get off work now, do you mind if I call you? Can I have your number?" The nice, thirtysomething telemarketer from Florida asked.

"Well, hell-o, you just *gave* me my new number." (This would have been my first clue that he was not the sharpest tool in the shed).

"Oh. Right."

"Yes, you can call me back."

We began speaking on the phone and eating through my new cell minutes. It seemed like a good idea to meet, so Chris booked a flight to the Atlantic City Airport and a hotel nearby.

When I picked Chris up from the airport, to my surprise, he was hot. I hadn't seen his picture because he said he didn't have one. (This was usually code for I'm unattractive so I'm not showing you a picture.) The other possibility, the one he claimed, was he had no camera. I had no camera, so I believed him.

I also believed him because he was making next to nothing as a telemarketer. I knew his son had died of cancer and that he and his then wife had spent every penny to try to save his life. I also knew they divorced after that, which was only a year ago or so. He was in the starting over phase of his life. I was taking a chance, true. I wasn't ugly, but I was at my heaviest, so I figured he caught me at a discount, so to speak. I had the personality, but the weight issue usually put men off. However, he was good looking and I was perplexed.

We were in his hotel room after dinner and I asked him questions about his personal life when the conversation turned to his son. I wanted to be his therapist. I wanted to help him because this was my m.o., you see. I'd already decided that this was why he was fucked up enough to pick someone up on the phone (while he was supposed to be doing his job). Why me? Because I was a little nice to him? (Which was probably uncommon since he was, after all, a telemarketer.) I quickly realized how broken down this man was.

He explained that he and his ex-wife were in the middle of a big lawsuit because the doctors did something wrong during the chemo. His four year old son might have lived. My heart broke for him. He said other medical opinions they had gotten were that his son could have survived if things were done properly. I wanted to shower him with empathy, but I couldn't fix this one. I could not bring back a dead son. This one was out of my league. His pain and angst turned to anger as he talked on. He cried and then he screamed at me.

"I don't want to talk about my son!" He yelled.

"I'm sorry." I felt so bad. I didn't know talking about it would cause him to blow up like this.

"I came here to get away from that!" It hit me that he was running away. He was trying to escape where it all happened.

"Okay, okay. We don't have to talk about that."

We both sat there in silence for a while. I thought what the hell have I gotten myself into? Where do I go with this stranger? I realized that there is no way Chris could escape the hell he had been living in. Certainly just coming to New Jersey could not get rid of that. Maybe though, we could still have some fun. I'd take him into NYC where he had never been, we'd fool around. I thought, *I have got to show this man a good time. For God's sake, he needs some fun!*

It was going well *until* I took him around NYC and played tour guide. We went to see the skaters at Rockefeller Center and looked at all the windows dressed up for Christmas. We walked everywhere so Mr. Florida could get the taste of NYC.

But there were a few problems.

First of all, he had no jacket. He came from Florida ill-equipped in that sense but he was, after all, from Florida. So, I cut him some slack and let him wear mine. Not a very big deal. Second, (and this was a big one), he had no money. I ended up paying for everything which was slightly annoying. The third, however, was much more serious. And, it was my fatal mistake.

"Let's go to The Village. It's a really cool section of the city." I took him into a quaint looking bar there. My first drink was a soda. I intended to stay sober and not pick up a drink, but the next thing I knew...

We were drunk and doing shots with another couple. There were two couches catty corner to one another. They were on one couch, we were on the other. All four of us were talking about starting a band. (Did any of us even play an instrument?) We were getting along like old friends. They seemed like good people. We were taking pictures with my disposable camera and having fun. I think.

Then I felt sick and wanted to go. We were out of money and there were only two trains left to get home. We had to catch one

I'M NOT CRAZY JUST BIPOLAR

of them because we couldn't afford a hotel in the city. Not even a fleabag hotel.

Mr. Florida leaned over and told me "hey, I got some stuff." He had a mischievous grin on his face.

"What do you mean, *stuff*?" I was already annoyed with myself for drinking. *"Stuff"* gave me the sneaking suspicion that Chris was even more fucked up than I thought.

"Some stuff, you know." He was still smiling, like he was the cat that ate the canary.

"Stuff? You mean like *drugs?* With what? I thought you didn't have any money?" I was pissed off he just bought drugs. I was also realizing at that moment , that I'd just spent all my money that day because he was supposedly broke and now, poof! Mr. Florida had money for drugs.

"I had a little money." He deemphasized, seeing how pissed off I was getting.

"What did you get?" I was praying for pot. It had been over two years since I had smoked pot. Then again, maybe it was something harder. I'd already fallen off the wagon by drinking. No, I should pray for something harder that I didn't want to do, so I wouldn't do it. Then I wouldn't relapse with drugs, too. None of this was good. Damn it!

"Crack."

"You got *crack*?" I could not believe my ears. "Where the hell did you get that?" I couldn't figure this all out. I looked over to the other couple who suddenly looked shady to me. Had he bought it from them? He wasn't even out of my sight except for when I went up to get drinks, or go to the bathroom. Or when *he* went to the bathroom. I stood up, put my coat on and said goodbye to the other half of our "band".

Mr. Florida followed me out of the bar. I had a very big problem on my hands and needed a solution. I ran to the corner to get some distance from him. What should I do? I wasn't exactly thinking clearly. I was drunk and now I had a madman with crack on my heels. Who could I call?

My one clear thought was to call my very level-headed friend Kim, who was my best friend since age seven. She even lived right in the city and could give me good, sound advice. I was freaking out because the clock was ticking before jackass would find me on the street corner. I pulled out my cell phone and frantically scrolled through the Ks.

"Hello?" Kim answered the phone. I had obviously woken her up.

"Kim?"

"Wendy?"

"Kim! Thank God! Listen…" I gave her the quick rundown.

"Leave him!" Kim, ever the voice of reason, said this immediately without any hesitancy whatsoever.

"I can't. He'll miss his flight. He'll be wandering around the city, homeless and broke and it will be my fault."

"Just leave him, Wendy!"

"I can't have that on my conscience! Plus, he's wearing my favorite jacket."

"Who *cares* Wendy? If he cared anything about you, he wouldn't have bought the crack or let you drink in the first place! *Leave him!*"

As much as I knew she was right, that it was the sane thing to do, I couldn't do it. I pictured him homeless and wandering around the city in my favorite red, fleece jacket. I knew he had no resources to get back to Florida if he missed his flight. Crack or no crack. No amount of anger could lead me towards taking such drastic action.

"Whatever." Kim gave up. "Just get home safe, but I'd leave him if I were you." She added that in a last ditch effort to breathe clarity into me.

We got a cab and, thankfully, made the last train home that left from Penn Station at two am. We walked back from the train to my apartment (he only had enough money to stay in a hotel for the first two nights). I told him on the train ride home he better get rid of the crack. I was terrified of ever seeing the stuff again. He agreed. Back in my apartment, we tried not to make any noise so we wouldn't wake up my roommate, who was usually passed out at that hour on a Saturday night anyway.

"Did you get rid of it?" I asked quietly.

"No, but I will." He responded.

"You *will?* Flush it now, Chris!" I was so annoyed I couldn't look at him. Why didn't I grab it and do it myself? I was drunk and terrified to go near it, much less touch the stuff. I didn't know if I'd ever get sober again if I smoked crack again. I pictured losing my job, my family, my friends and my apartment.

I passed out that night. The next morning I woke up and he was already awake next to me, propped up reading a magazine.

"So what did you do with the crack last night?" I presumed he would say he flushed it.

"I smoked it." He said matter-of-factly.

"You *what? Where?*"

"Here." He smiled like he had gotten one over on me, which of course he had. He went back to flipping through his magazine.

"Here where?" I asked. Surely he didn't mean here in my bedroom.

"Here. In bed."

"Right *next* to me? I told you to flush it down the toilet, Chris! You didn't even have the *decency* to smoke it in the bathroom?"

"I'm sorry." He wasn't. I knew it.

I was beyond pissed. I couldn't be mad at him too long, because I was equally as mad at myself. Of course he wasn't going to flush it, he was an addict.

I dropped him off at the airport and never saw him again. I would not return his calls. Many months later he called me and left a message saying the trial was over and that they'd won. As promised during his visit, he said he would take me on a vacation anywhere I wanted to go. I never called him back.

That was in December of 2001 and I'm blessed to say that I haven't had another drink since that night. I take it one day at a time and remain grateful for my sobriety.

The Great Depression

My Descent

My Roaring twenties were behind me and no longer visible in my broken rear view mirror. I had no idea what lay ahead in my thirties. I never would have guessed I would soon be in for the fight of my life.

I was complacent in my comfortable, local, predictable office job where I was a supervisor at a Fortune 500 staffing company. I was sober, on medication and going along at a steady pace. Then a few people I loved died and I had a really, *really* hard time.

The first death to shake me was my Uncle Rick's. He was diagnosed with melanoma (skin) cancer and it had quickly spread throughout his body. He had gone through chemo and tried to fight it, but lost the battle and within one year he passed away.

I was devastated. Uncle Rick was like a father figure to me because he helped me get sober so many times. We had that in common, being recovering alcoholics, and that was a very strong bond. I feel that he helped save my life.

He believed in me way back in the beginning, when I was thirteen and cleaned his house for camp money. I saw him get sober and marry my aunt and grow up emotionally in a way. He saw me try over and over to get sober. I was deeply depressed when he died, but hung in there. We were all a mess, my family, but comforted each other. He was the center of gravity for our family.

Time heals and a few years had passed since his death. I spent my days chained to my desk, eight or nine hours a day. I was living in an apartment in a hip little town in New Jersey, a few blocks away from my office building. My job was steady, still I oftentimes felt like quitting because the day in, day out was so boring. However, it paid the bills and kept me out of trouble, so I showed up. One thing I was not fond of was the constant phones. I felt like a phone operator.

The phone rang.

"----- Services, this is Wendy, how may I help you?"

"Hi, we just had someone quit. I need a clerk in our records department right away. Tomorrow morning at 8:00 am. I can't have it unattended and I have the guy from X-ray records covering there now. It throws everything off."

"Nancy?"

"Gosh, I'm so busy Wendy, I forgot to say my name!" She let out a little laugh. "Yes, it's me, Nancy." That was about as nice as Nancy ever got. And she really wasn't sorry. It was her attempt at being polite.

"Oh, hi. Okay, so you need another medical records clerk tomorrow?" Nancy was all business so you had to talk that way back to her. It wasn't 'how are you?' 'I'm fine, thanks.' Nancy had no time for chit chat. She was a big deal. At least she thought she was. She was the human resources manager for a hospital. Her job sure beat mine though, and undoubtedly paid more. I will give her that.

"Yes. And they *must* have experience with medical records. Of course, medical records in a hospital would be preferable." She always asked for everything under the sun, this woman. As if there was a pool of available medical records clerks, no, *hospital* medical records clerks, available and at our beck and call for not even twice minimum wage. That was a lot of responsibility for such crappy pay, I thought. And naturally, her hospital had to be at the very corner of the territory we covered so it was an added joy to try and get someone to travel that far. Shit!

"Sure, Nancy. I'll get back to you as soon as possible." She was the biggest bitch. Nancy never waited for the appropriate amount of time before hanging up the phone. She was the kind who pulls the I'm-so-busy-that-you're-getting-the-no-pause-slam type. The worst.

This was going to be difficult. It was one of the most impossible positions to fill. The person had to manage records in the basement of a hospital, and they had nobody to cover their breaks - except for lunch. Smokers were basically out. Plus, nobody wanted to work for $8.50 an hour. Who could blame them? That was a high turnover job, thus Nancy's call to me today. Great! Where was I going to find someone with a brain, who didn't want to get paid, didn't smoke and wanted a long commute?

"Kathy, who the hell are we gonna get for this?" I was stumped and counted on Kathy, my trusty, young redhead co-worker for help.

"I got it! Remember that kid who flunked out of college? What's his name? Dammit. Wait, let me find him. He signed up last May after college. But never went out for us all summer. Then he called us a few weeks ago saying that he was home and available. Remember, his parents were on his case to get out and work? He sounded desperate. He'd probably do it."

"Try him." I responded, relieved that she had someone in mind.

"Okay. I'll call him now." Kathy already had the phone in her hand. It was 9:15 and Nancy wanted us to check in around 11:00. If we didn't have someone by lunch she was going to call it out to her other staffing firm that she used. We *hated* those guys. They weren't very ethical. A lot of their employees had come to us after working for them and had given us an earful.

Kathy filled the job with the flunked out of college kid. His relieved mother had taken the call and, although he wasn't home, she assured us he'd take the job and also call us back promptly. He did. Job filled.

And that's what we continued to do. Hour after hour, day after day, until the days blended into meaningless weeks, and months into meaningless years.

Then one day, out of the blue, the bottom fell out.

I got the call I'll never forget.

"Wendy, are you sitting down?" Those are never good words. If people are going to tell you something good, they usually don't say this to you.

"Yes."

"Regina is dead."

"What?"

"Regina's dead."

"She's *what?*" I sat there unable to process what was just told to me. I mean, Regina, our office manager, had just called Kathy two hours ago to say she was going to be out sick.

"She's dead. I'm so sorry, Wendy. I know how close you were." I don't remember asking questions such as: what happened, where was she, or anything logical like that. I just remember holding the phone, frozen in shock.

I turned around and looked at Kathy, who was busy on the phone. Kathy got off the phone and spun around. She was about to tell me something, presumably about her phone call, when she stopped. She saw my frozen expression.

"Wen, what's wrong?" I looked up at her eyes opened wide in confusion.

"Kathy?" I paused, forcing the words out..."Regina's dead."

"What?"

"Regina's dead." I repeated in disbelief.

"She's *dead*? Oh my God."

We sat there in shock together.

After another call from somewhere, we found out that her husband went home for lunch and found Regina in the chair dead. Nobody knew why or what happened. I felt so badly for him.

Kathy and I sat there. It was very quiet. Soon after, we got calls from the regional office. They were worried about us. We were told we could go home if we wanted, but I couldn't imagine what I would even do. I wanted to be near Kathy because she knew Regina as well as I did.

One of the regional managers, Pat, who hired me, came down quickly and helped us get through the day. She may have stayed the week, I don't remember. I don't think I took any time off that week. I tried to keep going. I was in for the big crash though. I was trying to keep it together, but I was plunging downwards already.

I looked up to Regina and always admired her happiness. She seemed to have the life puzzle figured out and had gotten married just six months before. She was my mentor for life, not just business. Our small office wasn't a branch office of an old Fortune 500 company. It was a family of three that had operated together for two years with the synergy of a well-oiled machine.

Her cause of death was unknown. But a big part of me blamed the company for the pressure they had put on her. I knew whatever the cause of death turned out to be, there had to be stress behind it. Especially if it was her heart, which we were pretty sure it was. After all, she was a newlywed. With the exception of pressure from work, she was happy. Extremely happy. Maybe I needed someone to blame, to justify this unjustifiable tragedy, so I blamed my company. I knew in my heart that stress was a factor.

I went downhill quickly. This time it was very steep, and it took a long, long time to get back up. I was angry at God for taking her and I had survivor's guilt. I couldn't understand why He took Regina, who was so good and happy, and left miserable me. I knew I wasn't a bad person, but I had made a lot of bad choices in life. I had done a lot of irresponsible things. I had kept company with some very questionable characters. And I certainly wasn't happy like Regina was. Why did God keep me here? Why?

Regina constantly assured me through bad boyfriends, one after another, that it would get better. "Love is supposed to be fun, Wendy, I promise." She would give me a big smile and a little laugh and I would silently hope that she was right. She saw me through medication and doctor changes and yet another crappy used car breakdown. There were several apartment and roommate changes and sobriety relapses and she was always there to say that life would get better. And even though I didn't believe it to my core, I knew above all that she would never lie to me or steer me wrong. I believed that *she* believed and that helped me somehow.

I was trying to stay above water, but the weight of her sudden death pulled me under. It was hard to move or function. I was in a daze, picking up the phone and staring at the computer like a zombie. I carried on business for a few days but stared off at her desk like it was a graveyard. It ever reminded me we had lost our engine. We were a broken machine now.

One day, a few weeks after her death, Mike (our regional manager) came in for one of his branch visits. He had an unusual burst of energy that day. Then again, *anyone* compared to me seemed like they had enough energy to run a marathon. I barely had enough energy to hold and pull the trigger on the flare gun to begin the race.

He stood over Regina's desk. I could barely look over there, it was so painful. It was unfortunate that it was in my constant, direct view, this virtual cemetery.

"What's this computer used for?" Mike was pointing to the desk that was next to hers. It was empty and barely used. The computer sat there covered with dust.

He was hinting towards eliminating one of our archaic computers (it was even *older* than the one on my desk). I didn't want to lose another part of our office, so I stuck up for it.

"We use it sometimes." I said defending the poor, voiceless ancient piece of company memorabilia. It belonged in the company archives at corporate really, if there was such a thing.

He waved his hands around in a flurry.

"Get rid of it!" Since when did Mike make these snappy decisions? I was perplexed, stood up and walked over to defend it.

"Mike, our employees do their resumes on it." I lied to justify its existence. (Maybe one employee per month actually used the thing.) "And the printer works! Besides you can't just throw it out…it has an inventory tag on it."

"Just get it out of here!" He commanded. Not only was this odd for him to make such a decision, but to command in this fashion was, well, most unprecedented. He didn't wipe his ass without checking with two people above him on the ladder. One of those types, if you know what I mean.

"What do you want me to do with it?" I thought, *wow, he's really serious.* Then I thought, *since when am I in the computer moving business? Fucking small offices. What next?*

"I don't care, throw it in the dumpster." The dumpster? *Forget that*, I thought, *I don't have a computer!*

"I'll take it home."

"Fine." *Did he really just say fine? Holy shit! I have a computer!*

I disassembled that computer, monitor and printer so fast it would make your head spin and ran it out to my car before he changed his mind. I couldn't believe he was just going to have me throw it out in the dumpster. I also couldn't believe I now had a computer. And printer!

Since Mike had no balls, and this decision was clearly not coming from him, surely God or Regina, my new angel, had made the decision *through* Mike to give me this computer. I was meant to have it and I took it as a sign that I should start writing this book. (I stand by that to this day.)

Soon after the day I got the computer, the human resources manager suggested and approved a few weeks off for me. It was obvious I was losing it. It was considered "short-term disability." It started off as two weeks. Those two weeks turned into many more and eventually they downsized my position and closed the whole office. They decided to run operations for our territory from the next office north of us to save money.

Since I was on short-term disability when they downsized me, it qualified me to get full pay for one year. I really lucked out in that respect. At this point, I had a computer, printer, money and all the time in the world. So that summer, despite my deep depression, I began the rough (very rough) draft of this book.

Right after losing my job, I also lost my apartment because my roommate decided (due to a few rent hikes) not to renew the lease. I moved back in with my parents. Things were really bleak. I had lost my friend, my job and now my apartment.

I was in mourning and not just for the loss of my friend. Unfortunately, when I had lost my job, I lost my identity and my lifestyle, too. Who I was, was so wrapped in that job. For five years, forty hours a week, I knew where I was supposed to be and what I was supposed to be doing and thus, who I was. Now, I was floating out in space. A boat broken off its mooring, drifting and lost.

I know it could've been much worse. I did have full pay, a place to live, and the tools and time necessary to begin writing. But I felt so fucking bad that I wasn't seeing the silver lining at the time.

I spent a lot of late nights in my parent's basement in my new little makeshift "office." My archaeic PC sat atop this rickety old folding table I found in the cobwebbed corner of their basement. I taped inspirational quotes all over the monitor. Pictures were scattered around the desk, in an attempt to infuse hope, when what I really felt was hopeless. All the while, I was trying hard not to *completely* lose my mind.

The new piano keyboard I bought that was set up next to my "office" was an impulsive purchase. Inspired by the piano playing in "Clocks" by Coldplay, I decided to take piano lessons. I simply *had* to learn that sequence! Although the book was first on my list, I thought maybe I could start a band if I could get my piano playing up to par. However, learning or concentrating on *anything* when you're manic is tough. Since I couldn't be the piano whiz kid I was at age ten, I quit within a month.

I was teetering between mania and depression that summer, but tilted towards depression. It is what's called a mixed episode. I had lost my hold on reality in an effort to redefine myself. I was making my own set of dangerous rules. Well, no rules actually.

What compounded the problem was the shrink I had been seeing was not one of those doctors who listened to their patients. At least, he didn't listen to me. Another thing that was aggravating was he made a lot of references to me being overweight. This was not only obvious, it was infuriating. He must've weighed a hundred pounds max. What did he know of the pressures of being a single, overweight woman? Or about being overweight because of the very medications that are supposed to *help me* fight depression in the first place?

I really didn't care for Dr. Lin or his bedside manner. On this one particular day, I met my Mom at my appointment. I wanted my Mom to meet each shrink I went to so she was involved in my treatment. Every now and then, I also needed her help financially, so it was only fair to involve her. She offered to meet me at my appointment for moral support because I was struggling.

At this one appointment, Dr. Lin and I, with my Mom present, were talking about Regina's death again. I had brought it up before, but didn't think he was listening to me or understood the impact her death had on my depression. I explained they still weren't sure what had caused it. It was presumed to be heart related, especially since her father died relatively young of a heart attack.

"It must be drugs." The shrink said nodding, approving of his own diagnosis about a person whom he had never met.

"Are you kidding? Regina *never* did drugs!" I protested as I looked at my mother. She chimed in.

"Regina was not like that." My Mom shook her head. She looked at me like 'okay, Wendy now I really believe you, this guy *is* a moron.'

"Sounds to me like drugs." He repeated, nodding.

"There is *no* way. I mean she was a good 'ole Irish girl and liked her occasional beer, but she was clean as a whistle. She was *not* a drug addict!" I couldn't believe he had just accused my friend of dying of a drug overdose!

That was all I needed to hear. I knew skinny shrink was a bad doctor, now it was confirmed he was a jackass, too. I absolutely needed to go to him until I found a new shrink, though. Dr. Lin was it for now, like it or not. Great. It was time for shrink shopping again. Ugh.

Soon after Regina's death, I made the *disastrous* decision to go off my meds. Actually, it wasn't really my idea.

I was seeing a chiropractor at the time for the pain I was having with my back. He called himself "Dr. Steve." I guess it was a fantasy of his that he thought himself a doctor.

While in his office one day, he saw me take out my pill box and he was astonished at the size of it. Damn, caught red-handed!

"Whoa! That looks like my *grandma's* pill case!" Dr. Steve said, all smiles.

"Uh...well..." was all I could muster. I was mortified and wanted to crawl under the table.

"That doesn't look like a pill case for someone in their thirties!" He did a half smile, the kind that mocks you, which annoyed the crap out of me. Dr. Steve shook his head and went back to writing something down, presumably my weight as he had just weighed me. Humiliating!

"You should really look into taking vitamins. I take these *great* vitamins!" He launched into this fantastic explanation, as if he was starring in an infomercial. I tuned him out.

"I don't know, maybe."

"You know, I think a lot of your depression is because you're overweight." *Yeah, no shit.* Doctor Steve was looking down at me with pity. "Medications will do that to you." He added.

"Tell me about it."

I was tired of all these professionals telling me I was depressed

145

because I was overweight. Of course that was *part* of it. It was easy for them to say, not broke, fat *or* mentally ill. I was all three and it was not a good combo for success. I weighed 263 pounds, which was an all time high. And now I knew my number. Fucking great.

I gained a lot of weight on my current medications (note: not all medications cause weight gain, consult your doctor). It seemed logical enough: go off these meds, lose weight, take only vitamins and feel less depressed. I wanted to believe I could make it on my own. I followed Steve and saw where he was going with his logic. *Wellness*…it sounded so appealing! Lose weight, lose depression. Lose the geriatric pillbox. I liked how it sounded. I was a little hopeful for the first time in a long while.

I sat there looking at my gigantic pill box. It was ugly. I *was* too young to be on all these pills. Were they even working? Or will medication not help in times like these? I was too fat. Steve was right. I mean I did lose thirty pounds at Weight Watchers and had done well, but lost momentum. I was doing okay at the gym, but lost interest there, too. Was it when Regina died? I couldn't say. But I gained back those thirty pounds in just two months. Fucking meds! Enough was enough. No more fucking pills. I might still be depressed, but I'd be depressed and thinner! Dammit!

I was looking at my big belly. My grandmother had a big belly. We looked identical. *And* our pill cases matched. I didn't have to worry about getting old, *I already was old*. I might as well as move in next door to her at the old folks home. My boobs were sagging too, I noticed. And I barely *had* boobs, but what little I had already were already defying gravity. And forget about a love life. I *had* no love life. Not looking like this. Not feeling like this.

"Great news!" Dr. Steve whizzed in with the energy of a man who had just chugged ten expressos. His energy was starting to annoy me.

Mostly because I was jealous. I instantly sat up trying to minimize my big belly. Who was I kidding? Sitting up didn't help. Fuck it! I slumped back down.

"Jim has agreed to treat you for free! Isn't that great?" He smiled ear to ear, like he had just won the lottery and was going to split it with me.

I didn't know how Jim was going to treat me. Who the hell was Jim anyway? I was a little nervous because we seemed to be on different wavelengths.

"Jim is...?" I had begun to feel like I had walked into some kind of a trap.

"Jim is our hypnotist here." Dr. Steve declared like a proud father.

"Oh. Like the kind of people who help you quit smoking?" Just how much was this going to cost? Free never really means free.

"Well, yes, and he can help cure depression too." Cure depression? Was this guy for real? Could he walk on water too?

"Really?" Admittedly, I was more than a bit skeptical, but if this guy could help me, and was willing to do it for free, by golly, be my freakin' guest. I was down for it. I was down, period. But, I knew he couldn't bring back Regina or my Uncle Rick or make me un-bipolar or thinner. *Those* were my real problems.

"Yes, and he can see you right away! His office is at the end of the hall. He'll take your information and make an appointment with you."

I tromped down the hall to Jim's office. It was dimly lit and oddly calm. Jim was behind his desk waiting for me. In front of his desk, there was a relaxed-looking chair with another chair behind it. It looked like an ideal spot to take a nap or, I suppose, receive hypnosis. There was a modest bookshelf, and from the looks of it he was not a man of books. He was a man of many binders. That made me a little nervous. What was in those binders? Hmmm...

"Hi." The man behind the desk broke my train of thought. Jim was a very relaxed, better than average looking man. He stood up momentarily to shake my hand. He had dark hair and sparkling eyes, even though I couldn't tell what color they were. His perfectly white smile seemed to match that of his partner in crime, Dr. Steve. He had a calm disposition, like nothing could rattle him, not even an earthquake. Jim seemed like he was the kind of guy who floated through life.

"Hello." I felt awkward. Here I am: the fat, depressed, broke girl with the geriatric pill case at your service. Geez, I was a mess. I felt like I was in an unfamiliar alternative setting, which I was. This couldn't be any worse than the acupuncture I tried once, spent too much money doing, and cursed myself for driving so far to try.

"So, Steve tells me you're depressed and your medication isn't working."

"Well, yeah, I guess."

"I'd like to try meditation on you. If that's okay."

"Ok. But I'm pretty sure it's not covered on my insurance. And I really don't have the money. I'm sorry."

"Did he explain to you I'm willing to treat you for free?"

"Yes, but I just wanted to..." Oh, money was the bane of my existence. Did everyone struggle this much? It was so humbling to meet someone and right off the bat have them instantly know all my weaknesses.

"Don't worry. So...okay...let's set up a time." He had a gentle tone. Good for hypnotizing people, I thought. I wondered if this was going to work, but tried to remain open-minded. Maybe it wouldn't work if I had doubt in my mind? I tried to stay positive.

We set up the first appointment which was "an exercise." After a few sessions I did, according to Jim, achieve a hypnotic state. I don't remember details about my hypnosis. I wasn't trying for it *not* to work, but it didn't, because it certainly didn't cure my depression. Oh well. So much for Jim and hypnosis. At least it was free.

I never did tell my shrink that I stopped taking my meds, nor did I lose weight as a result. It was a *catastrophic* move! Dr. Steve, the great chiropractor, wasn't a medical doctor who knew anything about bipolar disorder. He had no business telling me what to do regarding medication. My Mom was absolutely *furious* when I finally told her where I had gotten my brilliant idea to go off all my meds.

Luckily, despite my poor decision, I had a great therapist at the time who was wonderful in helping me process Regina's death. I talked about it. I wrote about it in my journal. I wrote poems. I went to a women's group. I spent so much time and money on therapy, it was unreal. It all helped. But it did not bring back my friend, my job or the camaraderie we had there.

That summer, I would sit in my car late at night with a mini-tape recorder and speak into it while overlooking the river. (It was the beginnings of this book.) I'd later type what I had recorded. I also sat for many hours at a local church.

The church I frequented was the one in town that was open 24/7. It was a big, white Roman Catholic Church with tall, heavy red doors. The stained glass windows were old and beautiful, but dark at night. Sometimes there were flowers by the altar that permeated the air, even to the back pews where I often sat. The red carpeting created a unified ambiance, a paved safe haven for me to talk to my God.

Nobody was ever there. Not once did I run into a single soul. I would pray and cry and get angry and grieve, not only for Regina, but also for my Uncle Rick, who had died years before. I began to go back farther and also grieve the others I missed who had passed away over the years. I had lost a lot of people in the past decade. I was in a death spiral and Regina's death was also kicking up their memories.

I felt safe in that church, even at 2:00 or 3:00 am, when I would often go. It was as if God was wrapping his arms around me in his house of love. He was my captive audience there and sometimes I even sang. At first I sang quietly, gaining momentum at the idea that God would not mind if I sang louder. I sang *Fire and Rain* by James Taylor many times. Sometimes I stopped singing and I cried, unable to finish the song. Mostly, I talked to my God and my two main angels, Uncle Rick and Regina. Because I was alone, I even talked out loud.

At times, I found it easier to communicate with my angels than God. I don't know why, I just did. Maybe it was because I knew them. They had a face and memories and an embrace I had once felt. It wasn't that I didn't believe in God. I absolutely did. But I was struggling to believe in anything, to make sense of my life. I was grabbing onto anyone, anything, any spirit, any entity that I felt could help strengthen me because I felt myself going down.

All the while, I didn't have to work because I was receiving full pay for one year from my company. The problem was I didn't have to be anywhere at any time. I had no reason to get out of bed, no office to get to.

One day, Kathy and I decided to make our first trip to Regina's gravesite. Kathy was driving. I had no idea where we were; I didn't live near there. We were going by the directions the cemetery gave us over the phone and we were lost.

Then, something very strange happened to me.

I said in my mind, "Regina, God, Rick, *whoever* is listening, I have a doctor's appointment in forty-five minutes that I can't be late for, so you gotta give us some help. And fast."

While my eyes were still open, I saw a picture flash in my mind.

The picture was a huge yellow diamond shaped sign and to its left I saw the road dipped and curved and I knew the cemetery would be on the right.

I said, "Okay, Kathy you're gonna think this is weird, but I think pretty soon, we're going to see a huge, yellow diamond shaped sign. Then the road will dip and curve to the left. The cemetery is going to be on the right after that curve. Don't ask me how I know. Just trust me."

Kathy looked at me with wide eyes, but said nothing because before we knew it, there was our huge yellow sign. Right after that, sure enough, the road dipped and curved to the left. The cemetery was on the right and we found her grave.

I have never had a vision like that again.

First Suicide Attempt

Within two months of going off my medications, I made my first suicide attempt. I decided on New York City, my old workplace, a forty-five story hotel in Times Square. My mission was simple: to jump. While I worked there, several people had and, needless to say, they didn't survive.

It was a typical Saturday night in mid September 2003. I drove through the Lincoln Tunnel and into midtown. My car was on auto-pilot to the parking garage I had commuted to countless times before. The theater district was nearly deserted; the curtains were long closed. The city was still hopping somewhere, but not here.

I pulled into the garage across the street from the hotel. Although it had been eight years since I worked at the hotel, I still knew some of the attendants' faces. They knew mine too, and greeted me in their typical, friendly manner. One familiar veteran attendee approached me.

"How long will you be?" The attendee asked. He had my ticket in hand, ready to stamp and put on my windshield.

"Um…overnight. I think." Despite being asked this question every single time I parked there, it caught me off guard.

The attendant returned a puzzled look at first, but smiled back. As always, I kept my keys in the ignition and left it running. While he stamped my ticket, I made sure my rolled up $27 was visible in the center console. It was enough to cover parking plus tip. I didn't want to stiff them, certainly not on their tip.

"Have a good night!" He held out my half of the ticket as he slid into my car. They were always in a hurry, even with no cars behind me. They were programmed, we shared that quality tonight. I shoved the ticket into my purse, knowing I would not be returning. He sped away and with a slight screech on the turn, my tail lights disappeared.

I headed to the soda machine on my way out and fetched a dollar from my pocket. I fed it to the machine twice and out came my soda. I contemplated getting two Cokes, thinking I might need both, but only had room for one in my purse. It occurred to me I should've brought a bigger purse. I feared one soda might not be enough, but one would have to do.

I walked up the ramp towards the street, nervous, but with purpose. There wasn't much traffic. Sensing this, I crossed in the middle of the block without looking down the one way street.

I walked inside the hotel, but wasn't in the clear. First, I had to get past the security desk in order to get to the elevators. My snag was I had no key to show them, which was protocol. But I knew how this worked: walk fast, act like you belong here, smile and don't act nervous. They could be half asleep on their shift (and usually were), but if you were nervous, they would sniff you out like a dog on a crime scene and ask to see your room key. If they stopped me and I had no room key to show, I'd be screwed. My whole plan would fail.

I held my head high and smiled, giving my best rendition of an end-of-the-night-tourist-heading-to-their-room walk. Luckily, it worked. The guard nodded back and said nothing.

There was an open elevator to the left, ready and waiting to take someone to their floor. A nearby thirty something, happy couple headed towards it. They waited for me for a second, then pushed their button rather quickly and went back to holding hands. Polite, but in their own world. Just like me, I suppose. Minus the happy part, of course.

I walked past them in search of my own elevator and they went on their merry way. I guessed they were probably back from dinner, a show and perhaps a walk around Times Square before they realized all they really wanted was to be alone anyway. From the looks of it, they were a little tipsy, maybe wine with dinner or drinks at a bar afterwards. Maybe they were just goofy in love. New love, perhaps newlyweds. I didn't really care. All I knew was I had to be in my own elevator. The last thing I wanted was to make small talk with anyone.

I pressed button forty-five. Top floor. The doors to the glass elevator closed and without hesitation, it began to move fast. Really fast. For the hundreds of times I had taken them myself, it felt unusually quick and the speed scared me. Tourists came here all the time to ride them like they were rides in an amusement park. But there were no stops on the ride tonight.

Although I tried not to, I couldn't help but look down at the shiny, gray marble floor. It seemed hard, cold even, and with each passing floor, more treacherous. It sunk in. That's where I'd be landing. I stopped looking around the twentieth floor. It was becoming too real.

I eyed my bulging purse. It barely zipped shut because of the soda I'd jammed in there. I bought it so I could wash down the bottle of my strongest medication I'd brought along. I had a feeling that I'd need it to impair my judgment so I could go through with the jump. It was my Plan B.

I got off the elevator and walked over to the side I had picked out. I knew exactly where it had to be and I knew this long before tonight. I couldn't go to one side to jump because the front desk would see me land. (That had happened before when I worked there. It was a mess one of the front desk managers personally had to help clean up.) I went to the opposite side of the front desk.

The other two sides, the shorter of the two rectangular shaped sides, were out. The concierge "side" would have only been a fall of fifteen floors. Choosing the other side, would mean I'd land at the bellstand. I tried to pick the "best" side.

Despite the late hour, there were still guests coming and going at the nineteen hundred room hotel. The many glass elevators with giant bulbs and orange trim sped along at various intervals stopping and starting at different floors. People got on, swoosh, the elevator took them to their floor. It paused and then flew to its next destination swiftly. Up and down all night, the elevators were in constant motion. It was the one thing you could count on.

The atrium was quiet, as it always was at this hour, devoid of its usual hustle and bustle. The various fake plants kept all the cocktail tables company, not the one nuzzling couple or man glued to his laptop.

I felt strongly that I didn't want any employees or guests to see me jump and land. Although it might be unavoidable, I would try for the fewest possible witnesses. I would hate to see someone die. And die this way. I hoped the people in the atrium would be leaving soon. I had to do it soon or I would chicken out. I took off my purse and took my letter out.

My letter, which I had written, addressed and stamped, was to my parents. My intent was to drop it when I jumped, hoping some good Samaritan or hotel staff person would find and mail it. I also placed a business card of a good psychologist (who specialized in grief counseling) on my Mom's desk earlier that night. I had written on it: "Go see for grief counseling."

It was time to check everything and jump.

I had to time my jump so the elevators would be empty on my side, which was rare. I also had to watch out for the security guards who were roaming the floors. It was tricky, logistically speaking.

I stood up and turned around to watch the elevators, waiting for them to be clear of guests on my side. Simultaneously, I scanned the floors to make sure there were no security guards visibly walking them who might spot me.

Finally, my moment was here. I took a deep breath and put my hands on the wall.

I leaned all my weight forward and swung my right leg up on the wall. My left leg followed and I got to my knees clumsily. The stone embedded in the wall hurt my knees and hands. I took another look around for last minute clearance. I didn't think the plastic ivy that dangled through the metal grates was going to trip me, but if it did, it didn't matter. My goal was to fall anyway.

I stood up on the wall slowly, hunched over, and walked the two feet onto the metal grate. In a matter of a few inches, of a few seconds, I would be dead.

I took a deep breath and stood straight up. I couldn't believe how scary it looked when I leaned forward and looked all the way down. It was a long, long way down. I got scared to step out those last, few inches. Just before I did, I held my breath and told myself it had to be quick. Someone might see me soon.

I was ready to step out. I hadn't planned on actually jumping jumping. The grate I was standing on, the metal ledge, already put me a few feet from the wall. It would be more of a stepping out motion.

It was time. I moved my right foot off the grate and into the air. I looked down to where I would be landing in a few seconds and held my breath.

Then I spotted them.

The monkey wrench to my whole plan.

I saw two moving green things. What *were* they? I stepped back onto the grate and focused. Were they two people? What the hell are they *doing*? Oh my God, they were two employees from the hotel maintenance staff! Were they waxing the floors? In my spot? I couldn't believe they were in my exact, my *exact*, landing spot.

Dammit!

I crouched down for a moment, checking for security guards, people, elevators and looked back down to the lobby floor. They were still there! I had to get off this ledge before I was spotted. Dammit! The fucking floor waxers wouldn't move!

I hopped down from the metal ledge and stood in the hallway, befuddled. I couldn't believe it! What were the chances? I would have to wait until they moved. That's all. Then I would jump.

I considered moving for a moment, but knew I couldn't. It *had* to be the side I was on. I hoped they would move soon as I knelt back down on the hallway carpet. I faced the guest rooms and wondered: *what would a guest think if they came out of their room and saw me sitting here?* Would they put two and two together? Surely, it would look odd. Did I have a story ready if they asked? *Would* they even ask? I knew it wasn't likely someone would leave their room at 3:00 am. Still, I hoped no one would. Luckily they didn't.

I waited a bit until I thought the floor cleaners might be gone. It also gave me time to get myself together. I had to psych myself up. I didn't realize (until I was standing up there) exactly how much courage it was going to take to go through with it. And it only entailed stepping out a few, mere inches. Certainly a lot more courage than I had planned.

I peeked my head up slowly, timing the elevators for minimal guests, making sure there were no visible security guards roaming the floors and got my clearance. I stood up, leaned my weight onto the bumpy wall and swung my leg over the ledge again. I knelt, popped up, stepped onto the grate and leaned forward again. This time it was less awkward and I wasn't *as* afraid to be up there. But I was still afraid.

Were the floor waxers still there? I looked down.

They were! Fuck!

I couldn't go through with it with them there!

I got down again, half pissed off at myself for not being able to jump and half pissed off they were still in my spot. But I couldn't very well land *on* them! And I couldn't move down the hallway and land a few feet *away* from them either.

The other thing that held me back was my family. I got scared and thought, *if I do this, will I never get to see my family again in the afterlife? Is there an afterlife?* I had assumed, up until that point, there was and someday I'd be reunited with them. The pain was so great, I was willing to wait. But I suddenly questioned, what if taking my life meant I never got to see them again. Ever? I couldn't bear that thought. It hit me like a ton of bricks.

For the first time I also asked myself: *what if there is a Hell and that is where I would go?* The possibility of there being a Hell hadn't occurred to me. Until that moment where I was seconds from jumping, none of these thoughts entered my mind.

I hated what I was about to do. It was selfish. And make no mistake about it, I *knew* suicide was the ultimate selfish act. I thought of all the pain I was going to cause my family and friends. I hated resorting to this, but I didn't know how else to get out of the depression. Nothing was working. It wasn't going away; I wanted out of the pain. In hindsight, I don't believe *to the very core of my being* that I wanted to die. I just didn't want to keep living with my brain the way it was.

Since I couldn't go through with it, it was on to Plan B: pill impairment. It would take longer, but maybe by the time my pills took effect, the floor waxers would be gone. Then, maybe I could jump.

I sat back down and gulped my soda and pills. I was determined to take every last one. It was my strongest medication, an anti-anxiety that I'd stopped taking so I had nearly a full bottle. I took as many pills as I could stand without gagging, followed by big swigs of Coke. It had to be done quickly for maximum effectiveness. As I started to get to the bottom of my soda, I cursed myself for not getting the second one. The last few went down, barely, with what little soda I had left. They felt a little stuck in my throat, but they went down eventually. In no time, the entire bottle was gone. I waited a bit for them to take effect. Now it would be easier! And surely now, *now*, the waxers would be gone. It was an hour later, after all.

I checked everything from where I could see and waited for my perfect moment again. I got up on the railing, as I had before, and looked down to see if the waxers had moved yet.

But they *hadn't* moved!

I got back down quickly and cursed God. I *knew* He had put them there! He didn't want me to jump. I knew God was behind it. I knew this with every fiber of my being. Even with every *impaired* fiber of my being. Surely, I reasoned, He didn't want me to die. And He put the waxers there to stop me. Damn Him!

I repeated the process, one more time (that I remember). I peeked my head up slowly and carefully. I climbed onto the wall again and stood up.

I leaned over and looked down.

Fuck!

They still hadn't moved!

The entire time, going on over two hours now, they were waxing the same few little square feet of floor in the lobby. What were the chances of that?

Eventually, I switched to simply leaning over the wall and not standing up. I wanted to see the cleaners without having to get up on the ledge anymore. (I was really worried about being spotted by the security guards, or anyone for that matter.) I knew the more times I stood up on the metal grate, the greater chance I had of getting caught.

I knelt down on the floor and waited some more. I was starting to feel dizzy. The medication was seeping in.

I peeked my head up, slowly and carefully, a few more times over the wall.

But they never moved! For over two hours!

The *entire* time they were smack dab in my landing spot!

Dammit!

I cursed God again. There was no other logical explanation. No one at the hotel cleans the same few square feet for two hours. Not even the overnight shift. No one gets away with that. It doesn't happen. There are too many supervisors on every shift at that big hotel. I knew it from working there.

I finally gave up.

I left.

I have no recollection of leaving the floor, taking the elevator down or walking through the main floor. The next thing I remember is walking outside, through the same door I had come in.

I was surprised it was daylight already. I felt a woosh of air hit my face as I took in a deep breath of New York City air. It felt like the freshest air I'd ever breathed in, which I thought was ironic since it was, after all, city air.

I felt a deep sense of renewal. Like I was reborn in an odd, inexplicable way. It was as if I had confirmation from God that I was *supposed* to be alive. The floor cleaners were my signal. It was not my time. I literally felt a weight lifted off my shoulders. My steps felt lighter, too.

When I looked to my right, I noticed a popular chain coffee shop that wasn't there when I worked at the hotel. The employees were moving about inside. I walked up and tried to open the door, but it was locked. They motioned to the clock, which read 5:45 am, and went back to their routines. Their hours indicated they opened at 6:00 am, so I decided to wait the fifteen minutes. I was their very first customer when they unlocked the door and let me in.

Cheerfully, I ordered my favorite slushy cold coffee drink with whipped cream and extra caramel on top. In some fucked up way, my drink was a celebration to be alive. (You never would've guessed this was a girl who just spent all night trying to kill herself.) I sensed they were almost amused, in a we're-as-amused-by-your-cheery-attitude-as-we-can-be-for-the-opening-crew-of-a-coffee-shop, type of way.

That's the last thing I remember for over two hours.

I don't remember crossing the street. I don't remember getting my car from the parking garage. I don't remember driving through the Lincoln Tunnel into New Jersey.

Nothing.

When I came to, oddly enough, I was parked in front of the salon where I used to get my nails done. It was in the town I lived in, fifteen minutes from the city, when I worked and commuted to that very same hotel.

I don't know to this day if I had driven around for those two hours, or driven straight there and passed out. It's a miracle I woke up there, parked safely, and not killed someone or ended up in some ditch off the Turnpike.

At the time of the suicide attempt, I was living at home with my parents. When I woke up parked in front of the nail salon, it was 8:00 am and I knew they'd be waking up any minute. They would be worried, wondering where I was, especially my Mom. I called her and tried to pretend I was okay, but she knew something was wrong.

"Hi Mom."

"Wendy where *are* you?" Mom was obviously concerned.

"I'm at...ah... that place where I used to get my nails done."

"What?"

"You know, the one with the manicure/pedicure special for $25 on Mondays and Wednesdays. The one I still come to sometimes." (Now, this *may* have actually worked if it weren't for two things. One, it was actually Sunday. And two, I was never awake before 9am except for work. Oh, and three, I no longer had a job.)

"Wendy, it's Sunday. What's going on?" She was becoming annoyed.

"Um...Ah...Well..." I attempted to give her a lame explanation, but was caught off guard with it being Sunday. My speech had to sound off, but I was trying to act as if everything were perfectly normal.

"Wendy, come home." She obviously thought I was still okay to drive. How could she have known what kind of shape I was in?

"Okay."

Problem was: I didn't make it home.

The next thing I knew, I woke up somewhere else.

"What the hell?" I asked myself as I looked around. I was in my car, stopped, next to a concrete divider. It looked like an entrance or exit ramp of a highway. I had no idea where I was, if my car was damaged or what had happened.

I tried starting the car but it wouldn't start. (This was a blessing because I probably would have driven again if I could've.) I was really, *really* lucky. I dialed Mom again.

"Mom?" It was over an hour from the last time I called her. I should've been *home* by now. (It hadn't really hit me how I could've just *killed* someone or crashed my car.) I was more concerned about getting home because I knew my Mom was worried about me.

"Wendy, *where are you?*" This time her anger was clear.

"I don't know. My car won't start."

"Okay." She softened up, sensing I was in danger.

"I'm up against a concrete divider somewhere. I don't know where I am."

"Look around you. Do you see any signs?"

"Uh." I put on my detective hat. Slowly, I turned and saw a major highway to my right. I figured there must be a sign since I was on a ramp next to it. I turned to my left and saw a black and white sign with a circled number three on it.

"Do you see anything?" She repeated anxiously.

"I think I'm near an entrance or exit ramp to Route Three *somewhere,* but I don't know what town I'm in."

"Okay...keep looking." I looked to my left further and there was a huge blue sign that said "Welcome to Wayne."

"Wait...I'm in Wayne! There's a sign that says 'Welcome to Wayne' Mom!" I was relieved that there was a sign right there that told me where I was. I mean, what were the chances of that?

"Don't move!" She directed. "I'm calling the police to come get you."

"No! Wait...Mom...don't call...!" Click. She had already hung up the phone. I immediately began freaking out about the police. I hadn't gotten to the part where I outed myself. That I had downed a bottle of pills, attempted suicide and driven under the influence.

Shit! They are gonna see I'm messed up! Panic was setting in and I got out of the car to think. I decided I had to practice walking on the curb to get my balance. I talked to myself. *Pretend you're on the balance beam, Wendy, like you did in gymnastics when you were little.* It wasn't working. My coordination was horrible. I kept having to hold onto the side of my car. So much for walking a straight line and utilizing my balance beam skills.

I tried positive self-talk to calm down. I had to appear sober to the officers. I knew my license was in jeopardy.

Within what seemed like a few minutes, they pulled up and there were two of them! Great. Two cars and two officers. I stared at the flashing lights and started to freak out inside.

Calm down, I told myself.

Remain calm, Wendy.

I was standing by my car as they approached me. Their lights kept whirling in the background, making me feel dizzy. I had to refocus. Fast.

Focus, Wendy.

You can do this. Keep it together, Wendy. I kept reassuring myself.

One of the officers whipped out his pen and pad and with his head still down, began to write quickly. I couldn't tell if it was a ticket or a notepad, but either way, he had taken my license and was busy writing my information down. Then the policeman looked up and, just as he was about to launch into his string of questions, he paused. He looked at me suspiciously.

"Have you been drinking?" The officer accused.

Oh my God.

Think fast, Wendy.

Think fucking fast.

Keep your cool.

"No... I just...uh...took an extra prescription pill."

Phew...that was good thinking. Good thinking. They can't bust you for that. Can they?

Look right into his eyes.

He'll think you're lying if you look away.

Don't look away.

Don't back down.

Keep looking at him.

Don't look down.

Keep looking directly at him.

He paused for what seemed like an eternity. Hands down, the longest seconds of my life.

While he was deciding my fate, the annoying lights were taking away my attention. I saw my license flash before me. I saw my world flash before me and felt like I was going to pass out.

Don't look down.

Don't look at those flashing lights.

Keep looking at him.

"Well...you shouldn't do that!" He said in a scolding manner. After another moment of hesitation, he put his pad away. I wanted to take a huge breath, but had to keep my cool. My head was spinning.

I nodded my head in agreement, trying to act remorseful. Lucky for me I thought quickly on my feet, however, I didn't think I was in the clear. I still half expected him to whip out the handcuffs. I thought, surely it must be obvious how fucked up I was. Maybe he wasn't going to give me a ticket, but he was still going to arrest me and throw my ass in jail or something.

But I never got a ticket. I was never arrested. Nothing.

That's the last thing I remember.

The next thing I remember is being on the psych floor at my local hospital. To this day, I don't remember being admitted to the ER. Or how I even got to the hospital. The first memory I had was shuffling around endless white hallways and staring at the floors. I wasn't talking to anyone. Only staring at the floor, walking and thinking about everything.

The first feelings I recall were those of selfishness, shame and that ever-present depression. I felt a slight bit of relief that I couldn't go through with it. At the same time, I felt I was a failure for not being able to. And I threw that sense of failure on top of the bonfire. There's nothing like surviving a suicide attempt, then feeling *worse* because you don't have the balls to go through with it.

The guilt set in. What must my family think? I felt badly for them. I thought of my parents, my sister and all the kids in my immediate family. What kind of an example was I setting?

It certainly wasn't a cry for help. Not even for one split second. I *was* getting help. I *had* gotten help. *Nothing* was working and everyone knew it. It wasn't attention that I lacked, nor was it love or sobriety or help. It was the right *solution*. And all I kept thinking, was that I was going to be bipolar and miserable. Forever.

To me, science had failed, therapy had failed. Nothing was fixing me. Eventually it would, but depression doesn't let you see that it will get better. It only tells you that you'll always feel this way. And that's a horrible message to believe day in, day out. What I could *not* see (because of my depression blinders) was that I would get through the depression eventually. However, nothing anyone said to me could convince me of that at the time.

I noticed a few things since it was my first time being a patient in a hospital. It was very quiet. An uncomfortable quiet. A we're-at-the-hospital-and-someone's-about-to-die type of quiet. It didn't seem right and the lack of noise was very disturbing to me.

There was a lack of resources, too. There were no pamphlets lying around. Ones I could've used like: "You've Attempted Suicide and Failed. Now What?" Nothing helpful was anywhere to be seen. Not even blank paper to write on. (Not that I was in the mood to write.) Forget about therapy. There was nobody to help me discuss what was going on in my brain, or my life. Just a bed in a safe place and meds.

Music broke the painful silence. I begged for my CD walkman and when I got it, listened to my Pink CD over and over. Especially the song "Run" because that was exactly what I wanted to do. I felt it particularly helpful to have those lyrics in my head, handy, especially when a nurse was being bitchy. (Not that all nurses there were bitchy, there were some nice ones.) I'd sing the lyrics to myself to make me feel better and found solace that Pink knew how I felt. I had other CDs, but that one sticks out in my mind.

I didn't wear shoes most of the time. Why bother? It was not like I was going anywhere. They gave you those special hospital socks with the grippy things on the bottom: half sock, half shoe. A nifty invention, I thought. Sometimes, I elected to wear my own socks though, so I could just shuffle along easier and not get stuck, like I did in the hospital ones. That was the main downside to the hospital given shoe socks. You couldn't shuffle too well.

We had to earn the privilege of going outside for a fifteen minute break to smoke. Smoking just three times a day, once I got those privileges, was really tough. Waiting until you got privileges? Well that was *really* torture. You had to work up to that. I mean, you don't just try to kill yourself, get admitted to the psych floor and they say 'Sure go ahead outside and smoke. We trust you.' And wink and smile.

No, they think you're a flight risk, that you're gonna take off. So you have to prove yourself. You have to show good behavior. *Then* they let you out. Three times a day. I had forgotten air had a smell until I was locked up. It's funny the things you forget about, the freedoms you take for granted, until they're taken away.

I refused the nicotine patch. I wasn't going to quit smoking. Not then. It seemed ridiculous on top of everything else. The doctor told me nicotine was more addictive than heroin. Great. Maybe that was why I was extra irritable until I "earned" privileges to go out and smoke. Oh, those first few days were a joy! No music, no smokes, no privileges. Sheer torture, I tell you.

The other patients were surprised that I was thirty-three and had never been hospitalized for my bipolar disorder. I didn't know that was unusual. I gained a teeny tiny bit of pride knowing I had managed eleven years without institutions. They asked how I did it. I said I had always worked and kept busy. I also mentioned I came from a strong and loving family and that I was sober. 'Ah' they would say. I didn't realize at the time how large a part my sobriety played in my maintaining wellness. The magic ingredient was my sobriety. Not the steady work or strong family, although they certainly helped.

When I came out of my fog, I was desperate to find my sense of humor again. I had to, or I would go nuts inside those four walls. Once on the road to recovery, I needed to find others on my same wavelength and try, as best I could, to make light of *any* possible thing to pass the time. There sure weren't many things to do. I mean, even the deck of cards had some missing.

I avoided the puzzles. I figured the odds must've been high that pieces were missing. Wasn't it kind of cruel to leave an incomplete puzzle there for a psych patient to try and solve? Undoubtedly, some pieces had fallen on the floor over the months or years that it had been there. They probably got swept away when the custodians came to clean. We never bothered to play those games or do the puzzles. It was a given they were simply there on display to make the hospital seem like they had things for us to do. Essentially though, all you have is each other. The puzzles of each others' minds.

Again, there was no therapy, processing mechanisms or ways to get well in the hospital. I had to leave to do that. Being in the hospital was soley to be safe for us psych patients. That was it. It was for people who were suicidal. Also, for people who were so manic that they *might* be a danger to themselves or others. Those who needed to be brought down fast under strict medical supervision.

It was too expensive to be kept there. One week seemed to be the magic number for most, although I was there longer than that. People seemed to be coming and going, and the seriousness of my condition hadn't really sunk in. I had attempted to end my life.

I saw the people trying to deal with both addiction and mental illness at the same time and felt sorry for them. They were called "dual diagnosis" or "MICA/Mentally Ill Chemically Addicted" (over 60% of bipolars are in this category). That's actually me too, though at the moment I was dealing with only one, thankfully. At the time however, I had little gratitude.

I hung out with the two other women who I felt I had things in common with. They were well educated, dressed neatly and could hold a conversation of mutual interest. Both had also attempted suicide.

169

One girl was my age and married. She felt remorseful, talking about how wonderful her husband was and how badly she felt for him. I kept trying to reassure her that she didn't do it *to* him. I was trying to make her feel better. All the while, I was jealous that she had this wonderful husband who loved her.

The other woman I hung around with was named Paula. Paula had really curly hair that was just beautiful, the ringlety kind. When we started talking (as there's nothing else to do), she told me she'd written a book and said she'd help me edit mine. Talking about writing this book again gave me hope, a little purpose even.

Becoming friends with her got me through that hospitalization. The camaraderie gave us glimpses of moments where we could stand being in our own skin. When we all didn't feel so horrible about our lives, that maybe we could smile. Maybe. And it only happened with some people. Like Paula.

Paula had a very sarcastic sense of humor. She was in there for alcohol detox and had just gotten a DWI.

"I was only going to the store to get cat food. I *don't* drive drunk." Paula was the defensive, defiant type. Very intelligent. Probably too intelligent for her own good.

"Yeah, but Paula, did you drink *before* going to get cat food?"

"Well, yeah, I had like two or three beers."

"And then you drove?"

"Two blocks!" She declared.

"Well, then that's drinking and driving, right?"

"I guess. Technically. But it's so stupid." She sulked like a child.

"I don't get why you drove? Why not walk?" This part I didn't understand. Drinking and driving, I had done that. As bad as it was, I admitted to doing that before. But a few blocks? Why bother?

"And now I have to go to all these AA meetings and prove to the state that I went." She skipped right over my sensible question. "But I'm not even an alcoholic. It's not fair. *And* I have to go to stupid *bad driver classes*." She was very dramatic.

Everything was everyone else's fault in Paula's world. But it did take my mind off my problems to look at hers. Even though she did not stop complaining and it was a drag to be around her at times, I understood why she was depressed. She told me her Mom had died recently. She also told me about her divorce the year before. She may or may not have been an alcoholic. Like my Uncle Rick said, that was not for someone else to decide. I couldn't imagine losing my Mom. I couldn't imagine going through a divorce. Then again, I couldn't imagine being married.

"So, I still don't get it." I continued. "Why did you drive to get the cat food?"

"I didn't feel like walking." She looked at me blankly.

I burst into laughter. I couldn't help it. After holding back a little, she followed. That's how we knew we were getting better, when we could laugh at ourselves. Despite horrible circumstances, despite nothing being funny about what was going on in our lives, we had to laugh. Or we *would* have gone crazy in there.

Paula left a few days later but I was still stuck there. People came and people went. It seemed as soon as I thought of a nickname for them, they were gone.

"Wendy, you have a letter here," the nice nurse yelled across to me while waving a letter back and forth in the air. I was seated uncomfortably in the designed-to-be-uncomfortable standard issue hospital lounge couch.

"What? Me?" I thought there must be a mistake. Surely I wasn't getting mail here at the psych ward. Who knew I was here?

"Yes. You have a letter." She placed it on the top ledge at the nurse's station and went back to her business.

"Oh my God!" I looked at the handwriting and instantly recognized the script. "It's from my grandmother! My *ninety-two year old grandmother* has tracked me down! It's official. I have *got* to get out of here!"

It prompted me to play a game to kill time and not go crazy. This one wasn't terribly original. I ripped off David Letterman's popular "Top Ten" list.

My version was:

"Top 10 Reasons You Know You've Been at the Psych Ward Too Long:"

1. Grandma has tracked you down.
2. You've given everybody a nickname.
3. Patients who have checked out come back as visitors.
4. You know how to custom order food and get it.
5. You've learned to hide your cigarettes and smoke them illegally.
6. Your wrist band is so worn they give you a new one.
7. You know all the tricks for smuggling in food.
8. You know how to hide your snacks in the fridge using the vegetable/crisper drawer.
9. You know how to stock up on toiletry items by asking different staff members for the same items.
10. The cleaning lady knows your name.

Okay, so I was no David Letterman, but it kept me busy coming up with new ones.

It was during this hospital stay, when my psychiatrist suggested ECT (Electro Convulsive Therapy). I wasn't sure what the procedure entailed, but it scared me when I allowed myself to think about it. The idea seemed freaky and I had flashes of horror movies. Still, I had nothing to lose except maybe a few brain cells that weren't working very well anyway. And I knew in my heart that it would only be a matter of time before I found a plan that worked and I succeeded in killing myself. I couldn't do that to my parents, to my sister, my cousins, aunt, uncle, nieces and nephews, grandmother and friends. What did I have to lose? A little short-term memory? Well, the short term pretty much sucked anyway, so I thought: why not? Kill it.

Luckily, one of my closest friends, Laura had ECT. She was fine and that helped ease my fears. If I hadn't known anyone who had gone through it, I'm not sure what my attitude would have been. But I just wanted to die. And if you want to die so badly that you would jump forty-five floors, believe me, ECT would seem like a walk in the park. I'm not going to lie and say I wasn't worried about losing my *long*-term memory. I had great long term memories in life and I didn't want to lose them. The doctors assured me those would be in tact and I had no choice but to trust them. So I gave them the green light.

What the doctor *failed* to do was take me off one of my meds, which was an anti-seizure medication. (It's common for bipolars to be on anti-seizure type medications.) Because the purpose of ECT is to induce a short seizure, obviously an *anti*-seizure medication would block its effect. So, needless to say, the effectiveness of the treatments was a wash. I did lose a little short term memory and rack up some pretty high medical bills, but there was absolutely no benefit. I went through all those treatments for nothing.

I realize now we should've done some research. We simply trusted the doctor I was already going to, to administer the treatments. ECT deals with the brain, certainly one of the most vital organs; I strongly recommend you do careful research. If you need ECT, make sure you get the best doctor and facility possible. Period.

Someone Is There

My depression was getting worse while I received ECT, because my freedoms were disappearing. I couldn't work and on the days of the treatments, I also couldn't drive. Due to my short-term memory loss, this part of my life is hazy. (Again, not that they were good times that I really wanted to remember, anyway.) The real problem though, was not being able to work. I was *always* used to working. Now, I was out of work longer and going down further.

During this time, I was spending many nights writing and going to my favorite, local church. I felt peace there. And I would question God. *Why?* Why did He leave me and take my friend? Why was I born with mental illness? Why didn't He let me succeed at killing myself? I spent countless hours asking this pointless question.

Although it was a Catholic church and I'm not Catholic, I knew God did not mind where I spoke to Him. I felt comfort there. But in my mind, there was only *limited* comfort. It was fleeting, as the relief seemed to wear off moments after I'd walk out. Panic and depression would infiltrate my soul again.

Very late one night, I was watching TV (MTV to be precise) in the family room. I didn't want to wake my parents upstairs, so the volume was low. I was in complete anguish. The kind where you're rocking and moaning, but your pain is so intense, no noise is coming out. I think if I had been crying or screaming as loud as I wanted to, the whole neighborhood would've heard me.

Then I got mad. Really mad and my blood began to boil. I wanted God to hear me roar. Inside I was yelling at the top of my lungs to God. My anger had built up inside me and never, ever, had I confronted Him with such fierce rage.

I challenged God.

Why am I still so depressed?

Why am I bipolar?

Why did you make me this way?

I felt God had forgotten about me, his sick child. I'm not one to feel self-pity often, but that night I was drowning in it. I had morphed all my depression and self-pity into rage and was hurling it right at God.

If you are God, and you can do all things, why haven't you taken this depression away from me?

WHY?

Out of nowhere, I heard a man's voice.

"I never lied to you."

I abruptly stopped crying. Did I just hear a voice? *In my head?* Who *was* that? My anger subsided. I looked around but heard nothing except the sound of the TV.

I continued to question my sanity, until I heard the voice again.

"I never lied to you." The voice repeated. It was a beautiful, gentle voice.

I questioned myself: *did I really just hear a voice? Again?* This was not imagined. No, this voice was real.

It began to sink in. I heard a voice!

My shock wore off as I refocused on my questions. My anger returned.

That wasn't the question! I yelled to the voice.

I waited for a response.

Silence.

I desperately wanted the voice back. I knew it was gone, though. It was the sweetest, calmest voice I had ever heard. It was definitely a man's voice.

But who was that?

Was it God?

Jesus?

Was He really taking the time to speak to *me*? How could *I* be that important? Weren't there many more, worthwhile people He could be speaking to right now? Why me?

I didn't know what that meant exactly or who had said it, but I was instantly calmed and in awe of what had just happened. He wasn't answering my question precisely, but His presence comforted me. If only I could hear that voice again. It was the epitome of serenity.

It was one of my darkest hours emotionally, but I had been given a gift. A once-in-a-lifetime gift, this voice.

Someone was listening. I had proof.

Someone was listening.

Although it was comforting, I was still feeling little relief on a day to day basis. During this period of time, I was in and out of three different hospitals. Recently, I looked at my hospital records and added it up. I spent a total of three and a half months, locked up seven times over a fourteen-month period. It was a big blur, one that I'd like to forget ever happened.

All the while, everyone's lives around me seemed to be moving forward. Mine, in contrast, was at a standstill. It was the bleakest period of my life. There was no sunshine on the horizon for me, nor sunsets to look at. There was no color. All I saw was darkness. All I felt was constant despair. For fourteen months. One after another, a string of hospitalizations and suicide attempts blended into a gray haze. The abyss of weeks and months where I wished my life would end. That was my existence.

My second suicide attempt was the least severe of the three. It happened one night when I was up late thinking, spinning my wheels, as usual. (Clearly, being up so late was my first problem.) But my mind felt clearer late at night, with less interference, when the rest of the world was asleep. I liked *not* being around people at that time. Sometimes I'd drive to a local favorite spot of mine and park.

I decided to go to the local, municipal boat ramp where we had put our sailboat in the water many times when I was a kid. I didn't really have any deep connection to it, but it was close by. I loved the water. It was a calm place. Unlike my mind. I decided to drown myself. I was going to drive my car into the river. Driving off the boat ramp seemed like a good idea. On the night I had the nerve to do it, I drove the three short blocks it took to get there.

I had my car in position at the top of the ramp. I put each of my windows down slightly. As I was just about to drive forward, out of nowhere, came a light.

At first, I didn't see the boat. I only saw a tiny light off in the distance coming towards me, closer and closer. It seemed to be floating in the air, all by itself. Then I realized it was attached to the front of a boat. It was a small boat. Like the kind you'd motor around small rivers in. Except it made no noise. The motor wasn't on and there were no paddles. It just came slowly drifting in. Quietly, eerily drifting in.

The next thing I noticed was a dog in the bow of the boat. It looked like a black lab. Then I saw there was an older man in the stern. Each were looking off in different directions, neither at me. They were motionless. *Perfectly* still.

I thought this was particularly odd since I was right in their path. Wouldn't you think that if you saw a big, white car aimed at the water exactly where you were coming in to dock, you might stir? It was very strange.

I thought, 'Okay God, you're ruining this again!' It was around 3:00 am and there are never fisherman coming into that ramp at that hour. I had been parking there quite a bit and it didn't happen. Ever. It was freaky.

I quickly backed my car into reverse and got the hell out of there before he saw me or my plates.

Afterwards, I decided that they looked just like those ghost/apparitions in the Scooby Doo cartoons. Just floating quietly in the night. Even the dog was completely still, poised as if he were human, posing for a portrait. I'll never forget that.

They *must* have been real, but to this day I question it. It spooked me right out of there and I forgot all about my plan for the night. I went home and got into bed.

They literally scared me *out* of death.

Off the Tracks & ECT

Some time had passed and I tried to commit suicide again. Nothing was relieving my depression. Not medication, not ECT, not therapy, no combination of the three, nothing. I couldn't take it anymore and I saw no other solution: I wanted out. Only this time, it was much more serious. This time, I wanted to be sure I couldn't back out.

This was it. Last stop.

I drove to a nearby town to the place I'd picked out. I needed a dark, remote stretch of tracks to lie on. I parked my car at the end of the lot at the beginning of the trees, and left my keys in the ignition.

I cleaned out my purse, stuffing everything in the glove compartment. The only thing I left inside was my driver's license. I knew they would need it to be able to identify my body.

I nervously walked to the end of the lot and to the middle of the mini-forest. The train was nowhere in sight. It gave me time to position myself.

I laid down on the train tracks face down. The tracks were cold, hard and had that unpleasant metal smell. I stretched my arms out over my head, clutching my purse and waited. Many thoughts raced through my head, as several minutes, perhaps even ten or more, went by. Finally, I would be at peace. No more depression. No more mania. No more bipolar disorder. No more me.

I felt the vibrations of the train first and then saw the light in the distance. It would be over soon, I told myself. Soon.

I peeked my head to the right to see where the train was. It was moving along at a fast pace. The light was so bright it was nearly all I saw as the train zoomed torwards me.

Suddenly, the conductor saw me and leaned on the horn.

WOO WOO!

WOO WOO!

It was so loud it was DEAFENING!

WOO WOO!

WOO WOO!

In response, I jerked up and got off the tracks. It was in the nick of time. *Barely* in the nick of time.

I should've gotten run over. I was up and off the tracks before I even processed the thought to do so. I did not expect the conductor to see me. Nor was I expecting that horn.

The train was so close I cannot even tell you! It had to be no more than twenty or thirty feet. It may have been less. I shudder to try and recall how close it came to me. I don't like to think about it, even to explain it to you now. I really don't want to go back there in my memory and recreate the scene to figure it out. I try and my brain stops me.

I wanted to die. You might be thinking 'but she got up.' Let me assure you: someone who is lying on train tracks does not want to live. I can't figure out to this day why I got up, except to say the horn startled me. The next thing I knew, I was off the tracks. It's odd because I had every intention of dying that night. I had no desire to get up. That horn, that conductor, saved me. I suppose it was God, once again, because I can't explain it any other way.

I really should be dead. There is *no question* and I know it. Sometimes, on the very rare occasions when I think about it, I still can't believe I'm walking this Earth.

The strangest part is I still don't remember the exact spot where it took place. I don't remember where I parked my car that night. I have two guesses as to where it could be and I sometimes look down those gravel parking lots when I drive by the crossing. It was in between train stations, in a nearby town. I remember the long gravel parking lot near a little forest. But that's it. Which is bizarre because I was completely unimpaired. I was 100% sober, not so much as a drink or an extra pill in my system. Nothing.

I still remember the noise, even though I don't consciously think about it. Every time I hear a train whistle, something inside me gets alarmed to this very day. I'll wonder why I feel disturbed, then I realize: a train is coming somewhere.

The train attempt landed me in the hospital for a month. Surrounding all my suicide attempts, I was in and out of three different hospitals. However, I spent most of my time in a hospital/rehab called Princeton House. I had found my way there from a local hospital because of their excellent reputation for, notably, their "Women's Trauma and Addiction Program." It was the only one of its kind in the state. I went there three times a week, traveling an hour and a half each way, well after my inpatient stay.

In the beginning, I was assigned to "safety class." We were the worst of the worst. The bunch of us that were extremely suicidal, still self-mutilating and/or had eating disorders that were out of control. And we were stuck (rightly so) in safety class until our counselors deemed us safe again. Some of us were in there for many months. I felt like I was never getting out. On any given day, any one of us in there could've or should've been checked in for the state of minds we were in.

One Friday it was my turn. The other women were worried because I seemed especially suicidal that day. That was the type of week it was. (I remember frequently driving home from program with thoughts like: *if I turn right I'll kill myself, if I go left I'll go home.*) It was that bad. The women got together and told my counselor they didn't think I'd make it over the weekend. I never went home that weekend. I was in there for thirty days that time, too.

I found this entry in my journal from that time period:

Day after day
Hour after hour
I try to forget
My dream's slipping power.

This was where my head was. I felt nothing inside. Nothing except regret and emptiness.

One of the only things that made my stay there bearable was a group of guys. There were four of them, all guys in their thirties and forties.

Joey was the youngest in the group, still single and an idiot. With nice clothes and his thick, Italian hair, he was the baby in his family. I imagined him to be the son who could do no wrong. Joey thought himself to be the ringleader. Really, he was the only one with any energy.

Joey was in film, or so he said. He was trying to impress everyone. I thought, by the way he talked, that he was probably just a production assistant who worked for free. He was most likely full of shit. Well, either a P.A. or full of shit. Or both. Probably both.

We would sit around and talk. Correction. *They* would sit around and talk. I would listen, occasionally chiming in. One day we joked about how rehab would make for a great reality TV show (of course now years later, that has already been done).

"I have contacts at HBO." Joey beamed. Joey was in for cocaine. He was the token Mr.-Know-It-All in our little posse. Actually, *their* little posse. I was like their little sister who they didn't want around. They let me hang out on the periphery because they were tired of telling me to get lost. Plus, there was nowhere else for me to go. Here in the Rotunda, there was one giant TV and a bunch of uncomfortable couches and chairs. This was the standard, universal institutional policy. Let them sit, but for God's sake, don't give the patients a couch they could actually get comfortable on.

"Oh really? HBO?" Even though I couldn't stand him, I had to admit I was slightly impressed he knew anyone in TV, even though I tried my best not to show it. Nobody was paying much attention to him except me. The other guys probably thought, or knew, he was lying. I was pretty gullible and even *I* kind of thought he was lying. But it gave me something to do if I believed him. So I did.

"Yeah." Joey was very impressed with himself. He acted like it was top secret, this great job he had.

"Hmm. Interesting." I said. I tried to remain cool in the off chance he *was* in the biz and could make something happen down the road. You never know. Stranger things have happened than people making connections while in rehab or on the flight deck (take your pick). Which this place was, really, all of the above, with its beige walls and brown carpet and rotunda. It sure beat the white hues and cold tiles of the hospital. Plus, this place had good ice cream and better smoke breaks than your average hospital. A step up. It was my favorite (if I had to pick one) to be locked up in.

"If you think of any skits, write 'em down," Joey commanded from his chair.

"Okay," I replied flatly. Depression makes everything out of your mouth totally monotone. The same drip drab dribble day in, day out, pouring from your mouth when you do turn it on. Which you don't do often of course, because it takes too much effort.

We all talked about funny scenes out loud, off the top of our heads, and I wrote some stuff down for lack of anything better to do. It was all we could do from going insane in there. For me, it beat sitting alone in the art room watching TV. Or in my room on those noisy hospital beds that creaked every time you moved with their awful plastic mattresses.

It also beat the depressing shit I was writing in my journals. But I never showed Joey my skits or shared any of my ideas with him. I could just imagine him ripping my shit off and it becoming some popular show, an award-winning episode or something stupid. I don't know. I thought you never know and I wasn't about to do the work, then hand it over to Joey full-of-baloney, just in case he wasn't.

"What actress do you think could play her?" Joey asked the other two.

"I don't know." The one guy said, refusing to play, his eyes glued to the game on TV. But Joey was taking himself too seriously to throw in the towel that fast, so he threw out a few names.

"How about Scarlett Johansson?" Joey asked.

"No *way*, she looks *nothing* like her!" They both burst out laughing. They couldn't talk; they were hysterical for a good five minutes. Naturally, I needed this like a hole in the head. I actually had no idea who she was at the time, but knew I looked like no one in Hollywood.

"Well, then who?" Joey demanded. He was still on his quest for *someone* who could play me. As if he were some Hollywood big shot in need of a solution fast.

"I don't know. She doesn't look like anyone." One of the guys said, his eyes glued to the TV.

"Sandra Bullock." The other guy threw out. They broke out into laughter again finding this completely hysterical at my expense.

"Closer...but no." Joey's expression was very serious. "She looks more like her than Scarlett though." Joey was in deep contemplation.

"Thanks a lot you guys. I've had enough." I was over this ridiculous little exercise.

"What about what's her name?" They were talking amongst themselves again.

"She was in that movie last year, it came out around Christmas time...opposite that douchebag guy with the New York accent. Oh you know, what's his name? It was about the family that..." They were going on and on.

"Oh yeah. I know who you mean. Dude, *she's hot!*" One of the guys got all excited.

"Nah, she's got red hair and Wendy's got brown hair...and I mean, no *way*! They look *nothing* alike!" This game was giving me a complex. I threw my pen down.

"Ha ha. Very funny. You guys are hysterical." I said with the energy I could muster from all corners of my body, which wasn't much. This was doing wonders for my depression.

"What?" Joey defended.

"Kick me while I'm down assholes."

We all knew they were laughing because I didn't even look like a distant fucking relative of anyone in Hollywood. I was twice the weight, had acne and no boobs. Sure, I could buy boobs someday, but it would take forever to lose this fucking weight. Oh and what about this acne? Where the hell did this come from? Who in Hollywood has acne besides people who are spokespeople for skin care products? (And they *still* never looked that bad to begin with.) So to be on this quest to find a star who is either medically altered or possessing a mutant gene of near perfection, was not fair to do to this suicidal girl. No need for them to be so blatantly rude about it all.

"What? I'm just doing this so I can write the dialogue with someone in mind for your part." Joey explained. Ah, now he was a script writer. Interesting. Pretty soon he'd be directing it, too. "It's not who is actually going to be *playing* your part. It's just so I have an idea." Really? Even I knew that.

"Got it." I shot back sarcastically to Joey. The other guys had long since checked out of our conversation.

Still, all these antics diffused what was going on inside me. The laughter I observed while hanging around them (and occasionally joined in) was once again the only thing that helped me from going completely mad while being inpatient there.

Laughter *was* the best medicine. It helped me take my mind off getting ECT again. The guys made my month there bearable and gave me something *other* than myself to focus on. They took me out of my extreme introversion and I was eager for some new material starring anyone or anything else.

However, when I had the gumption to write in my journal, it was typically horribly depressing entries. Most of the journals I have since thrown away, but I still have two of them. I keep them, so on occasion, I can pull them out and read them to see how far I have come. These journals represent dark hallways I don't often wish to walk though. This is an example of why.

Here is my journal entry from 3/12/04:

"I'm waiting to see Dr. Smith. Are they going to put me inpatient again? There are a lot of people here. One lady who got her ECT last treatment was just sitting next to me. She was so nice and polite. Then there was this skinny girl named Erin who's back in again for heroin and she looks like hell. There's a red haired man hacking his lungs up asking for his Seroquel. I'm in a chair. I can't make decisions. The way I'm holding this pen has changed a gazillion ways since I've started writing.

I hate myself!!! I have to agree at this moment with Freud that there's really something to depression is anger turned in. I understand! But there's also a lot of chemical shit goin' on too. I am back to anger. I feel myself going under when all I really want is to go under for good. It's a trap though because that's how I feel permanently. This is fleeting but it is the ultimate sin and it is a selfish act. Nobody can save me. I know that I have to do it myself.

But I am scared and immature and there's no cure for bipolar or alcoholism or drug addiction or anything. There's no cure for anything. Death is not the answer but I don't know how to live. I hate how I think and nobody can solve that. The doctors can't solve the medication problem because I don't know how I feel. I feel nothing but disgust and hate. Occasionally I can feel love for family members but it is so fleeting. It is so rare that I feel at all that it doesn't matter.

People are so beautiful. It is so obvious how much everyone loves. They keep pain hidden well, or have released or been released from it. I can't seem to find that eject button."

When I stayed at that facility in particular, there were many characters who came and went. Since I spent so much time there (over two months collectively), I was able to observe many people. I found some amusement in everyone's idiosyncrasies. Plus, it helped pass the time and there wasn't much else to do.

There was one guy we nicknamed Corky. He *hated* the nickname we gave him. We even put a sign on his door just to annoy him and for something to do. Corky would always steal the fruit (which there was no need to because it was handed out freely). Corky loaded up his cargo pant pockets with it every night. He was an odd fellow.

There was also the "blouse man" from Brooklyn. He was a dear, older gentleman who sold blouses all his life. He'd recently lost his wife to cancer and, as a result, was there for depression. He used to recite poems sadly to me looking distant and lost. I felt so badly for him.

Then there was Erin. My strung out, stripper roommate Erin. Oh, she was a handful right from the start.

"Got any smokes?" She announced way too loudly as she plopped down on the couch next to me. She scared the crap out of me. Erin was the kind of girl who enjoyed scaring the shit out of you. We had known each other all of one and a half days, but because she was my roomie, I was stuck being her "go to" girl. How did I get so lucky? Couldn't I have gotten another suicidal person? Or, how about a manic chick? Maybe that would have a balance out effect? That was one for the comment box, I decided.

"Well, hello there." I said sarcastically back to her.

I knew that because Erin asked for smokes, this was also code for: *I'm broke.* Actually, you can just about guess 99% of the time the people walking through the doors at Princeton House for drug rehab are out of money. If they were hitting you up for smokes, then they were definitely not one of the 1% ers.

There were still some rich rehabbers here in existence, but it was pretty rare. Joey was a rich rehabber. You could tell he was still pretty well intact. He wore nice clothes and his hands still looked good, almost like he had just had a manicure. His was a civil family intervention. Joey hadn't been cut off yet. So he was a 1% er. Life for him was still good. Joey had all the cigarettes in the world.

Life for Erin was much tougher. She had burned through her

money with her drug of choice. I suspected her friends and family had probably, for the most part, turned their backs. Erin never had any visitors. Maybe the love was still there with some, but the 99%ers had been financially cut off. That's my theory anyway.

Erin was trying to kick heroin. I'd already been warned about her. And I knew this wasn't her first tour here; she had bounced in and out a few times. She looked like hell. Just one straw shy of death.

The addicts I knew from all my hospital stays were *always* the ones stealing. I knew she was going to steal from me. It was only a matter of time. You got the sense she was a pro.

"Smokes?" She repeated with her hand out. Apparently, she needed them this instant.

"Here." I fished out my smokes and hooked her up with a bunch. Why bother giving her one or two? She'd only steal them anyway.

Now there's something you have to understand about hospitals and rehabs: cigarettes were and still remain, the most valuable, legal commodity on the black market. If you're in there (especially for rehab), odds are, you're broke. If you're in there and you smoke, it's likely you can't afford to, but you gotta have your smokes! So I had gold in my pocket. Not that there was anything I wanted to trade it for, mind you. Except perhaps a magic pill to cure my depression (which obviously didn't exist or I wouldn't be there in the first place).

"What kind are they?" Erin asked. As if I said they were the no name, generic brand she would turn me down. Only to wait for a more generous, brand-name donor to come her way.

"Marlboro Reds." I replied, disgusted. I was pretty sure she knew what I smoked. She had already bummed two off me earlier. Now she was not just an annoying mooch, but a *picky*, annoying mooch. The worst kind. I felt like throwing them at her. Instead, I just handed her four. That would get her through the rest of our smoke breaks. She wouldn't have to bother me again all day. Done. I told her if she smoked in our bathroom I'd cut her off because they might think it was me. I didn't think she'd smoke in our bathroom because she'd already been thrown out of this place twice before. This would be her last shot, her third strike.

She was on thin ice as it was. She was homeless and hungry and from what I understood, had nowhere else to go. I suggested halfway houses to her and she made a face. She hated living with women, she said. Alrightythen. I stopped playing drug and alcohol counselor to her real quick after that. I returned to being roommate-waiting-to-be-stolen-from. I had $10 that I always kept. I had nowhere to spend it, but it was more comfortable to have a little cash. There was a reason they told us not to have money there. And it was because of people like Erin.

We sat there counting down 'til our next smoke break. It was that long lag in the evening after dinner and before bed time. There was absolutely nothing to do except watch TV and look forward to our last smoke break.

I started shaking the pretty sizeable tree next to me for entertainment.

"What are you doing?" Erin asked, looking at me sideways. She was sitting next to me, but only glanced at me for half a split second. Usually, like now, she was surveying the room. Erin was always looking around as if there was something exciting about to go down in the giant Rotunda. Which, of course, sadly there never was.

"Shaking for dead leaves." I said as I watched a few leaves fall on the couch, the floor and Erin's feet curled up on the couch next to me. She was still busy surveying the room. Like a secret service agent looking for a shooter or something.

"Is it real?" She asked absentmindedly. I looked at her to see if she was seriously asking me this, the dead ones plainly lying on her dirty socks. But she was too busy scanning the room to even notice them.

"Well, duh." I said, wide-eyed as I looked at her socks. (I didn't have enough energy to point. The tree shaking had taken it all out of me for the day.) Her gaze followed mine to her socks but quickly darted up again.

"Oh right." Erin responded halfheartedly.

Her eyes were glued to the fresh meat that had strolled into the Rotunda just now. Another strung out dude. Bullseye! She'd be talking to him in no time. He was kinda hot, in a young, tough streets kind of way. Now my stripper roommate had something to occupy her during her "sentence" here. I could guarantee that Erin would forget all about me, her virtual cigarette machine sitting inches away. She would stash the ones I had just given her and hit him up anyway just to talk to him.

Rehab romance. Totally predictable. Totally tragic. Been there, got the t-shirt. It shrank. It sucked. End of story.

They were always getting on Erin for her outfits. They had a rather strict dress code there (compared to some other hospitals and rehabs). Most people had no problem adhering to it. I certainly had no problem with it. But not Erin. She loved to show her too thin stripper body. (She probably did have a kick ass figure before heroin robbed her of it.) Erin was the poster girl for what not to wear there. They must have pamphlets printed up in the welcome packets now with her picture, half shirts, short shorts and a big red "X" through it.

The next day when Erin had checked herself out, my $10 had checked out, too. It was hidden in the back corner of my desk drawer. I don't know why I was surprised. I wasn't annoyed. I was more pissed off she took both packs of my smokes than my money.

191

I have to say, my Mom and/or Dad came every single day while I there. I was extremely lucky to have parents who were so supportive. I could've just rotted in there, for all I cared. But they gave me hope. My sister came twice when I was at the hospital close by, but never to see me at Princeton House where I had spent a total of two and a half months. Although that made me sad, to be fair, coming there was far for her. Still, I used to think that surely my sister could've come see me over the course of those stays.

However, I'm able to see it now for what it is: people deal with mental illness differently. Does it hurt? I won't lie; of course it hurts. But mental illness hurts and affects *everyone,* not just the person who has it. Recently, at a No Kidding Me Too (NKM2) fundraiser, I heard the statistic that 1 in 4 people are afflicted with some form of mental illness. What blew me away though, was the statistic that 4 in 5 are *affected* by it. I try to understand that today. I have met and spoken with people who have gotten little to no support from their families. I don't know where I would be if that were me. Probably dead.

Another journal entry from that time period:

> "I don't feel love inside me. I don't feel love coming back. I don't feel anything. It feels like my heart has turned to rock. I can't feel anything. I don't care about anything. I love my Mom so much. I love my family so much. I care about them so much and wish for them the best but wish for me the end. It is like a lonely, dark hallway and every door has been locked. I hate my fears and anxieties. I hate how uncomfortable I make people. I hate my insides. I hate my outsides. I hate the pity I feel for myself. I hate how tired I always feel. And so lethargic.
>
> I hate that I always feel such a lack of love towards anyone or anything. I can't be the person God wants me to be. I can't live

up to my own standards. I can't get well in this program because I am beyond human aid. I never have any energy. I only complain. I'm surrounded by beautiful people in my life and I'm the only one with an ugly rock heart."

Unfortunately, these were typical entries for a while. I wasn't writing consistently. When you don't have anything positive to say, you don't exactly want to pick up a pen and paper. When I did, it wasn't pretty. I sure as hell wasn't writing happy poems. Plus, I wasn't motivated. I had begun to feel like a cat. I slept a lot, ate some, walked around a little and cleaned myself once in a while.

A journal entry labeled "Sunday 6 pm:"

"I shaved in the shower earlier after lying in my bed all morning in clothes from the day before. As each day blends into the next day, with each dull chicken meal, a different t-shirt and my flip flops on. I lose track of the days and find myself shuffling along the hallways guided by the flow of foot traffic as opposed to the sense or understanding of the daily schedule.

Days blend into days and now weeks and I feel more and more institutionalized. Attending groups and crying remorsefully over my failures, regrets and current situation. I look with longing and jealousy at other women who care for themselves in any way about their appearances. The disgust I feel over my hopelessly flawed personality will not go and my numbed ambivalence won't go away."

Another read (brace yourselves, this one is really uplifting!):

"I feel inept, 100% irresponsible, ugly, scarred, a loser and unable to be social or trusting of hardly anyone. I feel I need someone to do all my finances and everything. I feel ungrateful for life. Even if it were close to perfect, I still feel I would be miserable because for so long I have been hiding behind the 'it will be okay' mask. My family and a few friends wish they could turn me off because I sound like a broken record.

I am so afraid of God or whomever. I cry every day. Sometimes to people, sometimes to myself, sometimes to you. Sometimes in my car. I cry at parties because I see others laughing with smiles and I feel I can't even fake that. Or something gets said that's offensive whether or not it's meant to be. I'm grateful I have a nice and loving family. At the same time, I wish I was homeless, knew nobody so I could die soon and that it wouldn't affect anyone.

I'm tired of what goes on in my head. I don't know what I can or can't control anymore. I'd love to laugh. I wish I could be genuinely happy. I despise myself so much that I know if self-love comes before you can truly love someone else, I'm gonna remain single. God, you could place in my path my soul mate but I'd only screw it up. I know I don't know what the future holds for me but I've spent enough years with me to know that it is going to take many many many many years and combos of pills to get this brain under control.

And finances. Unless there's a miracle, I'm a time bomb. Oh, about 6 wks from now I will not be getting another penny from disability. Social security denied me once but that was for welfare so who knows about SSD or SSA, the disability one. I dread living here too long and I dread moving out. I dread having to work and I dread having no job to go to. I need structure. I'm so sick of myself. I'm sick and tired of not feeling like I fit in anywhere. Blah blah blah. I'm tired of being afraid of pretty much everything all the time and being around everyone who seems to be getting better.

Everyone I know is happier than me. It's annoying. There can't be too many people who think as much as I do about all the constant comparisons as I do. That's it. It's sunny. Not an ounce of food yet. Princeton House called. New medication, again. Gotta go to CVS. Again. Hope that pharmacist who thinks she's a doctor is there again. My friend is at Carrier and was just diagnosed. Oh what a ride she's in for. I really feel badly for anyone who's bipolar. It's Hell. Purgatory. At Kathy's son's party (yup, cried there too!) her friend who shares the same birthday said to me that ...Oh shit...lost my train of thought! Feeling guilty because it's 4pm. No food in me yet! Still in robe. I don't know. Well I wrote. It's depressing. Do I feel better? Standard answer: I don't know."

They suggested I go for ECT treatments again. They hadn't worked the first time, but I figured I had nothing to lose. Clearly, all the combinations of medications they were trying were not working and my brain needed a jump start.

Princeton House is affiliated with Princeton University Hospital, which has one of the best reputations in the country for Electro Convulsive Therapy (ECT). It was a hundred times better than where I had been the first time, so I gave the procedure another try. I truly didn't care if I lived or died at the time. I did it for my family and that was my only motivation. I knew that chances were, sooner or later, I was going to succeed in killing myself. I owed it to them, especially to my parents, to try ECT again.

They helped us ECT patients into the Econo type van in the dark, early morning hour. As we rode the van in silence, I thought it oddly beautiful how our bodies swayed in unison around each turn and curve during the short drive to the hospital. There were only a handful of us in the van who came from Princeton House. A few others (who weren't inpatient) were there to have the procedure done on an outpatient basis and therefore checked in on their own. (I did this too when I had checked out from Princeton House weeks later.)

Everyone there was much older than me, elderly in fact. I looked around the waiting room and wondered how I had gotten there. These people were decades older than me. Where had I gone wrong in life?

Most of us were catatonically depressed and barely moving. I wasn't scared as much by the procedure as I was looking at these other people in the waiting rooms. It was tragic the way they were slumped over.

I wondered if this was what I had to look forward to. If I made it through this part of my life alive, would I feel this way again? Would I have to go through this again? I didn't linger in this thought process long, partly because the nurse was soon calling my name for me to lie down and begin. Partly because it was too unbearable to think I could end up this way again. And partly because I couldn't see out of the hole I was in to even *fathom* making it to that age.

I knew I had no options left. I was walking death. We were walking death. The other people looked shut down, like puppets without hands or strings to move them. I suppose I must've looked the same way. I knew we had one thing in common, all of us: we felt bone crushing bad. This procedure *had* to save us because there was nothing left to fix our depression. It was our last option.

The procedure was pretty simple. They checked you in and had you put on a fabulous gown. I always hoped nobody saw my ass; though even with their "wear two" method (one each way, back to back), someone was bound to see a little skin. I thought it couldn't be any worse than the saggy asses the old folks might be flashing and felt a little better.

The nurse in charge, Beth, had been the head ECT nurse for a long time and had it down to a science. I always felt I was in good hands. She had a bunch of degrees and initials after her name and knew what she was doing. It was comforting to know I was in the very best of care with the Princeton team.

I remember when they lay us down on the stretchers they gave us these warm blankets. They felt so good, although their warmth didn't last long though.

"Can I have another one?" I asked. The nurse smiled at me.

"I know. They feel so warm and cozy, don't they?" The nice nurse went and got me another one. She tucked me in and I felt all toasty again. It was definitely a highlight. Otherwise, it was freezing in there and my nose was always cold.

We all had our warm blankets and were lined up, ready to go. The anesthesiologist walked up. I thought, *not bad*. I was grateful he was kinda cute. Something fun to look at, anyway. Even if only for a minute.

"Okay, Wendy, count back from one hundred for me please."

The anesthesiologist was always very polite. He pulled the clipboard off the end of my cot. He was watching the monitor and the IV bag. It impressed me that he bothered to look up my name on my chart and get it right. A nice personal touch. They made a lot of money for such a short time, I thought. Then again, anesthesiologists also had a lot of responsibility.

I have to admit, I wondered: what if they didn't give me enough and I woke up in the middle of the procedure? How horrible. What if it was too much? Could I die? Doubtful. It was not as if I really cared if he did fuck up and I died. I was there because I was suicidal, after all. I was merely wondering these things for his sake and liability. *That* was why he was making the big bucks.

Still, I trusted this semi-young, good looking doctor. We were lined up in a row, one stretcher after another. He would inject us and quickly go to the next patient. You could tell with his speed this was no big deal for him. Despite my initial worries, it was quickly obvious this guy was a pro.

"Okay," I said.

"Now count for me please." He was writing, looking, talking, a very busy man indeed.

Suddenly I felt the slight burn of the fluid injected into me. Then I felt goooood. Yeah. It was a free high since I didn't do drugs anymore (not that I had ever been an intravenous drug user, mind you). The words from "Comfortably Numb" by Pink Floyd floated in my head. "Relax…just a little pinprick…" Reluctantly, I began to count.

"100…99…98…97…96…95…" I said slowly. I wanted to savor the feeling, every second. Oh I was an addict, there was no doubt. If there ever was, those moments confirmed it.

According to my records, my seizures lasted from thirty-six to seventy-six seconds. The doctor recorded the duration of each seizure and if anything abnormal occurred. Thankfully, nothing out of the ordinary ever happened during any treatment. I never felt a thing. The doctors were amazing, professional and very kind. I am blessed I went to a top place.

As far as the day of the treatment, I would get a headache which would go away hours later. I couldn't drive home because the anesthesia was still in my system. My parents or aunt would take me home once I was discharged from the surgi-center.

Initially, I received the procedure three times a week. Then it was tapered off to once a month for eight or nine months for what they called my "maintenance treatments."

Of course ECT is a huge disruption in one's life. But let's face it, so is depression. Especially depression to that degree. It was going to be hard to explain the gap in my resume, I thought. (Then again, my resume and job hunt at that moment were the *least* of my worries.)

Because they are putting you under, ECT is risky and never a first course of action when dealing with depression. However, it absolutely and *without question,* saved my life. I'm glad I know it exists because if it were to come down to it, I would absolutely seek the treatments again. Fuck the stigma. If something saves your life, you lean towards doing it. Short term memory loss or not.

True, those times are a little fuzzy in retrospect. In talking with friends, they remind me that I was panicking about my memory loss during the process. My friends tell me I was constantly asking, "Will this be permanent? What if it is?"

As the doctors and professionals had predicted and assured me, that was not the case. My long term memory has been fine. I don't advertise that I went through ECT because when I do tell people, they look freaked out. They look at me with a "One Flew Over the Cuckoos Nest" look.

You know, I feel like I hated life so much those months and years, why would I want to remember every single detail of those days anyway? I believe God left in my memory what I needed to remember and took away the things that didn't matter. I'm very grateful to the doctors and for the procedure.

I was extremely lucky my friend, Laura had the treatments ten years before. She knew exactly what I was going through and eased my fears. Laura helped take away the shame of my memory loss and stigma that were attached to the treatments.

I'll never forget, one day on the way to her house, I forgot how to get there. Despite having gone there hundreds of times, halfway there, I literally had to pull over because I forgot where to go. I panicked, felt ashamed and called her. Laura gave me directions. When I got there, she told me a bunch of things she forgot surrounding her ECT and we laughed about it. It really helped that my friend had been through it. I knew she was fine. And I knew if the ECT lifted my depression, I would be fine, too.

It seemed after a few treatments I felt some relief. However, I noticed every other day I felt crummy. I'd do well, then the next day I'd crash and be depressed again. The doctors said that was typical at first. I hung in there. Eventually, things turned around and I got better.

My journal entries began to change, too.

"The ECT treatments began turning me around. Finally, there was some relief! I began to feel differently. People began to notice a difference in me as well."

My next journal entry read:

"Since the ECT treatment I think I've been feeling better. Now with increased anti-depressant and added anti-anxiety meds, things are changing."

I started to read books that were suggested once the ECT had begun to make me feel better. I wrote out the exercises from those books to process everything. I examined how I felt and how I felt about how I felt. And one of the benefits about not being able to work was that I had a lot of time to get well.

I began challenging old thinking when I recognized it coming up. Not always, but I *worked* at it. I examined the notion that fear was slavery. I tried to keep in mind what I'd learned from my Uncle Rick, that when one door closed, another one opened. Instead of looking at my closed doors, I sought and kept an open mind to the new ones.

I accepted what the counselors were saying to my parents could be the best course of action. They suggested I not go home to their house; that I go to a place like Oxford House. It was for people who were starting over. I faced my fears of new beginnings. I opened my mind to the possibility and considered moving out of my parents' house again and starting from scratch.

I tried turning everything over to a God of my understanding and letting Him have the worries I was carrying. A huge weight was lifted off my shoulders. I tried to let go a little and practice what my uncle had repeated to me over and over in early sobriety. Without me knowing it at the time, I began to *accept* what was to come my way. Things were finally becoming aligned.

By June of 2004, when I had completed my ECT treatments, I was doing much better. I was feeling hopeful again. I hadn't made any decisions about what my next step was yet, but I felt I was on my way. It was time to say goodbye to Princeton House, which had served me so well and had gotten me back on my feet.

One afternoon, I had a meeting with my counselor, Vanessa. It seemed like our five-thousandth one.

"I want to graduate." I told her. "When do I graduate?"

"Wendy, you are not in a race." Vanessa said in her very soothing, yet nasal voice.

"I've made a lot of progress and I feel so much better!"

"This is *not* a race." Vanessa's voice was starting to annoy me.

"I think I'm done, Vanessa. I mean I'm talked out! We keep talking about the same stuff. Every week it's the same stuff. I feel better. I really, really do."

"You're doing *much* better. I think the ECT has really helped you. You're processing everything and working hard, yes. But you're not ready..."

"You don't understand. I *am* ready. I mean, if I hear one more time in Process Class that Allison blames her Mom for everything. If I hear the word Mom come out of her mouth *one more time*....I think I'm gonna snap! Everyone here is like a broken record! *I* am beginning to feel like a broken record. I'm processed out!" More calmly I added wistfully, "I will miss Art Therapy though. I mean, I'd love to make more hot plates, they went over big at Christmas and all." I switched gears and gained momentum "But I'm stick-a-fork-in-me DONE!"

"Wendy, keep the focus on you. This is not about Allison or anyone else in your classes." Nasal voice, nasal voice. "This is about you. And recovery takes *time*." Her soothing voice was continuing to annoy me big time. I wanted to blare some hard rock music in her office. It was too quiet in here. Suddenly everything and everyone in this place was getting on my last nerve.

It was the same soggy wet lettuce at the lame salad bar every day. It was the same women in my groups saying the same damn thing, day in, day out. Even the handouts were starting to look the same. The shit I was writing in my *journals* was sounding the same. I had to get out of there. At all costs. And fast, before I was sucked in forever.

"I don't know. I'm so tired of journaling and processing and talking. I feel like I've done enough for a lifetime!" I began to feel I could be there for a decade. My thirties flashed before my eyes. I was getting scared. I didn't care about a diploma. I just wanted to get the fuck out of there.

"It takes *time*, Wendy."

"But I've *spent* time here. I've spent a *lot* of time here. I've trekked across the state of New Jersey three times a week for God knows how long. I've done the work. I needed it. I know I did, but I'm done, Vanessa. I'm done. I want to join the human race. I wanna go back to work and feel like a normal human being again."

"You're *not* ready, Wendy." Her voice thing was irritating the crap out of me. What she was saying, however, was irritating me even more. She was saying, or inferring, I was still sick.

"Look, I have no insurance. This is costing me a fortune! I can't *afford* to get any more well!" I got up from my chair.

"I'm sorry." She said, shaking her head displeased. "I think you need more time."

"I'm done, Vanessa."

"There's no prize at the finish line, Wendy."

"I'm *at* the finish line."

I smiled to myself as I shut the door and walked down the hall. Already I felt twenty pounds lighter. Yes, leaving here was going to feel good. *Very* good indeed. I said my goodbyes and left.

Driving home that day I wondered how long they would still be there. Many of them were making a career at this program. Some lifers. I think many of those women didn't know *how* to be well. They were scared of it just like I was scared to go back to work and leave my parents' house.

Fear paralyzes. You carry a horrible burden, whatever it is, whatever the trauma. And the fear of getting rid of it almost paralyzes you into not getting well. That's not to say I or anyone else there didn't *want* to, but I believe we were all a little afraid of it. To be fair, a lot of the women had endured things far worse than I, so from where I was standing it was easy for me to judge. Some things were so horrific I would never know exactly what had happened to them. They never spoke about it to anyone other than their counselors or a choice confidante or two. I was one of the lucky ones and I knew it. Most of us had been raped or abused, some by acquaintances, some by strangers, others by family members.

Many had other issues stemming from those traumas, such as eating disorders or cutting. I couldn't imagine dealing with that on top of everything else. There were some women walking around who looked like virtual skeletons. Or they had slashes in their arms, symmetrical and planned. I felt so bad for them. There were so many beautiful souls there and I hoped they healed. I was just glad to be getting the hell away from all of it because if I had stayed, I would've gone backwards.

Truth was: there *was* a prize. The prize was that my outlook had changed. I had been restored to some type of sanity through ECT. And that enabled me to examine my depressed, distorted thinking and chip away at it. Gradually my thinking had changed. Being surrounded by so many women I viewed were stuck made me realize I not only *wanted* wellness, I wanted it more than anything else in the world. What I didn't want was to be near quicksand. Now that I'd climbed out, I feared I would sink, too. I worked hard in that outpatient program. I worked hard at challenging my negative thinking. I wanted to go back to work and get on with my life.

ECT had lifted the clouds, but I was flying my kite now.

My Manic Wendy

Wendy Walks on the Wild Side

It was the beginning of 2005 and I was happy and calm, at sea level. I was neither depressed nor manic. I was *finally* working. I averaged thirty hours a week doing retail. Then I switched to waitressing at a diner I had worked at on the weekends back when I was at the staffing company. I was productive, stable and back on track. Little did I know, mania missed me and was on its way.

Socially, I was better, too. I saw my friends and talked on the phone more. I compared notes with other bipolar women. I was sober, which was allowing my medications to do their job after ECT had reset me. I was comfortable and it was the best I'd been doing in two years.

I moved into an apartment across the street from the beach with a friend. Free and single, *finally* not depressed. I had my own place at last. The stars had not aligned like that for me in a long, long time. It was spring (which I've now come to learn is frequently a bipolar manic time).

But mania was waiting just under the surface. The lion was asleep but ever there, patiently waiting to make its move and attack. I don't know when I first thought I was getting manic. I was distracted with the move. That, with the spring spirit, masked my manic symptoms for excitement. I had new freedom being out of my parents' house. I could live the singles' life. I could sleep when I wanted, stay up when I wanted and wouldn't be scolded by my Mom for doing so. But there was a price.

I joined a new dating website I saw on a TV commercial. Back at my parents' house I had been on two different sites to try and find a boyfriend. They were the find-your-soulmate-here websites that were expensive and got me nowhere, except a couple of dates and frustrated.

It started out innocently. It had three sections: dating, relationships and intimate encounters. I had posted on dating and relationships but was getting few responses. I checked out the other one, intimate encounters. It sounded like a place where you could catch an STD. Still I thought: why not *see* what it's like? I didn't think I would actually *meet* anyone, but out of curiosity I posted there, too. The response was amazing! I loved all the instant messages and emails I received. I wasn't used to that. I really loved the attention more than anything.

Those emails and IMs turned into meeting guys from that sleazy website. I was honest with my most of my friends (well, I told them enough so that I *felt* I was being honest, but not everything so I would feel ashamed). At the same time, I knew I was playing a dangerous game. I kept justifying that I finally wanted to be intimate again. I was *celebrating* wanting to date and be sexual and finally no longer depressed. The only problem was that I wasn't being intimate, I was being promiscuous. How can you call it intimacy when there is no emotion? I was in denial and I let the reigns of mania go wild. *I* was going wild.

Meanwhile, a friend of mine, who is a professional in the mental health field, pointed out my pressure of speech. I reluctantly agreed with her. Still, I defended myself.

"Yeah, but we never get to talk. I'm talking fast so I can get it all in and catch you up!"

"Talk to your psychologist and your psychiatrist, Wendy. Tell them I said you have pressure of speech." She wasn't having my excuse. She knew better.

"I think it's just because I don't get to talk to you. Then when I do, I have to cram it all in to one twenty minute phone call. I'm sure it does seem like pressure of speech to you. But couldn't it just be that I'm trying to get it all in?"

"Just tell them what I said. I think it's pressure of speech and that you're getting manic, Wendy."

She reminded me that pressure of speech was a sign of mania. I cringed at the thought because I remembered when I first heard that term. It was back at Virginia Tech when I was pacing and talking fast my last semester of college. It scared me. At first I denied it because I was doing so well. Plus, who wants to be told they are manic? It's a buzz-kill. I mean after all, a *little* mania feels good, doesn't it?

However, extreme mania does not. That's the kind that interferes with your life and causes bad decisions that can put you at risk. It wrecks your daily, sane living and can put you in the hospital. And who wants that?

Mania is a dangerous game. When you're aware that you are manic, if you choose to ignore it, it often turns into trouble. If you ask any person with bipolar disorder which they prefer, mania or depression, I'm sure you'd find most of us prefer mania. Of course, we're not talking about the kind of mania that lands you in the hospital. That's a different story, although I'd still rather be in the hospital for mania than depression. It has taken less time for me to come down than to come up. And it's less, well, depressing.

For a while, I heard this from my friend: your pressure of speech is a sign that you are manic, your promiscuity is another sign and so on. Then I heard it from a bipolar buddy of mine. The questions kept coming: "Are you feeling a little manic? How are your meds? What are you taking?" We compared notes. The more I kept hearing it from people around me, the more I realized I had to accept it. I had to take action. I started to talk about it with my psychologist and see her more frequently. She said she was going to talk to my psychiatrist if I didn't get better and stop my behaviors. I had to get off that website. I had to change my sleeping patterns, go to bed earlier and get back into a routine.

After speaking to these men online through instant messages or emails (they would always contact me first), we would meet in public. I even brought back a few of them to the apartment. Some, I met at a local coffeehouse and we parted ways after having coffee. There was no physical or emotional chemistry, so it ended right there.

I met a guy from Portugal who I really liked. We saw each other twice. He liked larger women so I found that to be comforting. I was not used to that. I was less self-conscious when I was naked with him. He was getting his PhD at Rutgers, but his student visa was expiring soon and he had to go back to his country. I knew that, even though I liked him and he *seemed* to like me, we couldn't be in a relationship. He wanted to stay in the U.S. and I knew that if we were to settle down together, it would always be in the back of my head that he was using me to do that. He thought I was rejecting him.

"Don't you think your standards are too high?" he asked. Truth was I thought he was a great guy, but the circumstances were all wrong. (And I was manic and had met him on the sleazy website... details, details.)

"No. I don't want to settle down." I replied.

"I think you want too much." He said. We were holding each

other. He was caressing my back. I liked him, but couldn't trust him. I explained why we couldn't be together. He assured me that was not his reason.

"I could never believe that you like me for me. I would always think you wanted to be with me just to stay in this country." No, he wasn't dropping to his knee to propose. I was just jumping ahead in my mind to try to avoid heartache. I had enough of that in my life without starting the marry-me-to-avoid-being-an-illegal-alien program.

I didn't sleep with every man I met from the internet that spring/summer. Certainly not. I had standards and some of those guys I wouldn't want to share a cab with. What's the number? Well, it wasn't twenty or even ten men. It was nothing that extreme. But it was certainly out of character for me and mostly due to mania. (It was also because I had a newfound freedom being in my own apartment and I was *finally* not depressed.) However, since it was out of character, I realize it was manic-induced promiscuity. It was over the top. I do take full responsibility for my actions. I am not blaming my poor sexual decisions on my mania, merely pointing out the correlation between hypersexuality and mania. Again, when I'm not manic, this behavior would not only be uncomfortable, it would never happen.

I found a poem that I had written that summer that sums up how I felt:

> Pleasure doesn't last
> my mind tells me.
> I was only trying
> to set my body free.

> The summer of pleasure
> was fun yet bizarre
> I did it because I could
> that's my reason, there you are.

Of course I always used condoms with these men. I was not irresponsible. *Hypersexual during mania*, yes. *Completely stupid*, no. There are diseases you can catch. I'm fully aware of that, manic or not. And that's a good thing because I probably would've slept with a lot more men.

This was also the time I decided to liberate myself and go to the nude beach for the first time in my life. I lived my whole life one mile from it, but the thought of going never even occurred to me before then. Actually, the few times I thought of the nude beach, I cringed to be quite honest. I never in a million years would have dared to go there. But that summer I was in rare form. I went.

Instead of going home one day, I drove past my apartment off Ocean Avenue and kept going. As I headed for the nude beach, it occurred to me I didn't have a beach chair or bathing suit. Then I realized I was going to a nude beach after all, so who needed it?

As I walked onto the beach, all these families were leaving. I was disgusted at the thought of a nude family all hanging out together. Holy therapy bills these kids are gonna have! I stopped a lifeguard.

"Excuse me, is this the nude beach?"

"No. It's the next one down." The lifeguard responded.

"Oh, thank God!"

When I got there I took off all my clothes and jumped in the ocean. I felt liberated! I was making peace with my body that I had grown so ashamed of. It felt amazing and refreshing to be naked in the water. The waves swayed my body and I couldn't remember the last time I felt so in harmony with myself and nature. I felt confident. I did it!

I went back a handful more times that summer and what I loved was that I got approached and hit on every time. (Granted, there weren't too many single women there, however it was still an ego boost.) I always felt sexier when I left there. Guys would ask for a light or if I could put sunblock on their backs. Did I need it on mine? How was my book? You could see them coming from a mile away. Unfortunately, their penises would be eye level, practically in my face, making it awkward to say the least.

Going there helped me get over my hang up about my body and about nudity. There were other women whom I observed with bigger bodies than my own. Their obvious acceptance of themselves made them look more attractive. In turn, this made me feel better about my own body and feel more beautiful, too. It's hard to explain, but being around people who were secure enough to be naked in front of hundreds of other people somehow freed me.

There was one Brazilian guy. I never did get his name. Let's call him Prince. He kept calling me Princess. This one day Prince came up to my blanket.

"Do you have a light, Princessss?" He said in his very sexy South American accent. He hissed the end of the word out. No man had ever called me that before. It was a nice change and I was quite flattered, even if I probably was the only single woman for miles at the nude beach that day.

"Here." I handed him my lighter. It was hard to light in the wind. No sooner had I handed him my lighter when he took the liberty of sitting down on my blanket. *Sure, go ahead,* I thought. We did have some kind of weird chemistry. He was a bit of a Don Juan, I'll admit. An older one, yes, but with gorgeous eyes. I couldn't determine if they were blue or green, but they were his best feature. I was staring down at my belly and thinking I really had to do something about that. Would a thousand sit ups a day even make a dent?

"Thank you, Princesssssss." He handed it back once he finally lit his cigarette. By then I had pulled one out to join him. He leaned over to try to light me, but the wind was making it difficult. I took it from him.

"It's okay. I got it." I wondered what he thought about my boobs. Was he looking at them? Probably. They were right there in front of him. They were pretty small, not much to look at. Maybe he didn't care about small boobs. Why should I care? When was I going to see him again anyway?

We talked a little about nothing in particular when it started to get cloudy. Then it started to get very dark, like it was going to rain any second. Pretty soon it started pouring, I mean *pouring*, out of nowhere. I quickly began packing up. I put on my t-shirt and shorts, and pulled it away from my chest, thinking 'geez, this is total wet t-shirt! He can see me right through it.' Then I realized Duh! He just saw me totally nude!

"I'll be right back," he yelled over the rain.

"Okay." Although I wasn't sure why he was coming back. Clearly, beach time was over. He came back a little out of breath with all his gear, which wasn't much. Apparently, he travelled light.

"Can I carry your chair to your car, Princess?" It was pouring, so there wasn't time for contemplating this. I really didn't want to carry it, but I also didn't want him to see my car in case he was a total creep. I mean, he *was* a creep because he was hitting on me, but in case he was a *psycho* creep. He could get my plates and follow me, or rape me or kill me. You never know.

Then it started to hail.

I couldn't believe it. *Hail!* Had I ever been on the beach when it hailed? No and I had lived here at the beach all my life. Bizarre.

"Okay, hurry." It was pretty far to the parking lot.

We ran back to my car and took a minute to catch our breath. Obviously neither one of us were marathon runners, but it was a trek to the parking lot.

"Can we have a cigarette in your car?"

"Uh, sure." If it weren't raining, I doubt I would've said yes to sitting with a stranger in my car. Then again, I was at a nude beach and I had let this Brazilian dude already walk me back to my car. He had such nice eyes, though. He must have been a ladies' man, even if he was past his prime. After our cigarettes, he leaned over and kissed me. He didn't even ask me. I went with it because he was a really good kisser. We kissed for about ten minutes or so, until the storm was over.

"I'll be right back, Princessss. I have to go get something." He said.

"What are you going to get?" I inquired. I had a feeling about what he was going to get.

"I'll be right back."

"A condom? Don't even think about it. We're not having sex."

"No, Princessss." He flashed a smile and got out.

He never came back.

I didn't *always* use poor judgment that summer. Well, I suppose you might think kissing a stranger in my car who had picked me up at the nude beach might constitute poor judgment. To me, at the time, it was throwing caution to the wind. But that's mania and sex. They are a natural pairing in mania, like ice cream and hot fudge.

It wasn't as if I wasn't listening to my friends. I was. Well, sort of. And I kept appointments and I never (God no!) went off my medications. The important thing is to learn and be honest.

But I realize now, it was too late. I did admit to my psychiatrist that I was also hypersexual. I knew that was a sign of mania, so I was completely honest with him. It is essential that we be open and honest with our professionals in our network. If we aren't, what's the point of having them? I told him my psychologist and friend said they noticed I had pressure of speech. My psychiatrist was only seeing me for fifteen minutes on that particular day, so I had to fill him in on how I was doing the rest of the time. For example, how I wasn't sleeping well. And sleep is the other half of medication for bipolar disorder, according to my psychologist.

One day I was talking to a friend of mine who was also bipolar and I was telling her I was feeling manic. She asked what meds I was taking and I told her. She said, "Be careful, that drug spiked me into mania once. They had to adjust the dosage." I had no idea that an anti-depressant could spike someone into mania. I went to my psychiatrist with the story and asked him if we should adjust my meds, or that particular one, because I was feeling manic.

He said "drop it twenty milligrams." I did. However, it was already too late. Maybe it helped and I would've been worse off had we not done that. I don't know. But, I knew it helped to have a network of people and not just professionals. I was learning to listen to the people around me. I was learning how to handle my illness, realizing that I'm not always the one who knows best or sees a problem first. However, even talking about it *and* knowing what I'm doing wrong doesn't always mean I'm going to stop what I'm doing. Or stop it in time.

We are typically the last to know how severe our mania is. That is, until something really bad happens.

Cops, Cuffs and Straightjackets

My mania had turned into a full-blown episode by August of 2005. True to form, there was always a man in the cyclone.

Stewart was in his late forties, which was a little old for me, but I had gone out with older men before. I met him and was instantly convinced we were destined to be together. Just as I was sure every other time I was in a manic episode this *must* be "the one." That we should run away together and live happily ever after. (It wasn't until the episode was over that I thought what the fuck was I thinking?)

What I liked about Stewart (everybody called him Stu), was his sense of humor and the fact that he had lots of free time to spend with me that summer. Plus he was big like me, so I was less self-conscious around him. He was in my group of friends that summer; he was there when mania hit town.

The first night Stu and I spent together I *had* to have it on film. I called my Mom from the beach across the street for the sunrise. (Naturally, I hadn't slept all night.) I made her come down and meet us because she had a camera and I didn't.

"Hi, Mom!" I was excited. Love was in the air, the sun was about to rise, and time was of the essence. She had to get down there before the sun came up, which would be any minute now.

"Wendy?" Where are you? What's wrong?" A call from me before

9:00 am *always* meant something was wrong to my Mom. I was never an early bird.

"Nothing, Mom. Everything's perfect. Listen, I need a favor. Can you come down to the beach, Mom? Pleeease?" I waited for the inevitable argument. I was being demanding and I knew it. Stu was walking away, towards the ocean. He knew how this was going to go.

"Wendy, it's not even 7:00 am. What are you doing *awake?*" She knew instinctually that I hadn't been to sleep yet. She was onto me. I knew she knew, but had to press on.

"Mom, just please meet me down at the public beach across from my apartment."

"Wendy, I'm not awake yet. I'm going back to bed."

"Mom, please? It's reeeeally important! Oh and bring your camera. I want you to take a picture of me and Stu."

"Stu? Who is Stu?"

"He's the guy I'm dating. Mom, just please come?"

"Wendy I don't think so." I was not one to ask my Mom for a lot of favors. I thought if I kept going, maybe she would cave in.

"Mom, it's our first night together. I want to always remember it and the sunrise is going to be perfect! Please?"

"Okay, Wendy, I'll do it. But I'm *not* happy about this." I could hear my Dad stirring next to her.

"Great! Thank you so much! Don't forget your camera. And hurry, or you'll miss the sunrise!"

My Mom joined us at the beach. I couldn't believe she came down. As she walked on, digital camera in hand, she looked less than pleased. I don't know who was more embarrassed to be meeting this way, her or Stu. This was not the typical first meeting of your boyfriend to your mother, at sunrise when everybody should be asleep. She didn't even *know* I was dating anyone.

"Hi, I'm Wendy's Mom." My Mom put the camera around her neck and stuck her hand out to shake Stu's.

"Hi, Stewart, nice to meet you. You can call me Stu, though. Everybody calls me Stu." Stu was very cordial. I wondered what she thought about him. He was big. Bigger than any man I had ever dated. He looked like he was going to have a heart attack at any given moment. I knew my Mom was sizing him up. That's what mothers do.

We all stood there feeling awkward for a second. I was caught up in all the excitement. Here is the love of my life. Here is the man I might marry! Here are the *two* loves of my life now meeting for the first time. Exciting, exciting, exciting!

"Okay, Mom, now make sure you get the sunrise in the back with the waves."

"I'll try." My Mom was a trooper. I owed her big for this one. I was busy with my visions of this being the background picture for our wedding where everyone comes in and signs. I thought, *'How great if this were to be our first night together, captured on film, with the perfect sunrise behind us at the beach!'* I was desperately seeking love. I should have been desperately seeking sleep.

"Got it!" Mom seemed fine with just that one shot. I was concerned that if it didn't come out perfectly, we only had that one shot. "No, take a few. It has to come out right."

"Wendy, I'm taking two. That's it!" I knew she had been pushed to her limit, so I backed off.

She took another picture quickly. My enthusiasm was wearing off as I realized how annoyed she was with me. Two pictures would have to suffice.

"Nice to meet you, Stu." My Mom said, obviously tired. She turned to walk towards the parking lot.

"Nice meeting you too!" He returned, amused by the whole scene.

"Thanks, Mom, I really appreciate it." I gave her a kiss on the cheek and a quick hug, but she didn't pause for a long one.

"I hope so. Now I'm going back to bed," she said, irritated and tired.

Success! Our first night captured on film.

Now we needed a trip! Luckily, a bunch of our friends had organized a weekend camping/rafting trip. Two weeks later, Stu and I went on the trip to the Poconos with our friends. The trip started off okay, except that I was smack dab in the second worst manic episode of my life.

I had all these great ideas and plans swirling around in my head. Right next to the campsite was a strip of land that looked like a runway. I kept thinking how the Poconos area was booming and expanding. Surely, they'll need an airport! Do they even have one? I tried to convince Stu that we should look into buying this or other land and build an airport. I knew we didn't have the money. I wasn't 100% serious, but thought it was an excellent idea. (Plus, a little detail I didn't tell you about Stu. He was "connected," if you know what I mean. So I thought, with those *connections,* maybe someday our little airport could happen.)

Stu became concerned about me that weekend, and our mutual friend, who also had bipolar took him aside to fill him in. He gave him the bipolar manic rundown. Stu tried many times to get me to stop talking that weekend, so other people could get a word in edgewise. I kind of knew what he was doing, but kept going anyway. It was hard to stop. Almost impossible to shut my mouth, really. I felt a need to be heard and understood.

On what was to be our last night there, I couldn't sleep. Stu was still fast asleep and snoring away. I was wide awake and lost in thought. I left the tent and studied the clouds. I saw shapes in the clouds and thought of pictures they represented. (This may have been psychosis, I don't know. Were they pictures in the clouds? Or was my mind playing tricks on me? I'll never know.) I thought maybe someday I could go meet the Dalai Lama with my biological father, Bill. (After all, Bill had spoken to His Holiness in his hotel room in L.A. for three hours, years back.) Bill could introduce us! I would gain spiritually and bond with my long, lost biological father. Ideas and dreams like this were coming to me in rapid succession. Like a manic meteor shower.

Then the fateful decision.

After the weekend was over I decided to stay longer. Everyone else was packing and leaving, Stu included. My grand plan was to stay another week and hang out in the woods. Alone. (In hindsight, I realize I didn't want to deal with reality and come home.)

"Go ahead home, Stu. You can drive with Adam."

"What? Wendy, everyone's leaving today."

"No. I'm gonna stay longer. Just go. It's okay."

"I don't want to leave you here." Stu protested.

"Look, I'm sure you could use a break from me. I'm going to stay here. It's peaceful. I'm going to write and listen to music and be alone. I'll get some rest and come home later."

"When?"

"I don't know. A few days. Maybe a week?" I really liked it up there. Everything was so simple and tranquil. I loved being in nature and eating simply, out of a cooler. I liked lighting a fire at night and sleeping in a tent. It was easy living. Plus, everything was cheaper in Pennsylvania. When I went to the convenience store in town, I felt rich. The prices were half as much as they were in Jersey. My money would hold me for a bit anyway.

"I don't feel right leaving you."

"I'll be fine. I'm a big girl, Stu." I laughed. "I have everything I need."

"Did you make a reservation with the camp?"

"No, not yet. I'll go down there. It's dead. I'm sure they'll be glad for the business." It was only $5.00 a day. The price was unbeatable.

"I don't know, Wendy."

"Just go, Stu."

"Well, at least keep the map for when you drive home, okay?"

"No, you guys take it. I'll be fine."

"No. You keep it."

"I don't need it. Honestly. I remember how we got here."

"Wendy, we got lost coming here. Keep the map." Stu was insisting. He didn't want me to stay in the first place, but he *really* didn't want me to stay without a map.

"Just take it."

"Let's just tell her how to go. We'll take it but she can write it down before we go. It is pretty easy." Adam chimed in.

"Okay." Stu gave up and gave me the directions instead. Only, I wouldn't write them down. I was convinced I could remember them. I didn't *need* to write it down. It was my super-duper memory kicking in. (I was always overly-confident when I was manic.)

They left. All of a sudden, I had an epiphany. I *had* to catch up to them. I decided I must tell Stu I loved him. Mind you, we just started dating and I hadn't thought about telling him I loved him *before* that. Why I thought I could catch up to them, I don't know. My judgment was off and to top it off, I got terribly lost.

I stopped for gas and when I did, tried to convince the gas attendant to run away with me. (Nevermind that I was on my way to tell Stu I loved him!) I told the guy I had an idea that was going to make us rich. It had something to do with a hedge fund (I didn't even know what one was) and satellite radio (which had already been invented).

"I can't come with you," the cute, young gas attendant said to me. "I'll lose my job!"

"You won't *need* a job. We'll be rich!" I promised him.

"I can't!" He looked at me like he wanted to. I wanted him to. He was hot. Even at the time, I knew it was slightly crazy to be convincing this gas attendant to give up his job to be with a complete stranger. But I thought it was a *good* crazy.

"Come on, how much can you really want to be pumping gas anyway?" I persisted.

"I hate it," he admitted, "but I'm saving my money to get out of here. I don't know about hedge funds, but I do invest." Hmmm. I was surprised that this young, good-looking, gas pumping guy was also an investor. Impressive. Cute *and* saavy. Nice combo. Too bad I had to find one with some common sense who seemed grounded and not up for my great adventure. To where, I had no idea yet.

"Are you *sure*?" I didn't care about consequences, not for me, not for him, not for anyone or anything.

"I wish I could, but I can't." He took my credit card for the gas and I signed. I handed the mini-clipboard back to him. I thought, *damn I had to find a responsible, cute guy*. I wanted him to say the hell with it and be on the same wavelength as me.

"Okay. Too bad. Well, take care!" And I was off.

I was getting all these bursts of ideas and energies. It was exciting! I had dreams and plans. Always big plans in my manic episodes. It was like I was throwing all these ideas together without any rational thought to back them up. In hindsight, there was no logical way to connect the dots. But I wasn't, of course, in a rational frame of mind.

In addition to my racing mind, I was also crashing, missing my Uncle Rick. There was a song on that was making my tears flow. I kept playing that song over and over, inflicting a harder grieving time upon myself. Emotionally, I was all over the map. Of course, a map was exactly what I needed because I had gotten horribly lost.

I began to notice how lost I was. Am I going east or west? I should be going east, right? What did Stu say again? I should've written it down. I should've taken their map!

With no exit in sight, I realized I had to pull over.

I pulled off the highway onto the handle.

Cars zoomed past me and I tried to figure out where the hell I was, but there were no signs. I felt like I was in the middle of nowhere.

I decided my only choice was to pull back onto the interstate. I would have to get off on the next exit. From a dead stop on the side of the highway, I shifted from first into second and then second into third. My piece-of-shit car was accelerating like a turtle.

I wasn't going fast enough in the right hand lane. I didn't see the car when all of a sudden...

SCREEECH!

Fuuuck!!

I caused an accident.

Although we didn't crash, we came within inches. It was clearly my fault. My confusion and pathetic old car caused the near accident. A rage-a-holic-man covered in tattoos immediately jumped out of the passenger side of the car and started cursing at me. He called 9-1-1 while I checked on the woman and baby in their car. Everyone was fine (the baby was still sound asleep). Neither car was damaged and no one was hurt, but the police came. And that's when the trouble *really* began.

Now, let me preface this story. I have never had a problem with the police or been handcuffed or in jail. Nothing. I had speeding tickets and a few fender benders, but that was it. I have always known not to mess with three things: the police, the IRS and coloring my own hair.

However, that was not an ordinary day because I was in a full-blown manic episode. While I was extremely manic, borderline psychotic in fact, I was calmly sitting in my car waiting when the troopers first arrived.

I saw the police walk towards my car, two of them: one taller, one shorter. I was relieved! Someone was coming to protect me from the man who wanted to kill me.

Bang, bang, bang. The officer knocked on my window. It sounded like he was going to break it. I rolled it down, startled.

"Get out of the car!" The tall state trooper ordered. I was confused. My fear quickly shifted from the rage-a-holic to the trooper.

"Okay." I fumbled, rattled by their obvious impatience. I wasn't moving fast enough for them. When I got out of my car, the other trooper, the shorter one, stepped towards me. I prepared to give them my version of the "accident" and wondered if they were going to ask for my license and registration.

"Have you been drinking?" The tall one asked. Right off the bat, the interrogation began as they bombarded me with accusations. Like darts looming towards a target. And I was the target.

"No."

"Have you been doing drugs?" The short one asked. I turned to look at him.

"No. I don't do drugs. I've been sober for two years and I ..."

"Are you sure you're not high?" The taller one interrupted, leaning in. I couldn't keep up. The questions were coming too fast.

"Where were you coming from?" The other trooper demanded. *None of their business,* I thought. But I played along. I had to.

"The Poconos. I was..."

"*Why* were you in the Poconos?" The tall one snickered. This was getting personal; they were invading my privacy.

"I was on a camping trip. I was on my way back, I got lost, and pulled over to try to figure out where I was. Then I realized I didn't have a map...so I pulled out from the handle and that's when I..."

"Are you *sure* you're not high?" The tall, beefy one cut me off. Again.

"Yes. I'm sure. I was on a *sober* camping trip." (This response elicited more anger.)

"Are you going to Newark?" The tall one barked. He appeared to be the senior of the two. The ringleader or something. He asked more questions and was also the first one on the scene.

"*Newark?* I don't even know where Newark *is* from here. Or what road I'm on."

"Do you have drugs in the car?" The little one questioned. At that point, one of them flashed his light into the back of my car.

"Drugs? No, I have some camping stuff in there." I turned around and looked in the back of my car. I realized it looked pretty messy and that couldn't look good. Did I really look like a drug runner though? And where was the fuck was Newark, anyway? I had no clue where I even was.

"Are you *sure you don't have drugs in your car?*" The other one followed, as if he was giving me a second chance to come clean about some big stash of drugs I had.

"No, just stuff from my camping trip," I reiterated.

I will never forget how quickly they jumped to the conclusion that I *must* be a drug runner and therefore high, because I caused this "accident." (It was as if they had been briefed that night specifically to profile young women in older cars that were running drugs along the Poconos/Newark route. *Pathetic!*)

I continued denying the false allegations that flew at me, one after another. Before I knew it, the police then threw me against their car. Out came the handcuffs.

"Why are you handcuffing me?" I asked.

"Shut up, just shut up!" *Shut up?* How rude! I couldn't believe it. The questions and accusations? Wrong, but I could handle it. *Handcuffs?* This was *way* out of line! What the *fuck* was going on here?

"Wait! Are you *arresting* me?" I chuckled.

"Shut up." The shrimpy one chimed in.

"Why? All I did was cause an *accident.*" I was terribly confused as I felt the handcuffs tighten around my wrists. They were clamped down with not a millimeter to move.

"Ow! What about my Miranda Rights?" I watched TV. I knew a thing or two.

"We can read them to you later," tall cop mumbled.

"Later?" I was mad they were handcuffing me, but *enraged* they weren't even going to read me my rights. This was bullshit!

"At the station. We can read them to you there."

"Station? You're taking me to the *police station?" What the fuck?*

"Shut up!"

"Ow! These are really tight! Why are you handcuffing me? And so *tight!*"

"Just shut up!"

"I want a cigarette. Give me my fucking cigarettes!"

Somewhere in between calmly sitting in my car, waiting for the police to protect me from the rage-a-holic man and the handcuffing, I put away my manners and began to curse. Now ordinarily, if I *wasn't* manic, I *never* would've cursed at a state trooper. (By the way, I don't remember cursing until I was on the ground. I only know this because I watched the videotape months later.)

Still, no explanation came as to *why* I was actually being handcuffed or arrested. I had no idea what the difference was, or if there was a difference. Was I being charged? Or how I went from being in my car to being thrown and handcuffed against the side of the trooper's car.

Next thing I knew, somewhere in between the handcuffing and yelling back and forth, they threw me down onto the side of the road.

Hard.

Since I was handcuffed, and couldn't use my hands to soften the blow, my face hit hard too. My hair was spilled everywhere, like a giant bowl of spaghetti, I thought. I couldn't see a damn thing, except blades of grass. Which was also in my mouth. I spit out the grass and dirt.

I yelled and yelled until I was hoarse.

They yelled back.

"You're being videotaped!" One of the troopers yelled in a threatening manner. At this point, all I could see was the glare of bright lights from their cars and the grass through my hair. When I processed this statement, though, I was happy about it. I thought, *finally* I'd be able to prove how they were abusing me! I couldn't figure out where the camera was, though. That confused me profusely. I didn't know they had them built into police cars.

I turned my head to the left and looked over at the bushes. What fucking cameras were they talking about? I couldn't see one. Was this like Candid Camera or something? I was utterly baffled. But, if there were in fact cameras, they'd see the abuse. And I'd have proof of the injustice. Surely, having this on tape would be to my advantage.

"You're going to pay for this!" I threatened. "I'll see you on Oprah, motherfuckers!" It was the first time I remember cursing and I remember distinctly saying Oprah and motherfuckers. I let it all rip. Probably not the smartest thing to say, but I was pissed. Anger didn't describe what I felt. My rights were violated. I felt violated and was enraged! Without a doubt, I was going to press charges. Somehow, some way, I would make sure I'd get this tape. I would have to get a lawyer for sure. I planned to leak it to the local television channels first. I'd definitely put it in my book. Finally, I'd expose these evil New Jersey State Troopers and what they'd done to me on Oprah. (Which wouldn't be altogether impossible. I have a relative that works on her show. I knew there was a slight, admittedly *very slight,* but a chance nonetheless, that I could get it to her staff.) All of this went through my mind lying on the ground. Yes, all of it. It most certainly did.

"Yeah, okay, *Oprah.*" They had a good laugh, mocking me like five-year olds on the playground. The fact that they were laughing at me infuriated me. I realized it sounded a little crazy (even despite my mania), to pull out the Oprah word, but they had *no idea* who they were messing with! I was going to get back at them for this. I would get a hold of that tape and someday I'd expose them. Of that, I was sure.

I kept squirming and flinching. I knew I couldn't break free, still I was fighting it.

Then it came.

SLAM!

One of the troopers jammed his big boot in my back with all his force and I felt a pain I'd never known before. It felt like he'd broke my back in two. I was going to feel this for a long, long time. Fuck!

As soon as he did it, he blew it off, and acted as if it never happened. You could tell by their menial conversation neither one cared.

"So where are you going tonight?" The one trooper asked the other, his foot still on my back. (As if I was going to flee the scene.) Handcuffed, face down, big boot on my back, (back now injured), flee the scene. I was really going to make a break for it.

"Ah, I'm not sure." The other one said back. With my hair still in my face, I couldn't see anything. All I could do was hear voices. I wasn't sure if the big one was talking to the little one or what. So I wasn't sure who jammed their boot in my back, but I would get to the bottom of this. I *had* to get my hair out of my face, without free hands, to see who was in front of me. Which would mean the other trooper was the one who stomped on my back.

I shook my head and it moved a few strands to the side. Through the break in my hair, I saw the shrimpy cop in front of me. Aha! So, it was the big, tall beefy trooper who jammed his boot in my back. I should have guessed. Of course, he had to be wearing those big ass black combat boots, which must've weighed ten fucking pounds each. Fucking bastard.

My God, my back was killing me! These handcuffs were killing me! I couldn't believe I was lying face down in the grass, handcuffed like some dangerous, captured fugitive. Me! It felt surreal.

One of them chuckled. They were still discussing plans for the night and making small talk.

What the fuck was I still doing lying down? What had I done to be treated like this in the first place? I would get back at them. They were gonna pay for this. I mean, I was being treated like a convicted felon on the loose! I had flashes from the show Cops, of some derelict they'd just arrested. *I* was being treated like that derelict! Not some small town, harmless, sober girl. While I was not aware of how bad my manic episode was, I was aware of the abuse. And I knew I didn't deserve it. I felt a powerlessness like I had never felt before.

Then I had an epiphany.

I realized that if this *was* on tape, I should not be screaming or acting belligerent. The correct strategy for paybacks would be to lie still. Lie still like a dead fish. So I did. Perfect plan.

I heard the ambulance pull up.

Wait, *ambulance?*

The next thing I knew, the troopers got me up and over to the ambulance. The woman EMT helped put me in a straightjacket and then apologized for having to do so. She mentioned that it was procedure or something.

"I won't tighten it." Her eyes met mine kindly. "I'm sorry to have to do this" she apologized again. Finally someone nice! I was so grateful to be out of the possession of the police, I didn't care about the straightjacket. I was amused actually.

"That's okay. I always wanted to be in a straightjacket." I joked. Instead of laughing with me, the paramedics and EMTs half smiled. It was impossible not to notice. Still, I thought I was funny even if they didn't.

They knew how out of touch with reality I was at that point. I, however, did not. They also knew the tragedy in that. They treated me with understanding and experience, which was a sharp contrast than the state troopers. As evidenced by their kind eyes and the very different approach they took with me. This was extremely clear, even in my manic state.

When I got to the ER, they quickly drug tested me and the handcuffs came off. Finally! Of course, I was telling the truth about being sober and I passed the drug test. The troopers had both been lingering until the results came back. I felt their disappointment and shock when it came back clean. It was my only revenge, to prove those assholes wrong. Sweet victory had come! They quickly slithered away.

I noticed the marks on my wrists when the handcuffs came off and hoped they would go away soon. All of a sudden, I lost feeling on the left side of my body.

"Nurse?" I yelled.

No answer.

I began to panic. There was still no feeling on my entire left side.

"Nurse!" I screamed louder this time.

Silence. Panic had set in. It flooded my brain and made it hard to breathe.

"*NURSE!*" It was no time for the quiet yell. I gave it all I had.

"Yes?" She strolled in leisurely. Geez, move a little slower why don't you? What if I was having a heart attack? She looked at me, obviously ready to hear something she felt was going to waste her time.

"I can't feel the left side of my body! Please make a note of that." I was as concerned about that getting on my hospital record as I was about losing feeling in my body. I was gonna fry these bastards for doing this to me and it was imperative to have the proper documentation to do it. Something told me I would get feeling back, that it was a temporary thing. What they did to me emotionally though, and the memory of this night was, unfortunately, permanent.

The side I lost feeling on was the same side that was cuffed the tightest of my two arms. Then it hit me: *it was the side of my back the trooper kicked his boot into.* All of a sudden, I got really nervous thinking about that implication.

"Alright. Well, do you want any ibuprofen or something?" I had told them I was a recovering alcoholic/addict so they wouldn't give me anything addictive. I knew ibuprofen was going to be my only option, but I didn't see how that was going to bring back feeling in half my body.

"Okay."

"I'm sorry. I can't give you anything else until you see the doctor." I didn't think she was really sorry. She was just doing her job and it wasn't her job to be sorry. I also knew I wasn't going to be seeing a doctor any time soon. I was no emergency. Even with a severed limb, you still wouldn't be seen in this ER anytime soon. They were on island time.

"Can you mark that down in my record please?"

"I will." I was not so sure that was going to happen. I looked over at the padded cuffs again. Damn those fucking state troopers.

"Please don't forget." I reminded her.

"Um hm." She muttered as she walked out. Now I *really* wasn't sure it was going to happen.

Were those troopers going to get away with what they did? I was going to make sure that didn't happen. I was panicking, wondering if I would have any lasting damage. That would be horrible! I had never felt numb or paralyzed before.

Most of the feeling in my body came back later and calmed me down. Now it was just my hands and only part of my left side. Not great, but at least I was better off than I was. I stared at the red marks on my wrists. Fucking cops. I hated those state troopers.

I needed a cigarette but they wouldn't let me go smoke. I guess they thought I'd run away. To where? A cow pasture? Where the hell was I, anyway? The middle of nowhere. Correction: a hospital, next to a cow pasture, in the middle of nowhere, New Jersey. That's where I was. Hell.

A nurse came in, a different one than the one who wasn't much help earlier. She was very lively and seemed excited about something. I was skeptical.

"Hi. My name is Sandy." This one was a bit too cheerful. Something was definitely up.

"Hi." I was wondering where the last nurse went. So many nurses. This one was different; not even dressed like a nurse. She had a clipboard and pulled up a chair, like she was going to talk with me and stay awhile. I assumed this was not good. It wasn't.

"I want to let you know we have beds open on our psych floor."

"What? I'm not going on your psych floor."

"It's a really good facility." She nodded, attempting to be sympathetic. "I think you should consider it, we..."

"No way!" I interrupted. "I mean, where the hell *am* I, anyway?" I was still fixated on the fact that I had a car accident, been beaten up by the police and to top it off, I had no idea where the fuck I was.

"Well, this is County Hospital." She said quietly, still smiling.

"County Hospital? Where *am* I?" I was hostile and aware of it. She remained patient.

"We're in Flem-ing-ton." She broke it down slowly in syllables. Now she was talking to me like a retarded child, which I did not appreciate. Flemington... hmmm...I had been here before, when I was much younger. My parents had friends who lived there and we'd go visit them. They didn't have neighbors around for what seemed like miles.

It was confirmed; I *was* in the middle of nowhere. I could tell from where the accident took place. It was on a highway I'd never travelled before and there were hardly any cars, even though it was a Sunday night. In NJ, there were *always* a lot of cars on the highways. Except, apparently, near Flemington, in fabulous Hunterdon County.

"Get me out of here! I want to be transferred to a hospital near me."

"There are plenty of beds open." She kept pushing their psych floor. Plenty of beds here, get your fresh beds here. I felt like I was at a baseball game and she was pushing peanuts. I assumed they could probably use the revenue because we were in the middle of nowhere, and how many people came through here needing psych help anyway?

"I don't want to go."

"Well, you really should."

"You can't make me go. I'm not being committed, so I would be signing in voluntarily."

"That's true...but...you *need*..." I couldn't hear her take on what she thought I needed. She wasn't even a doctor or nurse. She was just a lady with a clipboard pushing beds on the flight deck.

"You can't make me."

"True." I could tell she hated to admit that.

"Nobody will visit me up here...it's too far. My parents will, but nobody else will. Nope. Plus, my doctor is down there. No way...I wanna transfer. I'm *not* staying here."

"They can visit you up here. It's not that far."

"No! I'm going down there."

"You can't just leave."

"Really? I can't? Why not?"

"You're not well. You need to be hospitalized."

"Then transfer me."

"Alright." She said sighing. She gave up and walked out. She had lost the battle. (Have you ever tried to win an argument with a manic bipolar? It's nearly impossible.) It was now in the wee hours of the morning in the ever so busy metropolis of Hunterdon County. And I was still stuck here, stuck in the ER. Ah, the medical system, so efficient.

A few hours even later, now early morning, (fabulous to have a manic bipolar miss an *entire* night of sleep), they had a private ambulance type transport company come for me. They took me to a local hospital closer to where I lived, over an hour away. (This time, no straightjacket. Thank God!)

The two EMT guys were young, rather cute and in their twenties. (I was going through a dating guys in their twenties phase). So I invited them to come to a party at our apartment. They smiled and said, 'okay sure.' Of course, as it turns out there was no party. They must've had no intentions on coming, as they were transporting a psych patient to a hospital. But they were good sports and played along.

I don't remember all the details about being admitted onto the psych floor at the hospital near home, but I remember feeling a little better that I wasn't on the committed floor. That was *not* where I wanted to be. (I am lucky I have never had to be involuntarily committed.)

On the voluntary floor, where I was, there were men and women in two hallways. Lots of people were drying out from alcohol and coming down from their drug use. Some were getting their first dose of being declared mentally ill. I began helping people and explaining our illness to those who had just been handed their bipolar diagnosis. It was okay at first. Then I started to get annoyed that I felt I was becoming a social worker. I had my own problems. My back had become a big one.

One night, I woke up in pain from my police injury and went to the nurse for help.

"Can I have some ibuprofen?"

"You should not be valking the halls. You need to be asleep." I couldn't place her foreign accent exactly, but it was definitely Eastern European. She was cold. Her bedside manner was the kind that should earn her permanent retirement from the profession.

"I can't sleep. My back is killing me." I complained.

"You vill vake the patients by being avake and valking in va hallvay." She was saying it slower and I could see this one had a temper problem. She was clearly a giant ball of anger and at any moment I felt all her apparent, inner rage was going to explode.

"If I could just have some ibuprofen, I promise I will only walk for a few minutes until it kicks in. Then I will go to sleep when I feel a little better. I *can't* sleep with this pain. I'm sorry I can't."

"You are keeping up the other patients now!" She was getting nasty. And loud.

"No actually, I was *tiptoeing in my socks in the hallway* and not waking anyone up. Your *yelling* is going to wake someone up!"

"Go to sleep *now!*" She said with a bit too much force. It was one notch below a yell and any second I imagined groggy patients, coming out into the hallways in confusion.

"No. I just want something for the pain. I'm allowed to have ibuprofen. It's my PRN."

"Do you need a tranquilizer?" Oh my God, did she just say that? Was she threatening me? With a *tranquilizer?*

"Are you serious? All I need is something for my back. I don't *need* a tranquilizer." I, at this point, was still not matching her loud tone. I was a few notches below.

"Do you need to go to the quiet room?"

"The *quiet* room?" I wondered what the hell she was talking about. Wait, was that like the *padded* room? Was there even one here? I never saw it, but it's not like it's on the tour or anything.

Nurse Von Bitch wanted to lock me in the padded room! Unbelievable! She'd never let me out. I envisioned the morning nurse would find me here the next day. I'd be hoarse and banging on the door, practically lifeless having expended every droplet of energy. I was about ready to throw *her* in the quiet room.

I was desperate and looked around for help. There was another nurse on the other side. Nurse Von Bitch was getting really loud, but I wasn't sure the nurse on the other side could hear her. Yet. I looked up and saw the patient Bill of Rights mounted on the wall behind plexiglass. Quickly, I scanned it for some protection. Surely, there had to be something on there that would shut this bitch the hell up. I found it.

"Section C, Title Eight." I read from the wall.

"Vat?" She questioned.

"Section C, Title Eight. The patient Bill of Rights." And I pointed to it there next to me on the wall because she looked utterly lost. Like I was talking Greek to her. I read it to her and broke it down slowly so she could pretend to understand.

Nurse Von Bitch raised her voice and I read out loud to her again. All of this started over wanting a pill. All I wanted was some freakin' ibuprofen and now I am reading the Patient Bill of Rights that the hospital writes up (that nobody even reads) just to get my stupid pill. Unbelievable.

"Zatz it! I am going to get ze ozer nurz!" She thought this was a monster threat, which I thought was funny.

What she didn't know was that "ze ozer nurz," Violet, knew my aunt from when my aunt worked on the ICU floor with her ten years ago. *Yeah, go get her bitch.* Violet even knew my grandmother who was a social worker for many years. She knew I was harmless because we had talked earlier that day. Surely Violet would side with me and see I was in physical pain. Surely she also knew her fellow nurse was a bitch.

Nurse Von Bitch disappeared to the other side. I thought it best to stay put. When she returned, Violet, the nice nurse followed. Violet took me aside.

"Wendy, the quiet room is really hot. The heat will be good for your back. I'll get your ibuprofen. You can go in there and just knock when your back feels better, okay?" Violet said quietly and kindly.

"Okay. Are you sure you'll be right..." Those visions of being forgotten in there swirled around in my brain again and I was reluctant.

"Yes. I'll be right here. I'll bring my paperwork over to this side. And she's going over to the other side."

"Okay." I took the two stupid ibuprofens and went in the padded white room. It was just like the ones in the movies, or how you'd picture them. I walked around. It was steamy hot and did help my back. I waved at her on the camera and knocked on the door when my back felt better. I did not want to stay in there any longer than necessary. Now I had been in a padded room *and* a straight jacket. What a week!

By this time, I had bruises on my wrists and face above my eyebrow. I made sure the doctor there examined me and that they also took X-rays of my back. (I would later find out that they took X-rays of my wrong side. Healthcare, what a nightmare!)

After four hellish days and a stint in the padded room, I wanted out of there. I was dying to get out of there. I went to the nurse's station.

"You can't sign yourself out." The male nurse said matter-of-factly.

"Really?" I said. "Because I voluntarily checked myself in, so that means I can voluntarily check myself out."

"That's going A.M.A. [Against Medical Advice]."

"I know."

"If you do that, you can't come back for six months."

"Where do I sign?" I would *never* come back to this hospital again.

But I wasn't free for long. Mom had other plans.

The next day my Mom and aunt drove me to the other local hospital. My mom had my aunt come for moral support. I did not want to check back in anywhere. I was protesting.

"I don't want to go to the hospital. I'm fine now." I was trying to convince them. My aunt was in the front passenger seat. She turned around to look at me.

"You *need* to be hospitalized, Wendy." My aunt said with a very serious look on her face, like someone was dying. My aunt was usually jovial. Her expression and the way she said that was a little bit of a wakeup call. I paid attention, but I still didn't like what I was hearing.

"I don't want to go back in. I'm not as bad as I was." I was not going down without a fight.

"You have to, Honey. I'm sorry, but you do." Mom said.

"No. I don't need to go." I was going back to incarceration. No smoking, no sunshine, no beach. Nada. And what must my job think? Plus, I had to get in touch with Stu.

"You *need* it Wendy." My aunt repeated. I couldn't see the reality of my situation. I was manic and belonged in a hospital. It was a good move that my Mom brought my aunt. Very smart.

It took us three and a half hours from when I stepped into the ER until I was on the psych floor. (That was with only two people in front of me too.) I remember pacing and thinking 'if I were in front of Congress and wanted to tell them how fucked up our healthcare system is for the mentally ill, this is what I would say.' I paced back and forth and practiced so when my day in Congress came, I'd be ready.

I'd yell at my Mom to leave me alone, to let me smoke in peace before they locked me up. She was losing patience and would come out from time to time just to make sure I was still there. She must've thought I'd run away. Truth be told, I remember looking up and down the road wistfully, half daring myself to make a break for it.

Finally, I was up on the psych floor after having talked to a handful of professionals. It was the psych/detox all-in-one floor again. We always seem to get lumped together.

Thankfully, it was a much better experience than the two other local hospitals. The staff was friendlier and there was a recreational therapist who even brought in his guitar one day. It turns out he was in a band so we lucked out. (Music is my thing!) It made all the difference in my stay. He also brought his karaoke machine in and we all made asses out of ourselves. Hospitals are not known for having any decent activities, certainly nothing *artistic*, so the music was a pleasant surprise.

Most of the other patients were depressed and had very little in their rooms. I thought I didn't have enough stuff, although my desk was covered! Books I had no intention of cracking were stacked up. Newspapers with store advertisements were littered everywhere. Every time I entered my room and looked at my desk, I felt pressure. As if I was neglecting all these things I was supposed to be doing. I couldn't focus or figure out which project to do, but they all lay there in my piles, silently fighting for my attention. You could just look at my desk and see where my head was at. When the nurses would come in to take my vitals, they'd look over at my desk.

"Wow, you have a lot of stuff with you!" The nurses nodded their heads and smiled. They were amused more than anything else. They were unaware of what potential I felt lay there amidst my heaps of crap.

I had a real estate magazine from the Poconos where I had just been. (There was a great house I could see fixing up as a B & B.) Also, from last week's circular, I had picked out this gigantic griddle on sale that I made Stu get me because I *needed* it, you see. I just *had* to have it. I mean, it was a great price of $20 and you never know when you would be making a bunch of pancakes for a host of friends. (Sure, I made pancakes on occasion, but never for more than myself.) All of these were my little projects. I had many things to do. Very busy indeed.

Completely opposite of me was my roommate. I felt badly for her. She was suicidally depressed. She had two cards out on her desk, from her kids and her best friend. That was it, nothing to read, nothing at all. She was a beautiful, married woman who found out her husband had cheated on her with her friend, another woman in town. It was a big scandal because it was a small town so everyone knew. Their kids played sports together. She felt humiliated.

"How can I face everybody, Wendy?" I couldn't even imagine. I knew how low she felt. I didn't know exactly how painful it was to be her at the moment. I'd never gone through that same situation, but I knew how it felt to want to die. When you thought that death was the answer, the only way out of pain.

"It *will* get better." I said and kept repeating it to her the whole week. I felt slightly guilty I was "up" and she was so down. I wouldn't trade places with her for the world, except that I was jealous that she had a family of her own. Even if her husband was a lying, cheating bastard, I was still jealous that she had children. (I was figuring out I was jealous a lot of other people in life.)

"How?" She asked. "How can I face these people? I mean, I'll always see them together. And everyone knows the story. Everyone knows they're together and he's leaving me for her." She always had tears welling up or coming down her face. I felt so bad for her. I wished his dick would fall off.

"I am so sorry. You will get through this."

"I wish I were dead. I don't want to be alive."

"Don't say that. Things will get better. Once you get rid of him, you have your kids. Fuck him. You'll find someone else. You will. You'll be happy again someday. You will." I was beginning to feel like a therapist, and thought I might actually make a good one. That was a nutty idea: *a manic therapist!*

"I still love him, Wendy. I know I shouldn't. I know he has ruined and humiliated me. Isn't that sad? I still love him. What am I gonna do?"

"You're gonna get through this. You will." Truth was, I didn't know how she was going to get through it. Diagnosis: depression from a broken heart. And there's no pill that can cure that.

When you're in the hospital for depression or mania, your appetite isn't your priority. The nurses keep an eye on how you're eating. To make this easier, once again, I did the custom ordering on the menus thing. I wrote in what I wanted. Mind you, there was no filet mignon with béarnaise sauce coming on my trays. But writing in chicken fingers or pizza saved me from having to determine what mystery meat lay before me. It assured me that I would have something at least familiar to eat. Eating while manic is challenging enough. You need all the help you can get.

My friend came to visit and, knowing my sweet tooth, brought me a huge bag of candy. It was a big score! (Especially since most of it was chocolate and she had spared no expense getting the really good stuff.) I had no idea how they let her in with it. No outside food is supposed to come in, but they were pretty lax with their security. I hid it in the cabinets that I knew just missed the cut offs for the security cameras. I let only the patients I really liked in on my candy stash secret. (The staff eventually found it days later but for a few days there, we were living large.)

I hid some of the extra desserts in the crisper/vegetable drawers in the fridge so the constantly-eating-everyone-else's-food guy wouldn't get to it. He never thought of going in there. Again, it was usually the near homeless, either alcoholic or drug addict, who you had to watch out for. He was the one who was used to fending for himself. It was always the guy with poor hygiene who never talked to the rest of us. We always wished they would take more showers and keep away from our snacks in the crisper drawers.

Sometimes we'd put some trap food like you would cheese in a mousetrap. Then we'd sit at the kitchen table playing cards with an eye out. Sure enough, we'd always catch them red-handed. There was *always* one. You could bank on it.

We would each smoke a cigarette while taking a shower. (It seemed the steam helped to get rid of, or at least mask the smoke a bit.) That one was my idea. I only let my two favorite people in on my ingenious plot to keep nicotine alive and well in our system. Naturally, I went first so by the time the nurses might've caught on, it would be one of the other two that would've gotten caught. If they said they got their cigarettes from me, they *knew* they'd never get another one from me again. Instant cut off for traitors!

You learn how to get by and deceive. We had a whole system going or at least I did. I hid my pack in the ceiling tiles in my room and my friends smuggled smokes in for me when they came to visit. Again, cigarettes are the highest ranking commodity you can have. It's worth more than money on the inside. Money is useless because you can't go out and buy anything with it. You're stuck in there.

We couldn't smoke at the hospital at all. Not even on our fifteen minute outdoor breaks. (It was a smoke-free hospital so we weren't supposed to smoke outside, either.) On our fifteen minute outdoor breaks we had to break off from the pack a little and hide it. The only way we made it through was to sneak 'em in *or* outdoors. It was hell! To be locked up, a prisoner of your mind *and* nicotine addiction is sheer torture, I tell you. The absolute worst.

When I left, they kept finding tubs of my stuff behind the nurses' desk. It was funny. They would be about to let me go and then "whoa here's some more stuff!" Out would come another pink, plastic tub with Wendy's stuff. I got a kick out of it. It surprised even me that I had so much crap sprawled out everywhere.

I left there after the formula amount of time: one week. I had no insurance at the time, so I knew this would cost more than a few thousand dollars. The bill came to $23,000 but I got an uninsured/low income "discount." They reduced it to $17,000. Fabulous. Some discount. For that amount of money I could've taken a vacation and hired a private doctor to treat me in paradise with *real* food! Yes, it did stop the mania with an arsenal of pills. It did force me to sleep, eat, and slow down. It was what I needed. I was where I was supposed to be. I'll never argue that.

Five years later, I just now finished watching the videotape of what happened that night of the accident. It was filmed from the police car on the side of the road after they arrested me. I had a lawyer subpoena it (but then couldn't afford to retain him). The lawyer let me have it since they'd mailed it to him already. The day I picked it up from the lawyers' office, he didn't look me in the eyes. I knew it was because of something on the tape. I knew it wasn't because I couldn't afford to retain his services.

I was horrified! It was not at all how I thought it went down. I was shouting nearly the whole time about needing "my fucking cigarettes." (Can you believe that? Saying the "f word" to a state trooper? I would never, ever, ever, do or say that to a police officer if I were mentally well.)

As painful as it was, I forced myself to watch the whole thing. My anger towards them lessened. It didn't take away the year and a half of back pain. Or erase the hours of physical therapy. They didn't need to handcuff me so tightly or jam their boot in my back.

I was convinced that my civil rights were violated that night they abused me. I had filed a Notice of Claim so that I could sue them. However, what I recalled happening was farther from the truth than I realized. Although they did hurt me, when I watched the videotape, I was aghast. I also played the copy of the 9-1-1 call the other driver made. Now I understand where they were coming from after seeing and listening to those tapes. As hard as that is to admit.

I feel like that wasn't even me. It was Manic Wendy. A Wendy I know nothing about because we never meet when I'm sane and I don't remember who she is until afterwards. And even then my view is skewed. It's as if my brain knows I can't handle it, so it blocks it out to protect me. My sister has always told me I have selective memory and it's usually about an event surrounding a time, or during a time, of acute mania or deep depression. She's right. I know that now. I'm learning that with each passing episode.

I'd like to think those officers weren't intentionally trying to hurt me. That they were just trying to do their jobs the best they could. I'd like to think that. I know people make mistakes on the job all the time. I have come to believe those officers had to take measures to keep me safe. However, they went too far and used unnecessary force to restrain me. (I mean really, could one woman hurt two strong state troopers?)

Long before I got the tapes, I made the personal decision to drop the case. One of the reasons was financial. I didn't have the money to pay the lawyer, not even in installments. The main reason though, was each time a piece of certified mail came from the State Police or my lawyer, it dredged it up again. I got tired of thinking about it and of fighting it. Initially, my lawyer filed the first Notice of Claim against the NJ State Police. Then I found out which trooper caused my back damage, and personally filed the Notice of Claim against him. It wasn't a huge settlement I was after or expected. I wanted it to be on their record, for them to not do it to someone else and to be forced to go to some training for the mentally ill. Those were my goals. But I gave up.

I only wish they had better training on how to handle the mentally ill, rather than make quick assumptions, such as the person must be under the influence of drugs or alcohol. I wish they hadn't used excessive force on me. I know it will happen again. Nearly every friend I have that has bipolar disorder has had an altercation with the police. I'd say at least half were the victims of unnecessary force. They usually get away with it because they are the police.

After watching the videotape, who would believe my side anyway? They would write me off as wackanoodle and say the troopers did what they had to do. Forget about her injuries. That they were only protecting themselves. Right.

However, for a brief (and I do mean brief) second while watching that tape, I found it ironic and borderline humorous that the videotape was the most effective tool to get me to see how manic I was. It felt full circle or something.

The shrink at Virginia Tech, was right!

The New Deal

From Then To Now

They say we learn from our mistakes. If that's true, I must know a lot. I can't say I've learned anything particularly fast. I can say that since I'm still alive, I've learned it in time.

There has been a lot that has happened (or not happened) since August of 2005. Let me fill you in. It has been six years since my last suicide attempt and depressive episode. It has been five years since my last manic episode. I have been hospital-free for five years and I've been sober for over eight years now.

All of these are miracles for any bipolar, especially one who is also an alcoholic/addict. In the past, if it wasn't my mental illness flaring up, it was my alcoholism/drug addiction. They often went hand in hand, making the double whammy twice as hard to overcome. Although I know I will never be cured of either illness, I am grateful I have been doing so well for so long. (Being sober really helps keep my bipolar disorder under control.)

Much of my success in recent years is my "team." By that, I mean everyone and everything in my world that keeps me going. I am fortunate to have the right professionals and medications that keep me afloat, a supportive family, a wonderful network of friends (many of whom battle bipolar and/or alcoholism/addiction as well) and the faith to get me through. It takes a lot of people to help me stay on track. Oh, it takes a village all right.

Through their support and my increased stability, my confidence has grown. I started to set and achieve goals for myself. There are things I always wanted to do, since my early twenties. Writing this book was one of them. Perhaps it was the biggest goal I achieved, but certainly not the only one.

I wanted to be real estate agent in my mid twenties, but opted for the safer desk job with benefits. When I was downsized, I went back to school, got my license and did it for several years. It was the worst time for the industry in three decades. (I never said I had good timing!) But I did it!

I also started a writers group to inspire myself and other authors, poets and bloggers. It has been a lot of fun and support. I made the decision and got my subbing certificate to see if teaching was something I wanted to do. I currently substitute teach at a local high school. It was another goal. I was afraid. But, again, I did it. With each goal I achieve, I pick up momentum. I prove to myself I can do it.

They can be baby goals. Goals such as what do I have to do for the week, or for the day. (I am a big list maker, otherwise I'll forget and it won't get done.) Or, it can be a big, massive goal. I never used to make anything happen, much less allow myself to dream about it. Big or small. But again, not all my goals will be to write my next book. There is much more in between.

I'm also proud to say I'm in a stable, loving relationship. It took me thirty-eight years to find love, or for love to find me, but I'm very happy. Everything has come together for me including falling in love for the first time in my life.

I decided to do something about my body. I was extremely overweight. I lost over forty pounds and got in shape. Once I had my first real estate commission, I gave a big chunk of it to my friend who is a personal trainer. She helped me get in shape and two years later, I look and feel completely different. I'll never be, or aspire to be, teeny tiny. But I'm thrilled not to be the plus size that I was. I was elated when my weight went below 200. For a girl who was once 263, that is monumental!

My greatest reward is I no longer feel or think like the Wendy who was suicidal. If you ask anyone, they'll agree. Even my psychiatrist sometimes shakes his head. He can't believe I'm the same person. Seven years ago, I was in his office constantly (when I wasn't in the hospital). Now, it is much less frequent. How often do I go to my psychologist? Well, that all depends upon what's going on in my life. I usually go every two or three weeks. If it's a rough patch, she'll see me a few weeks in a row until my kinks are worked out. I feel no shame in going more frequently if I need to. Absolutely none. There are lot of people (with or without mental illness) who aren't getting any help and need it. I look at it like I am improving myself. And that's always a positive thing.

In history, during the New Deal, FDR was building back our country. I look at my life as following this same pattern. For our country, it meant infrastructure and helping to restabilize the banks and agriculture. For me, it was stabilizing everything inside me, beginning with my brain. Though it has taken me a long time to get here, I realize now I had to go through my "Roaring Twenties" and "Great Depression" to arrive at my "New Deal." Those times *had* to happen for me to get to, and live in, recovery.

It's a process and one that did not come overnight. It has been a long, uphill battle. I am here to say it is not an impossible climb. But it is a climb. There will be setbacks. You pick yourself up and you keep climbing. Eventually you will get better skilled at *how* to climb and it won't seem to take as much effort.

And when you get the hang of it, the view is magnificent!

Acceptance

Acceptance was the hardest pill I've ever had to swallow. And like most bipolarians, I have swallowed a lot. None of this was easy to accept. I despised my label for a long time. I didn't have much time for denial though, the way it went down for me.

That's not to say I didn't go down without a fight. I certainly fought taking the medication off and on for a good five years. I was drinking and doing drugs and all of these things combined made for a very difficult cohabitation with my illness. But I learned how to get along with it over the years. Like an annoying roommate or irksome coworker. You manage. And, more importantly, I learned how to accept who I am. As is.

I'm blessed to have a devoted family that loves and accepts me despite the trials and tribulations this illness has caused all of us, especially my parents. Without them I know I would *not* be alive. Not everyone I love accepts this the same way; people do handle mental illness differently and I try to remember that today. It has though, at times, caused me great sadness with some friends and family members. I know it's impossible for everyone to fully comprehend how hard I have to work at simply staying sea level. I understand everyone is different and they may not totally "get" me. And that's okay today.

There are also a handful of supportive friends in my world who hung in there with me through the bad times. Luckily, I know a good number of people who also have bipolar disorder, so I don't feel so unique or alone. We compare notes; we laugh at ourselves. It's better than crying, but we do that too.

My grandmother Mimi used to say, "Never tell everyone on the East Coast everything." Clearly, I haven't stuck to her advice. But there was a reason for all this. I see it already. Even before this was published, the more I talked about the book, the more people have opened up to me. They told me about their child, their sibling, their parent, their neighbor, their girlfriend. I couldn't believe how surrounded I was and yet *I had no idea* until I told people about the book. We don't talk about it enough. I believe people *need* to talk. And talk more. We're just starting to open up and, as a direct result, things are beginning to change.

And it's not just us bipolarians who need to open up. It's those close to us who, oftentimes, are not the ones getting therapy, but they're extremely affected by our illness. It reinforced that I *should* tell everyone on the East Coast everything and hopefully more than just the East Coast. Hey, I'm not proud of everything I've done. But it's brought me to where I am today and for the most part, I'm a pretty content person. So how can I regret anything?

It's brought me to you. And it's helped me become more comfortable in my own skin, by shedding my old skin here. The shedding began with an article I wrote on having bipolar disorder and running it with my name and picture in the local paper. It removed all anonymity and escalated to using my real name on this book. (I had originally intended to use a pen name.) My own process of acceptance has been helped along through writing.

Regarding help. I do wish there were more resources out there, but there are some and it's getting better. This has been especially true for mental illness, because it carries a big stigma. Our insurance carriers aren't held accountable for the same coverage as other treatments and illnesses. We are making some progress, but we still have a long way to go.

Yet bipolar disorder, according to the World Health Organization, *is the 6ᵗʰ leading cause of disability in the world*. I was also shocked to learn one in five bipolar commits suicide. This goes beyond highs and lows and periods of inability to work. This is life or death, this is everywhere in the world, and we need more help. Research wise, we are one of the least funded brain disorders in the country. Yet, bipolar disorder affects one of the highest numbers of people of all the brain disorders categories. We are so behind and yet we are so big!

Slowly, we're shedding the shame. So am I. I *still* hold my breath when people ask me the title of my book. We're also just beginning to come out of the dark. I see famous bipolar people on magazine covers and on talk shows. That never happened ten years ago, much less five years ago. I have great hope for our progress. I know things will continue to get better for us. I truly believe this. It's also happening in Washington D.C., in our legislation. There is a shift. And it's only because we are shifting our attitude and energies towards our cause.

Hopefully, I will keep moving in that positive direction too. I'm no longer ashamed of who I am. God made me this way and as they say "God doesn't make junk." Yes, I *have* a mental illness, but it's not who I *am*. Thankfully, I understand that difference today.

I have a friend right now who's really, really depressed. She's where I was before, teetering between wanting to commit suicide and just being very depressed. She's in and out of the hospital and I worry about her a lot. Nearly every time we talk, she launches into her labels obsessively. Every conversation turns to:

"But Wendy, I am bipolar and ADD. I have PTSD and…"

"Stop!" I yell. "You *have* those things. That's not who you *are!*" I literally have to yell at her. Sure, I have those things too. A lot of bipolars have ADD. A lot of people, bipolars included, have PTSD. I still can't have pressure on the back of my head or my body goes into some kind of fight or flight mode without my permission. And I, too, felt the way she does for a long time.

We have to keep reminding ourselves, however, that this is only something we have. Who in the heck says, "I *am* cancer." Or "I *am* multiple schlerosis" or "I *am* diabetes." Of course, I understand her thinking because I also thought that way for many years. It's easy to get caught up in our labels. It can be a trap to think that's who we are. But it's not. It is just a piece of the pie (unfortunately that piece is in our brains, so it is a *complicated* piece of the pie.)

I am aware that this is a mental illness, and I'm not going to lie people and say that I have perfect acceptance about it all. There is a stigma attached to it and it's impossible to completely block that out 100% of the time. But I am caring less and less of what other people think of me. Mainly, I remember something Dr. Seuss said: "Those who mind don't matter and those who matter don't mind." I like that. I hold onto that one.

Can it be hard? Yes, but I don't view myself the way I did ten, five, or even two years ago. I suspect that will keep changing and evolving. My opinion of what others think of me will matter less and less. My opinion of what *I* think of me will continue to matter more and more.

Wellness

I got better and I want you to see that you will too if you hang in there, do the right thing and plug away. You are intelligent, higher than average. That's the good news. Hold onto that. You have to know that if you didn't before. Forget what grades you got or scores you didn't get. You are very smart, so feel better about yourself starting now. How does it feel, smarty pants? You can achieve so much. Just choose your goal and stay well in the process so you can get there safely.

There are things I did, and you can do, to get and stay well. I went to local DBSA (Depression and Bipolar Support Alliance) meetings. I found that being in the company of other fellow mentally ill sufferers was comforting. They understood. Those meetings were extremely helpful to me, especially in my darkest days when I felt nobody wanted to be around me.

NAMI (National Alliance for the Mentally Ill) has meetings in most areas of the country. NAMI also has an excellent twelve-week program for families that my parents attended and highly recommend. And they have a nine week Peer-to-Peer course for individuals with various mental illnesses.

There are also many twelve step programs for any addiction you might have. The contribution is only a dollar and that's only if you have one. People who are getting no help are doing that by choice, because there are plenty of resources. Are there enough? I'll never be satisfied and say we've solved that problem. But there is help out there and there is love. Go out and find it.

Another thing I have to do for myself is to keep up with my appointments for my psychiatrists, psychologists, and whatever other professionals I see on a regular basis. When I do go see them I have to be brutally honest, even if I'm embarrassed by what I have to say. They can help me only if I'm completely truthful with them as to how I'm doing, what I'm feeling, how my sleep is and all the details. It's crucial. If I'm going through a crisis, then I step up my appointments and go more frequently until I've gotten through it. Life can be really hard.

While writing this book, all within the span of a year and a half, a lot of tragedy happened all around me and I felt deep loss. Two close friends died, both of whom had bipolar disorder. I had my heart broken and also felt the tragedy of the shootings at Virginia Tech, my alma mater. I could've gone downhill for any one of these reasons, but I fought more fiercely than ever not to. It was not only extremely helpful to have wonderful professionals in my life to keep me "on the beam," it was *imperative*. I needed them to help me process it all. I didn't go under, but I easily could have.

That's how I know I'm getting better because I'm learning how to dodge the depression bullet despite tragedy. Even if you can't afford private care, there are clinics everywhere. I know there are a few in the county I live in alone.

Here's the biggie, one which can so quickly throw me for a loop. It's imperative for me, *as important as taking my meds*, to get the right amount of sleep. My psychologist tells me it is the *other* half of my medication. This is probably the one that I struggle with the most, as do my bipolar friends. I try really hard though, especially these last few years, for eight or nine hours a night. I aim to stay on the same schedule as well. The more I read and hear, the more I understand how sleep is proven to be closely linked to our disorder. I have learned to make this a top priority and guard it. When I stay up really late and throw off my clock, or don't get enough sleep, I know I'm playing games with mania. I am giving it a personal invitation to creep in, sometimes even after only one night. I don't want to get sick, so I work hard at this.

We are dealing with a fragile thing here, our circadian rhythm. I had never heard that sleep was so important to my illness until I started seeing my new psychiatrist and psychologist. They have both continually brought it up to me. The importance of sleep has been drilled into me. This has made a huge difference to my wellness. Why didn't anyone do this before? Do you know how many psychiatrists and professionals I have been to? Maybe they mentioned it, but these two current professionals keep an ongoing dialogue with me about how I am sleeping and keep me aware. In return, I am honest with them.

Even with this knowledge, while writing this book I would get on a roll and still stay up too late. I saw myself getting a little manic. It's a dangerous game. Sometimes it can be tempting to want to bring on mania to give us our creative edge. But we have to go against that desire and remain vigilant about our sleep. It's critical. I don't always do the right thing, but I know what the right thing is today, so that helps. I try. That's a big difference from sixteen years ago when I didn't care.

I have to work extra hard on my sleep in the spring. I *always* have a harder time sleeping when the spring comes. My psychiatrist tells me that's true of his bipolar patients. As the days are longer, there's more sunlight. Manic in the spring. It makes sense. Knowing this helps and with each passing year, I get better about anticipating mania and being on high alert with my sleep. I focus extra hard on keeping it routine. It's a challenge, though.

In keeping with that, I try to avoid caffeine late in the day and at night. I know it'll keep me up late. I'm a night owl, so caffeine looks attractive, especially at night. There are very few times I can justify it. I don't pretend I do this right all the time. But I try to pay attention, realize my mistakes and go on.

I'm a lot better at taking care of myself than I was. I try today. We have to if we want to strive for wellness and live with some peace. It's critical that we pay attention to these things. I don't want to be in the hospital for either mania *or* depression. Add not enough sleep, too much caffeine, miss a dose... pretty soon it could be WHAM! Mania! I've learned to be on high alert — just as much for mania as depression — because both are disruptive.

We're playing a serious game here. As you probably know, the wreckage of mania and depression can be extraordinarily horrible. It can tax our lives, families and jobs, running a tab we can't easily pay back. It takes away precious time that never returns. The longer I live with this illness, the more clearly I can see that. I have too much to lose. My mind is too valuable to me today. I have too many goals and dreams I want to accomplish; I can't afford to be on the side lines.

They say a moving target is hard to hit, and I believe that. I keep pretty busy between writing, working, being with friends and family, meetings, pottery class, my writers group, and (some) exercise. This means I don't have too much down time. When I was extremely depressed and suicidal, I had way too much time on my hands. I wasn't working. I didn't have to be anywhere and, as a result, I didn't *go* anywhere. I wasn't getting dressed up or even showering every day.

Too much time on my hands is a disaster waiting to happen. I've gone through periods in my life, especially in my early thirties, when I could not work. After a while though, I believe that also kept me in a depression, so it's a catch twenty-two. Depression is such a hard well to climb out of, even with a ladder and helping hands.

If you are depressed, challenge yourself to do something. I know this is easier said than done. But *try*. Humor me. Yell at yourself to move. Yell at those feet. Challenge your thinking. When you hear a negative thought in your head say something mean to you, when your head has turned on you and you are believing what it is telling you, I want you to challenge it. It's a big lie. It's not the truth, but you will think it is. Replace it with a good thought. I know it's hard, but try. That's the key: to try.

I was sitting in outpatient therapy when they taught me about these thoughts, so I could begin to recognize them (automatic thoughts, I believe they were called). Then when those negative thoughts popped up and came in, I began to notice them. Since I could notice and name them, I could begin to replace and change them. I had to challenge them, one by one and take back control. It was as if I were in a sword fight: fighting blade for blade, thought for thought. Stick up for yourself and tell those bad thoughts to take a hike. I don't care how corny that sounds.

Shower even though you don't want to. I used to drag my ass into the shower because I knew it would make me feel better even though it felt like it would take all the energy I had for the entire day to do so. Sometimes that was the *only* truly productive thing I did that day. It was a small victory but I did it. Then there were days, sometimes several days, when I never showered at all.

I remember one time when I was in the hospital, my friend came to visit me and saw my greasy hair. She took one look at me and she literally threw me in the shower with my clothes on and closed the bathroom door. I hope you have at least one friend who will do that for you. I know when I'm that down and out, I don't even want a close friend around, but let help in. Just try to let love in. At least let a friend come see you even if you think you will only bring them down. Maybe they don't care and they only want to cheer you up (or help get you clean)! Let them.

Listen to music. That *always* helped me. Whenever I was in the hospital, I always begged to have my CD player and headphones with me (this was pre iPods). Sometimes I had to earn the privilege, because the staff frequently gave me a hard time, but I convinced them it would help me. I fought. For me, being without music is like cutting off my arms. In outpatient therapy, they had us make a list of all the things that made us happy, that made us feel good. We were supposed to refer to that list and do something when we felt really shitty. It helped when I did it. Music was always at the top of my list.

About the middle. I'll notice when I'm doing well, on an even keel, I get a little worried. I wonder: when the other shoe is going to drop? Okay, life is good *now,* but what is going to happen and when? Will I have another episode and have to be hospitalized? When will I get manic or depressed again? Will it turn into a full-blown episode? I'm not used to things going well historically, certainly not for years at a clip as they are now. I practice living in the middle today and being okay with it. I'm getting better at enjoying the peace.

I know that as long as I learn to stay aware of my warning signs with this illness, and fix them sooner rather than later, I'm in good shape. Doing the best I can on my end helps the periods of calm last longer. I am enjoying these longer periods of wellness. I used to think they were boring. Not anymore. I do not miss hospitals. I do not miss ECT treatments. I do not miss trying medications at all different doses and combinations until we find the right mix. I do not miss my weight fluctuating so much that I could go up or down thirty pounds in any given few months because of all the medication changes. In short, I do not miss the chaos of this illness.

About medication. You know, it's only a piece of the puzzle for me, but it's a pretty *massive* piece. I'm sure there will be critics or even people with bipolar disorder that will look down upon medication or refuse it. I was once one of those people. I was also very sick then. This is my feeling and my journey. You will have your own.

The funny thing is, everybody seems to have an opinion about medication. Don't they? And whether or not we should be taking it. Maybe it's your spouse or boy/girlfriend or a friend or family member. I'd like to hear someone say to their spouse, "Honey why don't you try going without that heart medicine of yours. Let's see how you do." Don't listen to people who tell you to go off your medication. They're usually ignorant, have a motive or both. Your wellness is your business, not other people's who steer you wrong. If they don't have M.D. after their name, tell them to piss off.

There's exercise. This is a relatively new one for me. For many years I was so depressed I was barely moving. But when I got better I decided to do something. When I do I *always* feel better and the high I get from it lasts longer than one from chocolate! I walk with a friend who also suffers from depression. We get out now and then and walk along Ocean Avenue. Time flies. Then she started going through a really bad depression (she has bipolar disorder too). That's when I started to walk alone. Sometimes, I'd get a call and most of the walk I'd be talking to a friend anyway. Or I wouldn't bring my phone, only my iPod. Once, I even walked with nothing! I was shocked! I'm learning how to be okay with being at peace.

I'm lucky that my friend is a personal trainer. She cuts me a deal and even though I don't want to go, I go once a week. I'm never in the mood to exercise. I'm a slug working against my innate slugness. Although I loathe those sixty minutes, I always feel like a million bucks when I leave.

I've also gone to yoga here and there; although never regularly I'll admit. I see the value in it because it releases toxins and connects me all the way around: mind, body *and* spirit. When I first went, the instructor said "If you're pregnant you can try this variation." I looked around the studio realizing I was the only one over a size six in that whole place, so she was obviously talking about me. Oh well. So I can't do all the poses and I'm the biggest girl in there? So child's pose and downward dog are my faves? There are worse things. It helps me when I go, I love the calm music, the energy and I feel so...I don't know: Zen or something.

Meditation is my newest addition to the "Wendy Wellness Bag of Tricks." Although my friend Kim has been suggesting it to me for years, I have only recently begun to try it. My psychologist handed me a copy of *BP Magazine*. In it, there was an article on meditation. There have been a handful of studies done on mediation in this country and around the world. While these studies were not specifically for bipolar disorder, the findings were all positive, so I'm going to take that and run with it.

My friend's mom forwarded me a beautiful meditation from a Buddhist monk last night. I played it over and over. I went to that website and they have all kinds of CDs. You don't need a CD though; you can just be still and repeat a calming phrase. Or put on quiet music. Or do both. Sometimes I just sit there with my eyes closed and do absolutely nothing but breathe. The one I've been listening to has music in the background and the monk speaks during it, so it's considered a "guided meditation." It was beautiful and calming, and I can always use calm to quiet my unquiet brain. After hearing it for the first time, I thought of my biological father, Bill, who is a Buddhist. It sounded like something we heard when we were kids in his "mini-shrine." I had to laugh. Another full circle!

Another recent wellness trick of mine is to burn candles. I know, it might sound far-fetched as far as the wellness category, but not for me. Nighttime is the time of day when I do not feel my calmest. My mind clicks on at night. It truly does. I am at my *peak* from late afternoon until late evening. So, when the sun goes down, I light candles everywhere in my apartment. The big ones can get expensive, so I litter my place with the little tea lights. They burn for three hours and a bag of fifty is only a few dollars. You can't beat that! It has a wonderful calming effect *and* it saves on electricity!

Never underestimate the power of smell. How many times have you smelled a spray, oil or your favorite perfume and felt happier? Come on, admit it. I wear my favorite perfume nearly every day because it makes me happy. I don't save it for a "special occasion." It's expensive, but I don't care. I also keep lavender oil in the shower because I love the smell. You can get it at health food stores and it's not expensive. I even use lavender room spray. I recently purchased incense while on a camping trip in a cute, little store in town. It was only a dollar for each one. I picked out a couple scents I liked and every now and then, I burn those for something different. Never underestimate all the small things you can do for your wellness. It's the little things that go a long way. Candles and aromatherapy included.

There are positive readings you can do. I always listened to music until one day my CADC handed me *The Secret*. Listening to the CDs of the book *The Secret* has helped me a lot. It talks about how powerful meditation is and all about the Law of Attraction, which I believe helped me finish and publish this book. It helped me change my thinking in general. Other books like *Conversations With God* and *You Can Heal Your Life* have really transformed the way I view myself. (My psychologist brought up *You Can Heal Your Life* several times until I was forced to go buy it to get her off my back!) But I am grateful to all these books and CDs that were suggested to me. I brainwashed myself with them! They really helped me.

I am often stumped on what to do and where to go in life, but all three of these books have given me great insight on the world of possibilities that lie within each of us. I don't see only me anymore. I see me in a big universe of endless inspirations and opportunities. I believe, on my best days, that anything is possible.

My wish is that someday soon, you or your loved one will come to a relative peace with this illness. I know the journey will not always be smooth. There will probably be turbulence, as I expect more during my flight in life. When it is calm it will probably not be so forever. We must enjoy, learn to cherish and be grateful for calmness when we do have it in our grasp. I try not to look back or too far ahead, because it scares me if I do. I know these periods of peace have come and gone. It is likely that they will come and go again.

I hope this has shed some light. I hope you feel a little less alone. I hope you get the help you need and find some peace. Seek out whatever resources you need. Don't be ashamed of how you were made because you have many talents and you are, above all, a beautiful human being. Believe that as much and as often as you can. Getting help makes you strong, not weak. Throw away whatever negative beliefs have held you back. Life is hard enough without you fighting yourself, too.

Hang in there.
You are precious.

Please don't ever, ever give up.
Someone will miss you.
I will.

I may not know you
but I know who you are.
Stick around.
It gets better.
It might get worse.
But it *will* get better again.

Standing Still

As I strain looking out the tiny part of my kitchen window with a view of the ocean, I see only grey water and skies. I notice a flag across the street blowing every which way, not able to flow peacefully in one direction in the strong wind.

I think of the ocean, skies and weather and how similar their volatile condition is to life. Not just mine, but everyone's. I remind myself that even though today there are no blue skies or calm waters, there is a good chance there could be tomorrow. And just like the weather I see out my window, what I feel today will not necessarily be what I feel tomorrow.

I hear my cell phone ringing from the other room. It's my Mom and I'm running late to pick her up. I'm brought out of this moment back into reality, which is no longer a bad thing. I'm not always content with where I'm at in my life. But it's still a hell of a lot better than lying on train tracks and hoping the conductor doesn't see me.

On my way to pick up my Mom, I approach the bridge. It's the bridge I couldn't drive over for a long time after my friend Annie, who was also bipolar, committed suicide by drowning herself here a year ago.

Today I'm okay though, as the song "Lucky Man" by the Verve is blaring, reminding me how blessed I am to be alive. It's a bittersweet feeling because although I'm grateful to be alive, I'm also thinking of all the people I miss, especially whenever I drive over this bridge. For some reason today I remember a story about my Uncle Rick and I smile.

Before he passed away years ago, I went to see him. When I was newly sober, he was in the hospital, very sick with cancer. I had smuggled in a hot fudge sundae to him.

"You're the best, Wendells!" He thanked me, his mouth full of hot fudge and ice cream.

"I feel like I'm on a tightrope, like I'm holding my breath, waiting to fall." I was beside myself. We both knew I was talking about how I was worried I was going to relapse again. "I just want to run away, Rick."

"Wendells." He turned to look at me and got very serious, which was not something my Uncle Rick did very often. "The best things that've ever come to me in life, have come when I was standing still."

I stared back at him, waiting for an explanation, but none came. He simply went back to eating his ice cream while I sat there bewildered. I didn't understand what he meant and had no idea at the time that I'd ever remember that moment again.

Then it hit me as the wind was whipping my hair everywhere. I smiled a deep smile that radiated warm bits of energy to all parts of my body.

I realized that I too was standing still.

To The Parents & Families

Bipolar Disorder (Manic Depression) is a tricky, sneaky and tenacious disease. It took over and derailed Wendy at the prime time in her life (typically late teens, early twenties). This disease hit without any warning. It takes enormous patience, resources, knowledge, networking, and, yes, money to get through this.

For those of you wandering though this mess, I offer you just a few tips. Look for the signals:

The manic half:

- Going without sleep for days.
- Extreme overspending.
- Drinking and drugging to cover the highs (and lows).
- Cursing, blaming attitude.
- Grand thoughts and impossible goals.
- Going out with people they would never look at twice if well.
- Impulsivity and hypersexuality.

The depression half:

- Lack of interest in food, people, events.
- Unable to get out of bed or leave room.
- Hopelessness.
- Very dark thoughts day and night.
- Insidious suicidal thoughts.

As high as they go in mania; as low they will fall in depression-the most dangerous side of this illness. A mixed episode of mania and depression is when most bipolars commit suicide, so be on high alert for safety when they are exhibiting both.*

1. Know that all doctors are not created equal. Some do not have the expertise with bipolar disorder to prescribe the right combination of drugs to wrestle this disease to the ground. There are so many old and new drugs that must be delicately prescribed in the correct combination and strength. I will forever be grateful for Wendy's good friend who recommended Dr. Bransfield to us. He gets it. He led us through the right drug combinations to achieve wellness. When Wendy simply did not want to live anymore, I remember sitting in his office and feeling hope.

2. Be steadfast, firm yet remain compassionate, even though you are really mad. It will help your child survive this.

3. Make a contract with your child to promise that they will always take the prescribed drugs unwaveringly, no matter what. The up or manic feeling is intoxicating and causes many bipolars to go off their meds.

4. Lead the way and take good care of yourself. Find good resources for you and your loved one. Search and assemble the absolute best team you can of doctor/psychologists and any other professionals you need.

5. Join support groups. Educate yourself with as much as you can about this illness and the treatment. We went to the family NAMI program which really helped.

6. As far as treatment goes, I remember thinking that ECT was scary from the movies. Don't be afraid of this option. It actually saved her life.

7. Love unconditionally.

We are so proud of Wendy. She has battled this disease for 16 years. For much of the time she has had to dig deep inside to find out who she is, how sick she can be, and how to achieve wellness... and keep it. She has worked so hard.

May you find wellness with your loved one. Don't ever give up on them. Your help greatly increases their chances, whether you are aware of it or not.

Good luck to you!

-Wendy's Mom and Dad

*For more information on bipolar disorder, refer to NAMI and DBSA websites listed under Resources.

Author's Note

While editing this book, in the spring of 2010, I experienced my first episode since 2005. Though wellness is always the goal to avoid episodes, no one with this disorder is bulletproof. The cause of my episode was something out of my control. Worse: it's something that could happen to you or someone you know. Therefore, I felt compelled to add this in.

I had been on the same medication regime since 2005 and was doing great, despite life's twists and turns. Episode free for five years, which is an achievement for any bipolarian. I've worked very hard at it on a daily basis.

However, in an effort to cut costs, several months ago my insurance company refused to fill one of my medications in its brand form. I tried several generics to find one that worked and one generic of it caused me to get manic within ten days. Once I realized this (and it had to be pointed out to me), I immediately paid out-of-pocket and went back on my regular brand medication. But it was too late. It took several weeks to get rid of the mania.

We know what happens after mania: the crash. I experienced several weeks of depression afterwards. It just goes to show you what one generic can do. Beware. Some are fine. It depends on the generic manufacturer, the medication, the person, etc. For me, this particular one caused me a month of instability at a crucial time (while I was editing this book).

Wellness is attainable and I am back on track. Never give up hope. If I have one episode in five years, it's okay. It's still the best average I've ever had. This experience forced me to go on high alert, utilizing all my wellness tricks: getting my proper sleep, limiting caffeine

(I put myself on a caffeine blackout during mania), and stepping up my appointments with my psychiatrist and psychologist. We added an extra med to slow me down and all of it combined, helped me to get through it. Having people around you that are educated about your illness is also a *huge* help. They often are the ones who see the signs before we are able to recognize them.

Two appeals, several months and many faxes from my psychiatrist later, I just got word from my insurance company. They are going to make a formulary exception. Success at last! You know what they say about the squeaky wheel. Now I have my grease again.

Acknowledgements

(There are many who have kept me sane, loved me
and helped me with this book! Here goes...)

Mom and Dad: Thank you for always loving me,
believing in me, visiting me in the hospitals every day
and never giving up on me even when I had given up on life itself.
I'm alive because of you there's no doubt in my mind.
Thanks for always listening to me ramble,
letting me move back in when I needed it and
always, *always* loving me even at my worst.
I love you both endlessly!!!! xoxoxoxo

Auntie Carol: You're my loving aunt but most importantly,
a treasured friend always ready with a cup
of tea and a hug. luv you. xo

Nora: My Wife, My Editor-in-Chief
I am so glad you crashed on my couch and never left.
You are my moon and my stars.
I love you, turtle eyes. XOXO

Dr. Bransfield: AT LAST I found you! My
amazing psychiatrist!! You're a genius!
Thank you for keeping me sane, on the right
medications and even making me laugh!

Dev & Meg: My Birthday Twin Goddaughter
and Our Little Hippie Artist.
Never change. Rock on! "kiss kiss" xx

Sis: Thanks for being a great big sister.
I've always looked up to you.
You're so strong and sane *(darn you!)* love ya. xo

Katie, Parker and Seamus:
The greatest sound in the world are your giggles
and best sight, your smiles. I love each of you so much!! xxxooo

Becca: Thanks for believing in me from the very start!
You & Bryan made this book possible with
my 1st laptop & printer! xo love ya

To *all* my relatives, you're the greatest family a girl can have!

Kim: You're my best friend and have always been there for me.
Your constant encouragement has been one
of my greatest sources of inspiration.
Friend, editor, cheerleader...the list is long!
Your love never ends and I will always love you. xoxo

Heather Lennon: Where do I *start?*
Editor sent from the heavens...Mentor extraordinaire...
Thank you for helping me find my stride as a writer.
This book would be crap without you!! That is a fact!

Carol McC. I knew God hadn't given up on me when we met.
Thanks for your selfless, countless hours of love and guidance.
I'm so happy for you and Jamie. No one deserves
love twice more than you! xoxo

Mary and Jess: I'm so glad we've stayed friends since college.
Thanks for putting up with me over the years and
loving me despite my many faults. xxoo

Dr. Sharon Kamm: Thanks for saying you
never saw me on the back of a truck
and keeping me going through each death, break up & job change.
Your insight is invaluable to me! You're the best!!

Sandy Fritz: You've been so kind to me and are the example of the serenity I aspire to have. Thanks for your support & love always!

Brooke Borneman: Thanks for all your advice,
support, positive energy, guidance and love!
And for your zillions of emails back and forth. Love ya xo

Wendy Murphy: thanks for steering me to Corinda and Marion.
You are my amazing source! Where would I be without you??

Corinda Carfora, thanks for your smarts, time, guiding me to
Heather & impressing upon me that this is a business. And that
I had to do my 50 pages 6 more times to make this book!

Marion Lynch, thank you for publishing my first article and
giving me my big break. You not only helped me, you helped a
lot of other people with this illness and their families locally.

Rosie O'Donnell: Thank you for reading this
and for your advice summer 2009.

Joe Pantoliano: For your vision and starting your non-profit NKM2.
Thanks for reminding me that I can't afford to be anonymous.

To the Red Bank Writers Group:
Keep writing everyone! You can do it!!

Uncle Rick, Regina, Annie and Heidigirl:
You were shooting stars, now angels.
I was lucky to have witnessed your brilliance.
I know you're with me; I just wish you were still here.
Somehow, though, I know you are.

To Virginia Tech:
The school, my professors, the community, everyone.
You gave me a great education and supported
me, especially when I fell apart.
You had wonderful resources, when most schools back
then did not. I will forever be grateful to you.

To: Dr. Kay Redfield Jameson, Marya Hornbacher, Terry Cheney, Carrie Fisher, Andy Behrman and every bipolar author who has helped shed light on our illness, each with a different color.
Thank you for paving the way with your bravery and giving me courage.

To all my fellow bipolarians:
wherever you are.
Non-famous, famous.
Young, old and every age in between.
Especially the newly diagnosed and struggling.
Hang in there.
Don't ever give up.

Resources

NAMI (National Alliance for the Mentally Ill)
(800) 950-NAMI
www.nami.org

DBSA (Depression and Bipolar Support Alliance)
(800) 82N-DMDA
www.DBSAlliance.org

National Institute of Mental Health
(866)615-6464
www.nimh.nih.gov

AFSP (American Foundation for Suicide Prevention)
(800) 273-TALK
www.afsp.org

AA (Alcoholics Anonymous)
(800) 245-1377
www.aa.org

NA (Narcotics Anonymous)
(818) 773-9999
www.na.org

www.google.com
Google anything and everything you can.
Learn about your illness, your meds, facilities, doctors, etc.
Always educate yourself and learn. Read what other people have to say, just watch the source.

CPSIA information can be obtained
at www.ICGtesting.com
Printed in the USA
BVHW052139020922
646212BV00005B/36